FRIENDS OF GOD

Josemaría Escrivá

FRIENDS OF GOD

HOMILIES

This paperback edition in English is published in the United States for Scriptor, S.A. by Scepter Publishers, Inc.
www.scepterpublishers.org
info@scepterpublishers.org
800-322-8773 (US & Canada only)
1-212-354-0670
New York

This is a translation of *Amigos de Dios,* (1977, Madrid).

Printed in China
ISBN 9780933932838

With ecclesiastical approval

CONTENTS

THE AUTHOR

Saint Josemaría Escrivá was born in Barbastro, in northern Spain, on January 9, 1902. At the age of 15 or 16, he began to feel the first intimations that God was calling him and he decided to become a priest. He started his ecclesiastical studies in the Seminary of Logroño in 1918, and later, in 1920, in that of St Francis de Paula in Saragossa, where from 1922 he was a superior or tutor. In 1923 he began to study Civil Law in the University of Saragossa, with the permission of his ecclesiastical superiors. These studies did not interfere with his theological studies. He was ordained deacon on December 20, 1924 and became a priest on March 28, 1925.

He began his work as a priest in the village of Perdiguera, within the diocese of Saragossa, and afterwards in Saragossa itself. In the spring of 1927, with the permission of the Archbishop of Saragossa, he moved to the Spanish capital Madrid and there carried out abundant priestly work among all kinds of people, devoting attention also to the poor and destitute in the outlying districts of the city, and especially to the incurably sick and the dying in the hospitals. He worked as chaplain to the *Patronato de Enfermos* (Foundation for the Sick), a welfare organization run by the Apostolic Sisters of the Sacred Heart. He also taught at a university academy, and continued his studies for a doctorate in Civil Law, which at that time could only be obtained from the University of Madrid.

On October 2, 1928 God made him see clearly what up to then he had only inklings of; and Saint Josemaría Escrivá founded Opus Dei (in English, the Work of God). Under God's continuing guidance, on February 14, 1930 he understood that he must open up the apostolic work of Opus Dei to women also. As a result, a new path was opening up in the Church, to promote, among people of all social classes, the search for holiness and the practice of the apostolate, through the sanctification of ordinary work, in the midst of the world and without changing one's state in life.

From October 2, 1928, the Founder of Opus Dei directed his energies to the mission God had entrusted to him, with great apostolic zeal for all souls. In 1934 he was appointed Rector of the *Patronato de Santa Isabel* (St

Elizabeth Foundation). During the Spanish Civil War, at times putting his life at risk, he carried out his priestly ministry in Madrid and, subsequently, in the northern city of Burgos. Already in those years Saint Josemaría Escrivá experienced harsh and sustained opposition, which he bore calmly and with a supernatural outlook.

On February 14, 1943 he founded the Priestly Society of the Holy Cross, which is inseparably united to Opus Dei and which, as well as opening up the possibility of ordaining lay members of Opus Dei to the priesthood and incardinating them for the service of the Work, would later on also enable priests who are incardinated in dioceses to share the spirituality and asceticism of Opus Dei, seeking holiness in the exercise of their ministerial duties, while remaining exclusively under their respective Ordinaries.

In 1946 he took up residence in Rome, which was to be his home for the rest of his life. From there, he stimulated and guided the development of Opus Dei throughout the world, using all his energies to give to the men and women of Opus Dei a solid formation in doctrine, ascetical spirit and apostolate. At the time of his death, Opus Dei had more than 60,000 members from 80 different nationalities.

Saint Escrivá was a Consultor to the Pontifical Commission for the authentic interpretation of the Code of

Canon Law, and to the Sacred Congregation for Seminaries and Universities. He was a Domestic Prelate and an honorary Academician of the Pontifical Roman Academy of Theology. He was also the Chancellor of the Universities of Navarre (in Spain) and Piura (in Peru).

Saint Josemaría Escrivá died on June 26, 1975. For years, he had been offering his life for the Church and for the Pope. He was buried in the Crypt of the church of Our Lady of Peace, in Rome. Msgr. Alvaro del Portillo (1914-1994), who for many years had been his closest collaborator, was unanimously elected to succeed him. The present Prelate of Opus Dei is Msgr. Javier Echevarria, who also worked for several decades with Saint Josemaría Escrivá and with his first successor, Msgr. del Portillo. Opus Dei, which from its inception had had the approval of the diocesan authorities and from 1943, also the *appositio manuum* and subsequently the approval of the Holy See, was established as a Personal Prelature by his holiness Pope John Paul II on November 28, 1982: this was the canonical formula foreseen and desired by Saint Josemaría Escrivá.

The reputation for holiness which the Founder of Opus Dei enjoyed in his lifetime has spread after his death to the far corners of the earth, as can be seen from countless spiritual and material favors attributed to his intercession; among them, a number of cures which are medically inexplicable. Many letters from all the continents, and among them those of 69 Cardinals and nearly 1300 Bishops (more than a third of the episcopate worldwide), were written requesting the Pope to open the Cause of Beatification and Canonization of Msgr. Escrivá. The Congregation for the Causes of Saints gave its *nihil obstat* for the opening of the Cause on January 30, 1981 and this was ratified by Pope John Paul II on February 5, 1981.

Between 1981 and 1986 two processes took place, one in Rome and the other in Madrid, to gather information on the life and virtues of Msgr. Escrivá. Following the results of these two processes and accepting the favorable opinions of the congress of theological consultors and the Commission of Cardinals and Bishops, members of the Congregation for the Causes of Saints, the Holy Father, on April 9, 1990, declared the heroicity of the virtues of Msgr. Escrivá, who thus received the title of Venerable. On July 6, 1991, the Pope commanded the publication of a Decree declaring the miraculous nature of a cure attributed to the intercession of the Venerable Josemaría Escrivá. This act completed the juridical stages for the beatification of the Founder of Opus Dei, which was celebrated in Rome on May 17,

1992, in a solemn ceremony presided over by his holiness Pope John Paul II in St Peter's Square. Josemaría Escrivá was canonized on October 6, 2002.

From May 21, 1992, the body of Saint Josemaría rests in the altar of the Prelatic Church of Our Lady of Peace, in the central offices of the Prelature of Opus Dei. It is accompanied constantly by the prayers and thanksgiving of many people from all over the world who have been brought closer to God, attracted by the example and teachings of the founder of Opus Dei and by the devotion of those who turn to his intercession.

Among his published writings, apart from the theological and legal study *La Abadesa de las Huelgas,* there are books of spirituality which have been translated into numerous languages: *The Way, Holy Rosary, Christ is Passing By, Friends of God, The Way of the Cross, Loving the Church, Furrow, The Forge* (the last five titles have been published posthumously). Another book, which brings together press interviews, has the title *Conversations with Msgr. Escrivá.*

FOREWORD

God knows best. We men understand so little of his gentle fatherly way of leading us to himself. When I wrote the foreword to *Christ is Passing By* in 1973, I just could not have imagined that the holy priest who was its author would be going so soon to his heavenly home. Thousands of us, men and women all over the world, children of his prayer, his sacrifice and his generous abandonment to the Will of God, can apply to him, with immense gratitude, the same words of heartfelt praise that St Augustine wrote of our father and lord St Joseph: "he accomplished the fatherhood of the heart better than anyone else accomplished that of the flesh."[1] He departed this life on Thursday, June 26, 1975, at midday, in this city of the universal charity of the holy Church. As the bells of the Angelus were still echoing in our ears, the Founder of Opus Dei heard

[1] St Augustine, *Sermo* 51, 26 (PL 38, 348).

the words *amice, ascende superius,*[2] ("friend, come unto the joy of Heaven"), hearing them this time with their full and eternal meaning.

He left this world on an ordinary day, going about his priestly work, fully immersed in conversation with him who is Life itself. This is why he has not died, but is there at God's side. While he was busy caring for souls, there came to him the "sweet and gentle surprise" (as he puts it in his homily *Towards Holiness*[3]) of finding himself face to face with Christ, able at last to contemplate the beautiful Face he had longed so much to see: *Vultum tuum, Domine, requiram!*[4] ("Thy face, Lord, do I seek").

From the very first moments of his birth into his heavenly home, I began to receive testimonies from countless men and women, who had known his saintly life. They expressed, and continue to do so, feelings that now need no holding back. Previously, they had kept silent, out of respect for the humility of a man who considered himself "a sinner who is madly in love with Jesus Christ." I had the conso-

[2] Lk 14:10.

[3] *Towards Holiness*, no. 296. (The numbers here and in the quotations below refer to the numbers printed in the margin of this volume.)

[4] Ps 26:8.

lation of hearing directly from the lips of the Holy Father, Pope Paul VI, one of his many warm expressions of praise for the Founder of Opus Dei. Innumerable newspapers and magazines all over the world have published articles of appreciation, written by people nourished in the Christian faith and also by others who do not yet profess to believe in Christ but who have begun to discover him through the words and deeds of Msgr. Josemaría Escrivá.

"As long as I have strength to breathe, I will continue to preach that it is vitally necessary that we be souls of prayer *at all times,* at every opportunity, and in the most varied of circumstances, because God never abandons us."[5] That was his one and only concern: to pray and to encourage others to do likewise. That was why he brought about in the midst of the world a wonderful "mobilization of people," as he liked to call it, "who are ready to commit themselves to live Christian lives," by developing their filial relationship with God our Father. We are many who have learned, from this thoroughly priestly priest, "the great secret of God's mercy: that we are children of God."[6]

[5] *A Life of Prayer,* no. 247.

[6] *Getting to Know God,* no. 145.

In this second volume of homilies we have gathered together some texts that were published while Monsignor Escrivá was still with us here on earth, and others from the many which he left for later publication, because he worked unhurriedly and kept working to the end. He never set out to be an *author*, though he figures among the leading teachers of Christian spirituality. His teaching is both attractive and forceful, and is meant to be lived in the midst of our work, at home, in our dealings with other people, everywhere in fact. He had the art, humanly speaking as well, of giving more generously than one had bargained for. How well he reads! The directness of his expressions, the liveliness of his images, make him accessible to one and all, regardless of differences of mentality and culture. He did his schooling in the Gospel. It is here where he derives his clarity, his ability to strike at the depths of the soul, and his special gift for not going out of fashion, because he never bowed to fashion.

These eighteen homilies present a broad picture of the basic human and Christian virtues for all who wish to follow closely in the footsteps of our Lord. They are neither a theoretical treatise, nor potted hints for acquiring spiritual good manners. They contain living doctrine and combine a theologian's depth with the evangelical clarity of a good shepherd of souls. With Monsignor Escrivá, words turn into a colloquy with God—prayer—but without ceasing to be a heartfelt conversation completely in tune with the concerns and hopes of his listeners. The homilies are, therefore, a lesson in doctrine and in Christian life in which God is not only spoken of but spoken to. Perhaps it is in this that the secret of his great power of communication lies, because he always refers to the love of God as "looking at God without needing rest or feeling tired."[7]

Right from the first of these homilies we are reminded of one of the constant themes of Monsignor Escrivá's preaching, which is that God calls all men to be saints. Echoing the words of St Paul, "This is the will of God, your sanctification,"[8] he points out: "We have to become saints, as they say in my part of the world, 'down to the last whisker,' Christians who are truly and genuinely such, the kind that could be canonized. If not, we shall have failed as disciples of the one and only Master."[9] Further on he specifies what he means: "The holiness that our Lord demands of you is to be achieved by carrying

[7] *Towards Holiness*, no. 296.
[8] 1 Thess 4:3.
[9] *The Richness of Ordinary Life*, no. 5.

out with love of God your work and your daily duties, and these will almost always consist of small realities."[10]

What basis, what grounds do Christians have for nurturing such amazing aspirations in their lives? The answer comes as a sort of refrain, again and again, right through these homilies: it is the humble sense of daring "of the person who, knowing himself to be poor and weak, knows also that he is a son of God."[11]

Monsignor Escrivá sees a clear alternative facing every human being: "slavery or divine sonship, this is the dilemma we face. Children of God or slaves to pride."[12] Aided by the holy example of the faithful and heroic dedication of the Founder of Opus Dei, I have thought and prayed about this truth with even greater intensity since that day when our Lord took to his side the person I most dearly loved, that without the humility and simplicity of a child we cannot take a single step forward along the path of serving God. "Humility means looking at ourselves as we really are, honestly and without excuses. And

[10] *Ibid.*, no. 7.

[11] *Humility*, no. 108.

[12] *Freedom, a Gift from God*, no. 38.

when we realize that we are worth hardly anything, we can then open ourselves to God's greatness: it is there where our greatness lies."[13]

"He must become more and more, I must become less and less."[14] This was what John the Baptist, the Precursor, taught. And our Lord said, "Learn from me, for I am meek and humble of heart."[15] Humility does not mean being timid or inhibited. The humility preached by the Founder of Opus Dei is something alive and deeply felt, because "it means acknowledging our littleness in the eyes of God: a little child, a son."[16] Monsignor Escrivá has encapsulated this idea in an expression which may have been invented by him, when he speaks of "dynamism in our humility"[17]: because when a child, accepting his littleness, is helped by the all-powerful protection of his Father God, there is a dynamism in him which overflows into works of faith, of hope, of love, and of all the other virtues that the Holy Spirit infuses into his soul.

At no time does Monsignor Escrivá move away from the context chosen for his first homily, which

[13] *Humility,* no. 96.
[14] Jn 3:30.
[15] Mt 11:29.
[16] *Humility,* no. 108.
[17] *Living by Faith,* no. 202.

is ordinary life, normal situations, things that happen every day. In all the virtues he speaks of, he is always referring to Christians who live in the world because "this is their place, the place where God has wished them to be." It is here that the human virtues come into play: prudence, truthfulness, serenity, justice, magnanimity, hard work, temperance, sincerity, fortitude, and so forth. These virtues are both human and Christian, because, to take the virtue of temperance as an example, we see it is brought to perfection by a spirit of penance and mortification; and the human virtue which encourages the strict fulfillment of one's duty is enriched by the divine touch of charity, "which is like a generous overflowing of justice."[18] We live in close contact with the things we use, but detached from them, keeping our hearts pure.

Since "for those who busy themselves in affairs of souls, time"—more than gold—"is glory!"[19] The Christian has to learn to use time diligently, in order to show his love for God and for his fellowmen through "sanctifying his work, sanctifying himself in his work and sanctifying others through his work." He has to pay careful attention to small things, that

[18] *Open to God and Men*, no. 173.
[19] Cf. *The Way*, no. 355.

is to say, he must avoid useless daydreaming and must seek to practise the silent heroism, which is both natural and supernatural at the same time, of the one who lives his daily life with Christ. "Nowhere is it written that Christians should be strangers to the world. Our Lord Jesus, by his deeds and by his teaching, has bestowed praise on another human virtue which is particularly dear to me, the virtue of naturalness or simplicity. (...) What happens is that people tend to get used to what is plain and ordinary and, without realizing it, they begin to look for what is showy and artificial. You will have come across examples of this, as I have, as when for instance you remark on the beauty of some freshly cut roses, with delicately fragrant petals, and someone comments 'They look so perfect, they must be artificial!' "[20]

These words of the Founder of Opus Dei come to us with all the freshness of newly cut roses, yet they are the fruit of a whole lifetime spent in conversation with God and in carrying out an apostolate as vast as a "boundless ocean." Together with a great simplicity, there runs through all these writings the constant counterpoint of a passionate,

[20] *Human Virtues*, no. 89.

expansive love. We feel "our hearts profoundly shaken,"[21] urging us to "be in a hurry to fall in love,"[22] because "a whole lifetime would be little, to spend expanding the frontiers of your charity."[23]

And so we come to another of the great themes dealt with in his meditations: "the divine interlacing of the three theological virtues which form the backing upon which the true life of every Christian man or woman has to be woven."[24] He refers to this constantly: "let us live by faith; let us persevere with hope; let us remain very close to Jesus; let us really, really, really love him;"[25] "the certainty I derive from feeling—from knowing—that I am a son of God fills me with real hope;"[26] "the time has come, amid your ordinary occupations, to exercise your faith, awaken your hope, and revive your love."[27]

The three homilies on faith, hope, and charity are followed by one on prayer, although the need for us to have a close relationship with God in our lives is evident right from the very first pages. "Prayer ought to take root and grow in the soul little by

[21] *Towards Holiness*, no. 294.
[22] *In the Footsteps of Christ*, no. 140.
[23] *Time is a Treasure*, no. 43.
[24] *The Christian's Hope*, no. 205.
[25] *The Richness of Ordinary Life*, no. 22.
[26] *The Christian's Hope*, no. 208.
[27] *Working for God*, no. 71.

little,"[28] naturally, simply, and trustingly because we "children of God don't need a method, an artificial system, to talk with our Father."[29] Prayer is the thread of the fabric of the three theological virtues. All the things we do become one single thing: our whole life takes on a divine tone and our "union with our Lord does not cut us off from the world we live in. It does not make us strange beings, out of touch with what is going on around us."[30]

His precise and apt commentaries on Sacred Scripture and his frequent recourse to the treasury of Christian tradition are punctuated by expressions of love, breaking through like a river that has burst its banks. "How great is the love, the mercy of our Father! Whenever I think of his *divine extravagance* for us his children, I wish I had a thousand tongues, a thousand hearts and more, with which to be constantly praising God the Father, God the Son, and God the Holy Spirit."[31]

Why was his love so strong? Because God infused it in his heart, and also because he himself with his

[28] *Towards Holiness*, no. 295.
[29] *A Life of Prayer*, no. 255.
[30] *Ibid.*, no. 251.
[31] *Freedom, a Gift from God*, no. 33.

free will did all he could to make it grow and to pass it on to thousands of other souls. He loved and he wanted to love;* he wanted to respond to the graces that our Lord had placed in his soul. His love was so free that it became a passion: "I opt for God because I want to, freely, without compulsion of any kind. And I undertake to serve, to convert my whole life into a means of serving others, out of love for my Lord Jesus. It is this freedom which moves me to cry out that nothing on earth can separate me from the love of Christ."[32]

The path to sanctity which Monsignor Escrivá invites us to take, is paved with a deep respect for freedom. The Founder of Opus Dei relishes the words of St Augustine where the great Bishop of Hippo stresses that God "judged that his servants would be better if they served him freely."[33] This route to Heaven is, moreover, very appropriate for people leading ordinary lives in the midst of society, with a professional job of work to do, in environments which are sometimes indifferent or even hostile to the law of Christ. The Founder of Opus Dei is not addressing people who lead sheltered

* The author uses the two meanings ("to love" and "to want") of the Spanish word *querer*.

[32] *Ibid.*, no. 35.

[33] St Augustine, *De vera religione*, 14, 27 (PL 34, 134).

lives, but those who are fighting out in the open, in the most varied situations in life. In such circumstances, using their freedom, they come to the decision to serve God and love him above all things. Freedom is something they cannot do without. Through it, their love grows firm and develops roots: "People are not born holy. Holiness is forged through a constant interplay of God's grace and the correspondence of man."[34]

As a way of getting close to God, therefore, two passions are fostered: the passion of love and that of freedom. Their forces combine when freedom opts for the Love of God. The resulting torrent of graces, freely responded to, is so strong that it can withstand all difficulties: the *"psychological terrorism"*[35] which those who wish to be faithful to the Lord are subjected to; our own wretched failings which never disappear but which, through the freedom which repentance wins, can be converted into ways of reaffirming our love; the difficulties in our environment, which we can overcome by "sowing peace and joy around us."[36]

In the course of his comments on this divine and human interplay between freedom and love, there

[34] *The Richness of Ordinary Life,* no. 7.

[35] *Towards Holiness,* no. 298.

[36] *Humility,* no. 105.

are moments when one catches a glimpse of the sufferings which were a constant feature of Monsignor Escrivá's life. They were sufferings brought on by his love-sorrow for the lack of response on man's part to the mercy of God. When one met him, it was difficult to detect that he suffered. Few people have gone through life as cheerfully or as good humoredly as he, with his sense of youthfulness and his ability to get the most out of every instant. He felt nostalgia for nothing, except the Love of God. But he did really suffer. Many of his children who knew him at close quarters later commented to me: "How was our Father able to suffer so much? We always found him so happy, so attentive even to the smallest details, giving himself entirely to us all."

He has given us the answer, indirectly, in some of these homilies: "Do not forget that being with Jesus means we shall most certainly meet with his Cross. When we abandon ourselves into God's hands, he frequently permits us to taste sorrow, loneliness, opposition, slander, defamation, ridicule, coming both from within and from outside. This is because he wants to mold us into his image and likeness. He even tolerates that we be called lunatics and be taken for fools."[37]

[37] *Towards Holiness,* no. 301.

Because he had learned to embrace our Lord's Cross passionately, Monsignor Escrivá was able to say "my life has led me to realize in a special way that I am a son of God and I have experienced the joy of getting inside the heart of my Father, to rectify, to purify myself, to serve him, to understand others and find excuses for them, on the strength of his love and my own lowliness."[38] He was always docile to the inspirations of the Holy Spirit, in order that his own conduct might reflect the beautiful image of Christ. His faith was such that he took the Master's words quite literally, and he was often under attack from people who seemed unable to bear the thought that one can live by faith, with hope, and with love. "Perhaps someone will think I am naive. It doesn't worry me. Although I may be labelled as such, because I still believe in charity, I assure you I will believe in it, always! And, while God gives me life, I shall continue, as a priest of Jesus Christ, to work for unity and peace among those who are brothers, by the very fact that they are children of the same Father, God. I shall continue to work with the aim of getting men to understand each other, and to share the same ideal, the ideal of the Faith!"[39]

[38] *Getting to Know God,* no. 143.
[39] *Open to God and Men,* no. 174.

The passion of love and freedom and the conviction that we are meant to operate in the divine atmosphere of faith and hope, lead on to the apostolate. One of the homilies—*That All May Be Saved*—is entirely dedicated to the subject. "We find Jesus by the Lake of Genesareth, with the crowds pressing upon him, eager 'to hear the word of God' (Luke 5:1). Just as they do today! Can't you see? They want to hear God's message, even though outwardly they may not show it. Some perhaps have forgotten Christ's teachings. Others, through no fault of their own, have never known then and they think that religion is something odd. But of this we can be sure, that in every man's life there comes a time sooner or later when his soul draws the line. He has had enough of the usual explanations. The lies of the false prophets no longer satisfy him. Even though they may not admit it at the time, such people are longing to quench their thirst with the teachings of our Lord."[40]

A living spirit of apostolate, which is a passionate communication of God's impatient love for mankind, runs through every page of this book. Our task is to "bring peace, genuine peace, to souls" and to

[40] *That All May Be Saved*, no. 260.

"transform the earth."[41] To emphasize this Monsignor Escrivá constantly turns his attention to our Lord, who taught men to speak of everlasting happiness by treading our earthly paths with his divine footsteps. I cannot resist quoting a passage from *Towards Holiness*, in which the Founder of Opus Dei comments on a Gospel scene he loved so much, the one describing the apostolate that Jesus carried out on the road to Emmaus with the two disciples who seemed to have lost all hope.

"They were walking along at a normal pace, like so many other travellers on that road. And there, without any fuss, Jesus appears to them and walks with them, his conversation helping to alleviate their tiredness. I can well imagine the scene, just as dusk was falling. A gentle breeze was blowing. All around were fields ripe with wheat, and venerable olive trees, their branches shimmering in the soft glowing light."[42]

Christ is Passing By. The two men, when they saw that Jesus was making as if to continue on his journey, said to him, "Stay with us, it is towards evening, and it is far on in the day."[43] "That's just like us. Always short on daring, perhaps because we

[41] *Towards Holiness*, no. 294.
[42] *Ibid.*, no. 313.
[43] Lk 24:29.

are insincere, or because we feel embarrassed. Deep down, what we are really thinking is: 'Stay with us, because our souls are shrouded in darkness and you alone are the light. You alone can satisfy this longing which consumes us.' "[44]

This longing for God, which we all have within us, offers Christians daily opportunities for doing apostolate. We men are crying out for God, and we look for him even among doubting consciences and outlooks which are fixed on earthly things. "And Jesus stays. Our eyes are opened, as were those of Cleophas and his companion, when Christ breaks the bread; and though he vanishes once more from our sight, we too will find strength to start out once more—though night is falling—to tell the others about him, because so much joy cannot be kept in one heart alone."[45]

I go back with my memory to a day that is ever present for me, I never forget it, to that June 26, 1975, the day Monsignor Escrivá was born in a definitive way to the Love of God, because his heart by then needed an eternal Emmaus, where he could be forever close to Christ. In the homily, *Towards Holiness,* he had written, "A thirst for God is born in

[44] *Towards Holiness,* no. 314.
[45] *Ibid.*

us, a longing to understand his tears, to see his smile, his face. (...) The soul goes forward immersed in God, divinized: the Christian becomes a thirsty traveller who opens his mouth to the waters of the fountain."[46] Further on he says, "I love to speak of paths and ways, because we are travellers, journeying to our home in Heaven, our Father's land."[47]

He dwells there with the most Blessed Trinity; with Mary, the Holy Mother of God and our Mother; and with St Joseph, whom he loved so well. Many of us, all over the world, entrust our prayers to him, in the sure knowledge that God, our Lord, will listen favorably to someone who desired to be, and indeed was throughout his life on earth, a "good and faithful servant."[48]

The writings of the Founder of Opus Dei published to date, notably, *The Way, Holy Rosary, Christ is Passing By,* and *Conversations,* run to more than five million copies and they have been translated into more than thirty languages. This second volume of homilies is being published with the same purpose in mind: to help souls draw closer to God. The Church is going through difficult times and the Holy Father never tires of urging his children to pray, to

[46] *Ibid.,* no. 310.
[47] *Ibid.,* no. 313.
[48] Mt 25:21.

have a supernatural outlook, to be faithful to the sacred deposit of the Faith, to have brotherly understanding, and to promote peace. In these circumstances we cannot be disheartened; it is time to put into practice, even to the point of heroism, the virtues which define and express the true image of the Christians, of the children of God who strive that "our heads should indeed be touching Heaven, but our feet should be firmly on the ground,"[49] as we walk through the earthly city.

The life of the Christian who decides to behave in accordance with the greatness of his vocation is, so to speak, a prolonged echo of those words of our Lord, "I do not speak of you anymore as my servants; a servant is one who does not understand what his master is about, whereas I have made known to you all that my Father has told me; and so I have called you my friends."[50] When we decide to be docile and follow the Will of God, hitherto unimagined horizons open up before us. Monsignor Escrivá delights in emphasizing this beautiful paradox: "There is nothing better than recognizing that Love has made us slaves of God. From the moment

[49] *Human Virtues*, no. 75.
[50] Jn 15:15.

we recognize this, we cease being slaves and become friends, sons."[51]

Sons of God, *Friends of God*; this is the great truth that Monsignor Escrivá wanted to engrave on the hearts of those who knew him. His preaching is a constant effort to stop souls thinking of "friendship with God only as a last resort."[52] Jesus Christ is truly God and truly Man, he is our Brother and our Friend. If we make the effort to get to know him well, "we will share in the joy of being God's friends."[53] If we do all we can to keep him company, from Bethlehem to Calvary, sharing his joys and sufferings, we will become worthy of entering into loving conversation with him. As the Liturgy of the Hours sings, *calicem Domini biberunt, et amici Dei facti sunt* ("they drank the chalice of the Lord and so became friends of God").[54]

Being his children and being his friends are two inseparable realities for those who love God. We go to him as children, carrying on a trusting dialogue that should fill the whole of our lives; and we go

[51] *Freedom, a Gift from God*, no. 35.

[52] *A Life of Prayer*, no. 247.

[53] *Towards Holiness*, no. 300.

[54] Response to the second reading in the Office of the Dedication of the Basilicas of the Apostles, Sts Peter and Paul.

to him as friends, because "we Christians are in love with Love."[55] In the same way our divine sonship urges us to translate the overflow of our interior life into apostolic activity, just as our friendship with God leads us to place ourselves at "the service of all men. We are called to use the gifts God has given us as instruments to help others discover Christ."[56]

Those who see a rift between ordinary life, temporal affairs, the events of history on the one hand, and the Love of God on the other, are simply deceiving themselves. Our Lord is eternal; the world is of his own making, and he has put us here so that we may pass through it doing good, until we reach our final homeland. Everything is important in the life of a Christian because *everything can be an occasion for meeting our Lord* and can therefore acquire everlasting value. "Men lie when they say 'forever' about things on earth. The only true, totally true 'forever' is that which we say with reference to God. This is how you ought to live your life, with a faith that will help you to taste the honey, the sweetness of Heaven whenever you think about eternal life which is indeed 'forever.' "[57]

[55] *For They Shall See God*, no. 183.
[56] *That All May Be Saved*, no. 258.
[57] *Living by Faith*, no. 200.

Monsignor Escrivá now has direct knowledge of this sweetness and beauty of God. He has entered into eternity. His words, including those of the homilies in this volume, have now taken on an even greater force, if one can say this; they penetrate more deeply into our hearts and are more compelling. I shall finish with a quotation which can help to win us over to another of his dominant passions:

"Love the Church; serve the Church with the conscious gladness of one who has committed himself to this service for Love's sake. And if we should see any one travelling without hope, like the two men on the road to Emmaus, let us approach them full of faith—not in our own name but in Christ's name—to reassure them that Jesus' promises cannot fail, for he is always watching over his Spouse and he will never abandon her. The darkness will pass away, because we are children of the light (cf. Eph. 5:8) and have been called to life everlasting."[58]

Alvaro del Portillo

[58] *Towards Holiness*, no. 316.

THE RICHNESS OF ORDINARY LIFE*

I remember, many years ago now, I was 1
going along a road in Castile with some friends, when we noticed something in a field far away which made a deep impression on me at the time and has since often helped me in my prayer. A group of men were hammering some wooden stakes into the ground, which they then used to support netting to form a sheep pen. Then shepherds came along with their sheep and their lambs. They called them by their names and one by one lambs and sheep went into the pen, where they would be all together, safe and sound.

Today, Lord, my thoughts go back specially to those shepherds and their sheepfold, because

* A homily given on March 11, 1960.

all of us who are gathered here to converse with you—and many others the world over—we all know that we have been brought into your sheepfold. You yourself have told us so: "I am the Good Shepherd. I know my sheep and my sheep know me."[1] You know us well. You know that we wish to hear, to listen ever attentively to your gentle whistling as our Good Shepherd, and to heed it, because "eternal life is knowing you, who are the only true God, and Jesus Christ whom you have sent."[2]

The image of Christ with his sheep at his right and left means so much to me that I had it depicted in the oratory where I normally celebrate Holy Mass. Elsewhere, as a reminder of God's presence, I have had engraved Jesus' words, *cognosco oves meas et cognoscunt me meae*,[3] to help us consider constantly that he is at our side, reproaching us, instructing us, and teaching us as does a shepherd with his flock.[4] The Castilian scene I have recalled is very much to the point.

[1] Jn 10:14.
[2] *Ibid* 17:3.
[3] *Ibid* 10:14.
[4] Cf. Ecclus 18:13.

God wants us to be saints

You and I belong to Christ's family, for "he himself has chosen us before the foundation of the world, to be saints, to be blameless in his sight, for love of him, having predestined us to be his adopted children through Jesus Christ, according to the purpose of his will."[5] We have been chosen gratuitously by our Lord. His choice of us sets us a clear goal. Our goal is personal sanctity, as St Paul insistently reminds us, *haec est voluntas Dei: santificatio vestra* [6] ("this is the Will of God: your sanctification"). Let us not forget, then, that we are in our Master's sheepfold in order to achieve that goal. 2

Another thing I have never forgotten, though it took place a long time ago, was once when I had gone into the Cathedral in Valencia to pray and I passed by the tomb of the Venerable John Ridaura. I was told that whenever this priest, already very advanced in years, was asked how many years he had lived, he would reply with great conviction, in his Valencian dialect, *Poquets,* ("Very few! Only 3

[5] Eph 1:4-5.
[6] 1 Thess 4:3.

those I have spent serving God"). For many of you here, the fingers of one hand are still sufficient to count the years since you made up your minds to follow our Lord closely, to serve him in the midst of the world, in your own environment and through your own profession or occupation. How long is not all that important. What does matter is that we engrave, that we burn upon our souls the conviction that Christ's invitation to sanctity, which he addresses to all men without exception, puts each one of us under an obligation to cultivate our interior life and to struggle daily to practise the Christian virtues; and not just in any way whatsoever, nor in a way which is above average or even excellent. No; we must strive to the point of heroism, in the strictest and most exacting sense of the word.

4 The goal that I am putting before you, or rather that God has marked out for us all, is no illusory or unattainable ideal. I could quote you many specific examples of ordinary men and women, just like you and me, who have met Jesus passing by *quasi in occulto*,[7] ("hidden as it were"), at what appeared to be quite

[7] Jn 7:10.

ordinary crossroads in their lives, and have decided to follow him, lovingly embracing their daily cross.[8] In this age of ours, an age of generalized decay, of compromise and discouragement, and also of license and anarchy, I think it is more important than ever to hold on to that simple yet profound conviction which I had when I began my priestly work and have held ever since, and which has given me a burning desire to tell all mankind that "these world crises are crises of saints."

Interior life. We need it, if we are to answer 5
the call that the Master has made to each and everyone of us. We have to become saints, as they say in my part of the world, "down to the last whisker,"* Christians who are truly and genuinely such, the kind that could be canonized. If not, we shall have failed as disciples of the one and only Master. And don't forget that when God marks us out and gives us his grace to strive for sanctity in the everyday world, he also puts us under an obligation to do apostolate. I want you to realize that, even looking

[8] Cf. Mt 16:24.

* *Sin que nos falte un pelo*, that is "down to our finger tips" or "every inch of us" (Translator's note).

at things humanly, concern for souls follows naturally from the fact that God has chosen us. As one of the Fathers of the Church points out, "When you discover that something has been of benefit to you, you want to tell others about it. In the same way, you should want others to accompany you along the ways of the Lord. If you are going to the forum or the baths and you run into someone with time on his hands, you invite him to go with you. Apply this human behavior to the spiritual realm and, when you go towards God, do not go alone."[9]

If we do not wish to waste our time in useless activities, or in making excuses about the difficulties in our environment—for there have always been difficulties ever since Christianity began—we must remember that Christ has decreed that success in attracting our fellowmen will depend, as a rule, on how much interior life we ourselves have. Christ has stipulated that our apostolic endeavors will only be effective if we are saints; rather (let me put it more correctly) if we strive to be faithful, for while we are on this earth we shall never

[9] St Gregory, the Great, *Homiliae in Evangelia*, 6, 6 (PL 76, 1098).

actually be saints. It may seem hard to believe, but both God and our fellowmen require from us an unswerving faithfulness that is true to its name and is consequent down to the last detail, with no half measures or compromises, a faithfulness to the fullness of the Christian vocation which we lovingly accept and caringly practise.

Some of you might think I am referring only **6**
to a select few. Don't let the promptings of cowardice or easygoing ways deceive you so easily. Feel, instead, God urging each one of you on, to become another Christ, *ipse Christus*, ("Christ himself"). To put it simply, God is urging us to make our actions consistent with the demands of our faith. For our sanctity, the holiness we should be striving for is not a second-class sanctity. There is no such thing. The main thing we are asked to do, which is so much in keeping with our nature, is to love: "charity is the bond of perfection;"[10] a charity that is to be practised exactly as our Lord himself commands: "Thou shalt love the Lord thy God, with thy whole heart, and with thy whole soul, and with thy whole mind,"[11]

[10] Col 3:14.
[11] Mt 22:37.

holding back nothing for ourselves. This is what sanctity is all about.

7 Certainly our goal is both lofty and difficult to attain. But please do not forget that people are not born holy. Holiness is forged through a constant interplay of God's grace and the correspondence of man. As one of the early Christian writers says, referring to union with God, "Everything that grows begins small. It is by constant and progressive feeding that it gradually grows big."[12] So I say to you, if you want to become a thorough-going Christian—and I know you are willing, even though you often find it difficult to conquer yourself or to keep climbing upwards with this poor body of ours—then you will have to be very attentive to the minutest of details, for the holiness that our Lord demands of you is to be achieved by carrying out with love of God your work and your daily duties, and these will almost always consist of small realities.

[12] St Mark the Hermit, *De lege spirituali*, 172 (PG 65, 926).

Little things and the life of childhood

Thinking of those of you who, despite years 8
of experience, still go about dreaming—with vain and childish dreams, like those of Tartarin of Tarascon—imagining they are hunting lions in the corridors of their homes, where the most they will find are mice, if that; with, I insist, such people in mind, I can only remind you how great a thing it is to be accompanying God through the faithful fulfillment of your ordinary daily duties, coming through struggles which fill our Lord with joy, and which are known only to him and to each one of us.

Rest assured that you will usually find few opportunities for dazzling deeds, one reason being that they seldom occur. On the other hand, you will not lack opportunities, in the small and ordinary things around you, of showing your love for Christ. As St Jerome writes, "Even in small things, the same (greatness of) spirit is revealed. We admire the Creator, not only as the framer of Heaven and earth, of sun and ocean, of elephants, camels, horses, oxen, leopards, bears, and lions, but also as the maker of tiny creatures, ants, gnats, flies, worms, and the like, things whose shapes we know better than their names: and in all of them (big or small) we reverence the same skill. So too, the person who is dedicated to Christ is equally earnest in small things as in great."[13]

9 When we meditate on the words of our Lord, "And for them do I sanctify myself, that they also may be sanctified in truth,"[14] we clearly perceive our one and only end: sanctification, or rather, that we have to become saints in order to sanctify others. Then, like a subtle temptation, the thought may come that there are very few of us who have really taken to heart this divine invitation. Moreover, we see that those of us who have, are instruments of very little worth. It is true; we are few, in comparison with the rest of mankind, and of ourselves we are worth nothing. But our Master's affirmation resounds with full authority: Christians are the light, the salt, the leaven of the world and "a little leaven leavens the whole batch."[15] That is precisely why I have always taught that we are interested in each and every person. Out of a hundred souls we are interested in a hundred. We discriminate

[13] St Jerome, *Epistolae*, 60, 12 (PL 22, 596).
[14] Jn 17:19.
[15] Gal 5:9.

against no one, for we know for certain that Jesus has redeemed us all, and that he wishes to make use of a few of us, despite our personal nothingness, to make his salvation known to all.

A disciple of Christ will never treat anyone badly. Error he will call error, but the person in error he will correct with kindliness. Otherwise he will not be able to help him, to sanctify him. We must learn to live together, to understand one another, to make allowances, to be brotherly and, at all times, in the words of St John of the Cross, "where there is no love, put love and you will find love;"[16] and we have to do this even in the apparently uninspiring circumstances that arise in our professional work or in our domestic and social life. You and I must, therefore, seek to make use of even the most trifling opportunities that come our way, to sanctify them, to sanctify ourselves, and to sanctify those who share with us the same daily cares, sensing in our lives the sweet and inspiring burden of the work of co-redemption.

I wish to continue this conversation with our **10**
Lord with an observation I made use of years

[16] Cf. St John of the Cross, *Letter to María de la Encarnacion*, 6-VII-1591.

ago, but which is just as relevant today. I had noted down some remarks of St Teresa of Avila: "All that passes away and is not pleasing to God, is worth nothing, and less than nothing."[17] Now do you understand why a soul loses all sense of peace and serenity when it turns away from its goal, and forgets that it was created by God to be a saint? Strive never to lose this supernatural outlook, not even at times of rest or recreation, which are as important in our daily lives as is work itself.

You can climb to the top of your profession, you can gain the highest acclaim as a reward for your freely chosen endeavors in temporal affairs; but if you abandon the supernatural outlook that should inspire all our human activities, you will have gone sadly astray.

11 Allow me a short digression. In fact it is very relevant to what we have been saying. I have never asked anyone who has come to me, about his politics. I am just not interested! My attitude here demonstrates a fundamental fact about Opus Dei, to which by the grace and mercy of God I have dedicated myself completely, in order to serve our holy Church. I am not

[17] St Teresa of Avila, *Life*, 20, 26.

interested in the subject because, as Christians, you enjoy the fullest freedom, with the consequent personal responsibility, to take part as you see fit in political, social, or cultural affairs, with no restrictions other than those set by the Church's Magisterium. The only thing that would worry me, for the good of your souls, would be if you were to overstep these limits, for then you would have created a clear opposition between your actions and the faith you claim to profess, and in that case I would tell you so, clearly. This holy respect for your opinions, so long as they do not lead you away from the law of God, is not understood by those who are unaware of the real meaning of the freedom which Christ won for us on the Cross. *Qua libertate Christus nos liberavit*[18] ("Such is the freedom Christ has won for us") by the sectarians at either extreme: those who seek to impose their temporal opinions as dogmas; or those who degrade man, by denying the value of the faith and putting it at the mercy of the grossest errors.

But to return to our subject. I was saying just **12**
now that though you might achieve spectacular

[18] Gal 4:31.

success in society, in public affairs, in our own careers, if you neglect your spiritual life and ignore our Lord, you will end up a complete failure. As far as God is concerned—and in the last analysis that is the only thing that matters—victory only comes to those who strive to behave as genuine Christians. There is no middle way. That is why you find so many people who from a human point of view ought to be ever so happy, yet they go about uneasy and embittered. They appear to be overflowing with happiness, but just scratch beneath the surface of their souls and you will discover a bitterness more bitter than gall. This will not happen to us, provided we really try, day in day out, to do God's will, to give him glory, and praise him and spread his kingdom to all mankind.

Genuinely Christian lives

13 It makes me very sad to see a Catholic—a child of God, called by Baptism to be another Christ—calming his conscience with a purely formal piety, with a *religiosity* that leads him to pray now and again, and only if he thinks

it worthwhile! He goes to Mass on holy days of obligation—though not all of them—while he cares punctiliously for the welfare of his stomach and never misses a meal. He is ready to compromise in matters of faith, to exchange his faith for a platter of lentils, rather than give up his job...And then he impudently or scandalously seeks to climb up in the world on the strength of being a Christian. No! Let us not live on labels. I want you to be genuine, solid Christians; and to become such you will have to be unswerving in your search for suitable spiritual food.

Personal experience shows, and you have often heard me tell you so, to warn you against discouragement, that our interior life consists in beginning again and again each day; and you know in your hearts, as I do in mine, that the struggle is never ending. You will have noticed too, when making your examination of conscience just as I do (excuse these personal references, but even as I am speaking to you I am going over the needs of my own soul with our Lord) that you often experience little setbacks, which at times perhaps may seem to you enormous, revealing as they do an evident lack of love, of self-surrender to God, of a spirit of sacrifice, of refinement. Well, strengthen your yearning for reparation, with a sincere act of contrition, but please do not lose your peace of mind.

14 Way back, in the early forties, I used to go quite often to Valencia. I had no human means at the time and, with those who were gathered around this penniless priest, as you are now, I would pray wherever we could, some afternoons on a deserted beach. Just like the first friends of the Master, remember? St Luke writes how, when St Paul and he were leaving Tyre on their way to Jerusalem, "they all of them, with their wives and children, escorted us until we were out of the city; and there on the beach we knelt down and prayed."[19]

Well, late one afternoon, during one of those marvellous Valencian sunsets, we saw a boat approaching the shore. Some men jumped out, swarthy looking and strong as granite, dripping wet, stripped to the waist, so weather-burned that they might have been made of bronze. They began to haul in the net that trailed behind the boat. It was laden with fishes, all shining like silver. Their feet sank into the sand

[19] Acts 21:5.

as they pulled away with amazing strength. Then all of a sudden a little boy appeared, all sunburnt too. He came up to the rope, seized it with his tiny hands and began to tug away with evident clumsiness. The tough, unsophisticated fishermen must have felt their hearts soften, for they allowed the child to join in, without chasing him away, even though he was more of a hindrance than a help.

I thought of you and of myself. Of you, whom I did not know as yet, and of myself; of our daily tugging away at the rope, and of many things. If we come before God our Lord like that child, convinced of our weakness yet ever prepared to second his plans, we shall more easily reach our goal. We shall haul the net onto the shore, bursting with an abundant catch, for the power of God reaches where our strength cannot.

Sincerity in spiritual direction

You well know the obligations of your **15**
Christian way of life; they will lead you safely and surely to sanctity. You have also been forewarned about the difficulties, or practically

all of them, because you can already get a rough idea of them at the beginning of the road. Now I wish to emphasize that you must let yourselves be helped and guided by a spiritual director, to whom you can confide all your holy ambitions and the daily problems affecting your interior life, the failures you may suffer, and the victories.

Always be sincere in spiritual direction. Don't make allowances for yourselves without checking beforehand; open up your souls completely, without fear or shame. Otherwise this smooth and straight road will become tortuous, and what at first was trivial will end up strangling you like a noose. "Do not imagine that those who are lost fall victims of a sudden failure. No, each went astray at the outset or neglected his soul for a long spell, so that the firmness of his virtues was gradually undermined while his vices grew little by little, and so he came to a wretched downfall...A house does not fall down suddenly by some unforeseen accident. There was either something wrong with its very foundations, or the neglect of those dwelling in it was so prolonged that what at first were tiny defects ended up corroding the firmness of the structure, and so when storms came or torrential rains fell, the house tumbled inevitably and in so doing brought to light the years of neglect."[20]

Do you remember the story of the gypsy who went to confession? It is only a story, a joke, because we never talk about confession and, besides, I have a very high opinion of gypsies. Poor fellow! He was very sorry for what he had done. "Father," he said, "I have stolen a halter." Nothing much to worry about there, is there? "And with it there was a mule...and then, another halter...and, another mule." And so on, up to twenty. My children, it is the same with us. Once we give in and steal the halter, the rest follows, a whole string of evil inclinations, bringing wretchedness, degradation, and shame. Something similar can happen in our dealings with others: at first there is a small, cutting remark, and in the end people can end up cold shouldering each other, and living in an atmosphere of icy indifference.

"Catch the foxes, the little foxes, that spoil **16**
our vineyards, our vineyards in bloom."[21] Be faithful, very faithful, in all the little things. If

[20] Cassian, *Collationes*, 6, 17 (PL 49, 667-668).
[21] Cant 2:15.

we try to live thus, we shall also learn to run trustingly into the arms of Mary, as children of hers. Did I not remind you, at the beginning, that we are all really very young, only as old as the years we have lived since we decided to come very close to God? That being so, it is understandable that our wretchedness and littleness should find strength in the greatness and holy purity of the Mother of God, who is also our Mother.

There is another story, a true one, which I can tell you since it took place many, many years ago; and because the expression used is so startling that it will help you reflect. I was giving a retreat at the time, to priests from several dioceses. I invited them, in a friendly way because I wanted to help, to come and have a talk and unburden their consciences, because we priests too need brotherly help and advice. I began to speak to one of them. He was somewhat rough in manner, but a worthy and honest man. I tried to draw him out a bit, gently but firmly, so as to heal any wound there might be inside his heart. All at once he interrupted me, more or less with these words: "I'm very envious of my donkey. It's been working in seven parishes and you can't say a thing against it. If only the same could be said of me!"

Examine your conscience sincerely: perhaps 17
neither you nor I deserve the praise that country priest had for his donkey. We have worked so hard, held responsible positions, you have won success in men's eyes in such and such a job...But, in God's presence, is there nothing you regret? Have you truly tried to serve God and your fellowmen? Or have you pursued your own selfish plans, your personal glory, your own ambitions, seeking a purely earthly success that will dwindle pitifully into nothingness?

If I am speaking to you somewhat bluntly, it is because I myself want once again to make a very sincere act of contrition, and I would like each one of you to do the same. As we call to mind our infidelities, and so many mistakes, weaknesses, so much cowardice—each one of us has his own experience—let us repeat to our Lord, from the bottom of our hearts, Peter's cry of contrition, *Domine, tu omnia nosti, tu scis quia amo te*[22] ("Lord, you know all things, you know that I love you, despite my wretchedness")!

[22] Jn 21:17.

And I would even add, "You know that I love you, precisely because of my wretchedness, for it leads me to rely on you who are my strength:" *quia tu es, Deus, fortitudo mea.*[23] And at that point let us start again.

Seeking God's presence

18 Interior life. Sanctity in our ordinary tasks, sanctity in the little things we do, sanctity in our professional work, in our daily cares...; sanctity, so that we may sanctify others. A friend of mine was dreaming once. (He is someone I've never really managed to get to know!) He was flying very high, but he was not inside the plane, in the cabin. He was outside, on the wings. Poor soul, how he suffered! What anguish! It was as if our Lord was showing him that just such insecurity and danger faces apostolic souls who would fly up to the heights of God, but have no interior life, or else neglect it. They are full of anxiety and doubt, and in constant danger of coming to grief.

[23] Ps 42:2.

I really do believe that a serious danger of losing the way threatens those who launch out into action—activism—while neglecting prayer, self-denial, and those means without which it is impossible to achieve a solid piety: receiving the sacraments frequently, meditation, examination of conscience, spiritual reading, and constant recourse to our Lady and the Guardian Angels...Besides, all these means contribute in a way that nothing else can, to making the Christian's daily life a joyful one, for, from their hidden riches, flow out the sweetness and joy of God, like honey from the comb.

In our inner life, in our external behavior, **19**
in our dealings with others, in our work, each of us must try to maintain a constant presence of God, conversing with him, carrying on a dialogue in a way that does not show outwardly. Or, rather, which as a rule does not express itself in audible words, but which certainly should show itself in the determination and loving care we put into carrying out all our duties, both great and small. Without such perseverance, our behavior would hardly be consistent with our status as children of God, for we would have wasted the resources which

our Lord in his goodness has placed within our reach, in order that we may come to "perfect manhood, unto the measure of the fullness of Christ."[24]

During the civil war in Spain I travelled a lot to offer priestly care to many young men at the front. In a trench one day near Teruel, I heard a conversation which I have never forgotten. A young soldier was saying of one of the others, apparently a somewhat indecisive and weakwilled person, that he wasn't *all of a piece!* I should be very sad if it could seriously be said of any of us that we are inconsistent: people who claim to be striving to be genuine Christians, saints, yet despise the means of becoming such, because when they carry out their duties they fail to show God the constant affection and love that he deserves from his children. If our behavior could be so described, then neither you nor I would be Christians who are *all of a piece.*

20 Let us try to foster deep down in our hearts a burning desire, an intense eagerness to achieve sanctity, even though we see ourselves full of failings. Do not be afraid: the more one

[24] Eph 4:13.

advances in the interior life, the more clearly one sees one's own faults. Grace works in us like a magnifying glass, and even the tiniest speck of dust or an almost invisible grain of sand can appear immensely large, for the soul acquires a divine sensitivity, and even the slightest shadow irritates one's conscience, which finds delight only in the limpid clarity of God. Speak now from the bottom of your heart: "Lord, I really do want to be a saint. I really do want to be a worthy disciple of yours and to follow you unconditionally." And now you should make a resolution to renew each day the great ideals which inspire you at this moment.

Oh, Jesus, if only we who are united in your Love were truly persevering! If only we could translate into deeds the yearnings you yourself awaken in our souls! Ask yourselves often, "What am I here on earth for?" It will help you in your efforts to finish all your daily tasks perfectly and lovingly, taking care of the little details. Let us turn to the example of the saints. They were people like us, of flesh and bone, with failings and weaknesses, who managed to conquer and master themselves for love of God. Let us consider their lives and, like bees who distill precious nectar from each flower, we shall learn from their struggles. You and I shall also learn to discover so many virtues in the people about us, who teach us by their hard work, their self-denial, their joy, and we shall not dwell too much on their defects; only when it is absolutely necessary, in order to help them with fraternal correction.

In Christ's boat

21 Like our Lord, I too am fond of talking about fishing boats and nets, so that we may all draw clear and decisive resolutions from the Gospel scenes. St Luke tells us of some fishermen washing and mending their nets by the shores of Lake Genesareth. Jesus comes up to the boats tied up alongside and goes into one of them, which is Simon's. How naturally the Master comes aboard our own boat! "Just to complicate our lives," you hear some people complain. You and I know better, we know that our Lord has crossed our paths to *complicate* our existence with gentleness and love.

When he has finished preaching from Peter's boat, he says to the fishermen, *duc in altum et laxate retia vestra in capturam*[25] ("launch out into the deep and let down your nets for a catch")! Trusting in Christ's word, they obey and haul in a wonderful catch. Then turning to Peter who, like James and John, cannot hide his astonishment, the Lord explains, "Fear not; henceforth you shall be fishers of men. And having brought their boats to land, leaving all things, they followed him."[26]

Your boat—your talents, your hopes, your achievements—is worth nothing whatsoever, unless you leave it in Christ's hands, allowing him the freedom to come aboard. Make sure you don't turn it into an idol. In your boat by yourself, if you try to do without the Master, you are—supernaturally speaking—making straight for shipwreck. Only if you allow, and seek, his presence and captaincy, will you be safe from the storms and setbacks of life. Place everything in God's hands. Let your thoughts, the brave adventures you have imagined, your lofty human ambitions, your noble loves, pass through the heart of Christ. Otherwise, sooner or later, they will all sink to the bottom together with your selfishness.

[25] Lk 5:4.
[26] *Ibid* 5:10-11.

22 If you agree to let God take command of your boat, if you let him be the master, how safe you will be!...even when he seems to have gone away, to have fallen asleep, to be unconcerned; even though a storm is rising and it's pitch dark all around you. St Mark tells us how once the apostles were in just such circumstances and Jesus "when the night had reached its fourth quarter, seeing them hard put to it with rowing (for the wind was against them), came to them walking on the sea...'Take courage,' he said, 'it is myself; do not be afraid.' So he came to them on board the boat, and thereupon the wind dropped."[27]

My children, so many things happen to us here on earth!...I could tell you so many tales of sorrow, of suffering, of ill treatment, of martyrdom—and I mean it literally—of the heroism of many souls. In our mind's eye we sometimes get the impression that Jesus is asleep, that he does not hear us. But St Luke describes how the Lord looks after his own. "When they (the disciples), were sailing, he slept. And there came down a storm of wind upon the lake and they began to ship water

[27] Mk 6:48, 50-51.

perilously. They came and awakened him saying, 'Master, we perish!' But Jesus arising, rebuked the wind and the rage of the water. And it ceased and there was a calm. And he said to them, 'Where is your faith?' "[28]

If we give ourselves to him, he will give himself to us. We must trust the Master completely, place ourselves unreservedly in his hands; show him by our actions that the boat is his; that we want him to do as he pleases with all we possess.

Let me finish with these resolutions, asking our Lady to intercede for us: let us live by faith; let us persevere with hope; let us remain very close to Jesus; let us really, really, really love him; let us live out and enjoy our adventure of Love, for we are in love, in love with God; let us allow Christ to come aboard our poor boat, and take possession of our souls as Lord and Master; let us show him sincerely that we are going to try to live in his presence always, day and night, for he has called us to the faith: *ecce ego quia vocasti me!*[29] We are coming into his fold, drawn there by his call, his gentle

[28] Lk 8:23-25.
[29] 1 Kings 3:9.

whistle as our Good Shepherd, certain that only in its shelter will we find true happiness both here and in eternity.

FREEDOM, A GIFT FROM GOD*

I have often reminded you of that moving scene in the Gospel where Jesus is in Peter's boat, from which he has been speaking to the people. The multitude following him has stirred the eagerness for souls which consumes his heart, and now the Divine Master wants his disciples to share his zeal. After telling them to launch out into the deep, *duc in altum,*[1] he suggests to Peter that he let down his nets for a catch. 23

I am not going to linger now over the details of what happened, although there is much to be learned from them. What I would like you to consider with me is how the Prince of the

* A homily given on April 10, 1956.
[1] Lk 5:4.

Apostles reacts to the miracle he has just seen: " 'Lord, depart from me,' he says, 'for I am a sinful man.' "[2] This is true and I am quite sure it applies perfectly to the personal situation of each one of us. Nevertheless, I assure you that having witnessed during my life so many marvellous works of divine grace performed through human hands, I feel moved, and more so each day, to shout out, "Lord, do not depart from me, for without you I can do no good at all."

Precisely because of this, I readily understand those words of St Augustine, Bishop of Hippo, which ring out like a wonderful hymn to freedom, "God, who created you without you, will not save you without you."[3] Every single one of us, you and I as well, always has the possibility, the unfortunate possibility of rising up against God, of rejecting him (perhaps by our behavior) or of crying out, "we do not want this man to rule over us."[4]

[2] *Ibid* 5:8.
[3] St Augustine, *Sermo* CLXIX, 13 (PL 38, 923).
[4] Lk 19:14.

Choosing life

We have learned with gratitude, because it makes us realize the happiness we are being called to, that all creatures have been created out of nothing by God and for God: both men, who are rational creatures, although we so often act unreasonably, and the irrational beings who roam the surface of the earth, or burrow in its inmost recesses, or sail the azure skies—some soaring so high that they come face to face with the sun. But in all this wonderful variety, it is only we men (I am not referring now to the angels) who can unite ourselves to the Creator by using our freedom. We are in a position to give him, or deny him, the glory that is his due as the Author of everything that exists. 24

This possibility makes up the light and shade of human freedom. Our Lord invites us, urges us to choose the good, so tenderly does he love us! "See, today I set before you a choice between life and death, good and evil. If you pay heed to the commandments of Yahweh your God which I command you this day, by loving Yahweh your God, by walking in his ways, and by keeping his commandments and his statutes and his ordinances, then you shall live...Choose life, that you may live."[5]

Ask yourself now (I too am examining my conscience) whether you are holding firmly and unshakably to your choice of Life? When you hear the most lovable voice of God urging you on to holiness, do you freely answer "Yes?" Let us turn our gaze once more to Jesus, as he speaks to the people in the towns and countryside of Palestine. He doesn't want to force himself upon us. "If you have a mind to be perfect...,"[6] he says to the rich young man. The young man refused to take the hint, and the Gospel goes on to say: *abiit tristis*[7] ("he went away forlorn"). That is why I have sometimes called him the "sad lad." He lost his happiness because he refused to hand over his freedom to God.

25 Consider now the sublime moment when the Archangel Gabriel announces to the Virgin Mary the plans of the Most High. Our Mother listens, and asks a question to understand better what the Lord is asking of her. Then she gives

[5] Dt 30:15-16, 19.
[6] Mt 19:21.
[7] Mt 19:22.

her firm reply: *Fiat!*[8] ("Be it done unto me according to thy word")! This is the fruit of the best freedom of all, the freedom of deciding in favor of God.

This hymn to freedom is echoed in all the mysteries of our Catholic faith. The Blessed Trinity draws the world and man out of nothing, in a free outpouring of love. The Word comes down from Heaven and takes on our flesh, an act which bears the splendid mark of freedom in submission: "Behold I have come to do thy Will, O God, as it is written of me in the scroll of the book."[9] When God's appointed time comes to save mankind from the slavery of sin, we contemplate Jesus Christ in Gethsemani, suffering in agony to the point of sweating blood.[10] He spontaneously and unconditionally accepts the sacrifice which the Father is asking of him: "Like a lamb that is led to the slaughter, like a sheep standing dumb before its shearers."[11] He had already told his disciples that this was to happen, in one of those conversations where he would pour out his

[8] Lk 1:38.
[9] Heb 10:7.
[10] Cf. Lk 22:44.
[11] Is 53:7.

heart so that those who love him might know that he is the Way, the only way, to approach the Father. "This is why my Father loves me, because I am laying down my life to take it up again afterwards. Nobody can rob me of it; I lay it down of my own accord. I am free to lay it down and free to take it up again."[12]

The meaning of freedom

26 We will never fully understand Jesus' freedom. It is immense, infinite, as is his love. But the priceless treasure of his generous holocaust should move us to ask, "Why, my Lord, have you granted me this privilege which I can use to follow in your footsteps, but also to offend you?" Thus, we come to appreciate that freedom is used properly when it is directed towards the good; and that it is misused when men are forgetful and turn away from the Love of loves. Personal freedom, which I defend and will always defend with all my strength, leads me to ask with deep conviction, though I am well aware of my own weakness: "What do you want from me, Lord, so that I may freely do it?"

[12] Jn 10:17-18.

Christ himself gives us the answer: *veritas liberabit vos*[13] ("the truth will set you free"). How great a truth is this, which opens the way to freedom and gives it meaning throughout our lives. I will sum it up for you, with the joy and certainty which flow from knowing there is a close relationship between God and his creatures. It is the knowledge that we have come from the hands of God, that the Blessed Trinity looks upon us with predilection, that we are children of so wonderful a Father. I ask my Lord to help us decide to take this truth to heart, to dwell upon it day by day; only then will we be acting as free men. Do not forget: anyone who does not realize that he is a child of God is unaware of the deepest truth about himself. When he acts he lacks the dominion and self-mastery we find in those who love our Lord above all else.

Convince yourselves that to get to Heaven we must commit ourselves freely, with a wholehearted, constant, and voluntary determination. By itself, however, freedom is insufficient: it needs a guide, a pole-star. "The soul cannot proceed without someone to guide it; this is

[13] *Ibid* 8:32.

why it has been redeemed in order that it may have as its King, Christ, whose yoke is easy and whose burden is light (Matt 11:30), and not the devil, whose rule is oppressive."[14]

Reject the deception of those who appease themselves with the pathetic cry of "Freedom! Freedom!" Their cry often masks a tragic enslavement, because choices that prefer error do not liberate. Christ alone sets us free,[15] for he alone is the Way, the Truth, and the Life.[16]

27 Let us ask ourselves once again, here in the presence of God: "Lord, why have you given us this power? Why have you entrusted us with the faculty of choosing you or rejecting you? You want us to make good use of this power. Lord, what do you want me to do?"[17] His reply is precise, crystal-clear: "Thou shalt love the Lord thy God with thy whole heart and with thy whole soul and with thy whole mind."[18]

Don't you see? Freedom finds its true meaning when it is put to the service of the

[14] Origen, *Commentarii in Epistolam ad Romanos*, 5, 6 (PG 14, 1034-1035).

[15] Cf. Gal 4:31.

[16] Cf. Jn 14:6.

[17] Cf. Acts 9:6.

[18] Mt 22:37.

truth which redeems, when it is spent in seeking God's infinite Love which liberates us from all forms of slavery. Each passing day increases my yearning to proclaim to the four winds this inexhaustible treasure that belongs to Christianity: "the glorious freedom of the children of God!"[19] This is essentially what is meant by a "goodwill," which teaches us to pursue "good, after having distinguished it from evil."[20]

I would like you to meditate on a fundamental point, which brings home to us the responsibility we have for our own consciences. Nobody else can choose for us: "men's supreme dignity lies in this, that they are directed towards the good by themselves, and not by others."[21] Many of us have inherited the Catholic faith from our parents, and, by the grace of God, supernatural life began in our souls from the moment we were baptized as newborn infants. But we must renew throughout our lives, and every day of our lives, our determi-

[19] Rom 8:21.

[20] St Maximus the Confessor, *Capita de caritate*, 2, 32 (PG 90, 995).

[21] St Thomas Aquinas, *Super Epistolas S. Pauli lectura, Ad Romanos*, cap II, lect III, 217 (Marietti, Turin 1953).

nation to love God above all things. "He is a Christian, a true Christian, who subjects himself to the rule of the one and only Word of God,"[22] without laying down conditions to his obedience, and being ever ready to resist the devil's temptings by adopting the same attitude as Christ did: "Thou shalt worship the Lord thy God, and serve none but him."[23]

Freedom and self-surrender

28 God's love is a jealous love. He is not satisfied if we come to meet him with conditions. He longs for us to give ourselves completely, without keeping dark corners in our heart, where the joy and happiness of grace and the supernatural gifts cannot reach. Perhaps you are thinking, "if I say 'yes' to this exclusive Love might I not lose my freedom?"

Aided and enlightened by our Lord, who is presiding over us in this period of prayer, I trust that this question will become clearer for you and me. Each one of us has at some time or other experienced that serving Christ our

[22] Origen, *Contra Celsum*, 8, 36 (PG 11, 1571).
[23] Mt 4:10.

Lord involves suffering and hardships; to deny this would imply that we had not yet found God. A soul in love knows however that when such suffering comes, it is only a fleeting impression; the soul soon finds that the yoke is easy and the burden light, because Jesus is carrying it upon his shoulders as he embraced the wood of the Cross when our eternal happiness was at stake.[24] But there are people who do not understand. They rebel against the Creator, in a sad, petty, impotent rebellion, and they blindly repeat the futile complaint recorded in the Psalms, "let us break away from their bondage, rid ourselves of their toils."[25] They shrink from the hardship of fulfilling their daily task with heroic silence and naturalness, without show or complaint. They have not realized that even when God's Will seems painful and its demands wounding, it coincides perfectly with our freedom, which is only to be found in God and in his plans.

Such people barricade themselves behind **29**
their freedom. "My freedom! My freedom!" they cry. They have their freedom, but they

[24] Cf. *Ibid* 11:30.
[25] Ps 2:3.

don't use it. They look at it, they set it up, a clay idol for their petty minds to worship. Is this freedom? What use is this treasure to them, if there is no commitment guiding their whole lives? Such behavior goes against their very dignity and nobility as human beings. They are left aimless, with no clear path to guide their footsteps on this earth. You and I have met such people. They then let themselves be carried away by childish vanity, by selfish conceit, by sensuality.

Their freedom turns out to be barren, or produces fruits which even humanly speaking are ridiculous. A person who does not choose, with complete freedom, an upright code of conduct, sooner or later ends up being manipulated by others. He will lead a lazy, parasitic existence, at the mercy of what others decide. He will let himself be blown to and fro by any wind whatsoever, and it will always be others who make up his mind for him. "These are waterless clouds, carried hither and thither by the winds, autumn trees that bear no fruit, doubly dead and rootless,"[26] even though they may try to disguise their lack of character,

[26] Jude 12.

courage, and honesty behind a smokescreen of constant chatter and excuses.

"No one is forcing me!" they obstinately repeat. No one? Everyone is coercing his make-believe freedom which will not run the risk of accepting responsibility for the consequences of his own free actions. Where there is no love of God, the individual and responsible use of personal freedom becomes impossible. There, despite appearances to the contrary, the individual is coerced at every turn. The indecisive and irresolute person is like plasticine at the mercy of circumstances. Anyone and anything can mold him according to its whim, and especially his passions and the worst tendencies of his own nature wounded by sin.

Remember the parable of the talents. The **30**
servant who received one talent could have put it to good use, as his fellow servants did. He would have set to work with his own abilities. He could have made sure that his talent bore fruit. Instead, what is on his mind? He is worried about losing his talent. Fair enough. But, then? He goes and buries it![27] The talent he received bears no fruit.

[27] Cf. Mt 25:18.

Let us not forget this man's sickly fear of putting to honest use his capacity for work, his mind, his will, *his whole being*. "I'll bury it," the poor fellow seems to be saying, "but my freedom is safe!" Not so. He has turned his freedom towards something very definite, towards the most miserable and arid barrenness. He has taken sides, because he had no alternative. He had to choose, but he has chosen badly.

It is utterly false to oppose freedom and self-surrender, because self-surrender is a consequence of freedom. Look, when a mother sacrifices herself for love of her children, she has made a choice, and the more she loves the greater will be her freedom. If her love is great, her freedom will bear much fruit. Her children's good derives from her blessed freedom, which presupposes self-surrender, and from her blessed self-surrender, which is precisely freedom.

31 But, you might say, when we have attained our heart's desire, our search will be over. Does freedom vanish then? I assure you that it will then be more active than ever, because love is not content with a routine fulfillment of duty. Love is incompatible with boredom or apathy.

To love means to renew our dedication every day, with loving deeds of service.

I insist, and I would like to engrave this deep in your hearts, that freedom and self-surrender are not contradictory. They sustain one another. Freedom can only be given up for love; I cannot conceive any other reason for surrendering it. And I am not just playing with words or phrases. When people give themselves freely, at every moment of their self-surrender, freedom renews their love; to be renewed in that way is to be always young, generous, capable of high ideals and great sacrifices. I remember how pleased I was when I was told that the Portuguese term for young people is *os novos* ("the new ones"). That is just what they are. I tell you this because, although I have been around a good many years, when I pray at the foot of the altar "to God who gives joy to my youth,"[28] I feel young and I know that I will never consider myself old. If I keep true to my God, Love will constantly vivify me. My youth will be renewed like that of the eagle.[29]

[28] Ps 42:4.
[29] Cf *Ibid* 102:5.

It's because we love freedom that we tie ourselves down. Only pride sees such bonds as a heavy chain. True humility, which is taught us by the One who is meek and humble of heart, shows that his yoke is easy and his burden light:[30] his yoke is freedom and love and unity; his yoke is the Life which he won for us on the Cross.

Freedom of consciences

32 Throughout my years as a priest, whenever I have spoken, or rather shouted, about my love for personal freedom, I have noticed some people reacting with distrust, as if they suspected that my defense of freedom could endanger the faith. Such faint-hearted people can rest assured. The only freedom that can assail the faith is a misinterpreted freedom, an aimless freedom, one without objective principles, one that is lawless and irresponsible. In a word, license. Unfortunately, this is what some people are advocating, and their claim does indeed constitute a threat to the faith.

[30] Cf. Mt 11:29-30.

This is why it is inaccurate to speak of *freedom of conscience*, thereby implying that it may be morally right for someone to reject God. We have already seen that it is in our power to oppose God's plans for salvation. It is in our power, but we should not do so. If someone adopted this attitude deliberately, he would be sinning, by breaking the first and most important of the commandments: "Thou shalt love the Lord thy God with thy whole heart."[31]

I defend with all my strength the *freedom of consciences*,[32] which means that no one can licitly prevent a man from worshipping God. The legitimate hunger for truth must be respected. Man has a grave obligation to seek God, to know him and worship him, but no one on earth is permitted to impose on his neighbor the practice of a faith he lacks; just as no one can claim the right to harm those who have received the faith from God.

Our Holy Mother the Church has always **33**
spoken out in favor of freedom and has always rejected fatalism, both in its ancient and more

[31] Dt 6:5.

[32] Leo XIII, Enc. *Libertas praestantissimum*, 20-VI-1888, ASS 20 (1888), 606.

modern versions. She has pointed out that each soul is master of its own destiny, for good or ill: "and those who have been true to the good will go to eternal life; those who have committed evil, to eternal fire."[33] I have always been impressed by this awesome capacity which you and I have, which all of us have, a capacity which indeed reveals the nobility of our state. "So true is it that sin is a voluntary evil, that in no way would it be sin if it did not have its origin in the will. This affirmation is so evident that the few wise men and the many fools who inhabit the earth are agreed upon it."[34]

Once again I raise my heart in thanksgiving to my God and Lord, because there was nothing to stop him from creating us impeccable, irresistibly drawn towards the good. Nevertheless, "he judged that his servants would be better if they served him freely."[35] How great is the love, the mercy of our Father! Whenever I think of his *divine extravagance* for us his children, I wish I had a thousand tongues, a thousand hearts and more, with which to be constantly

[33] Symbol *Quicumque.*
[34] St Agustine, *De vera religione*, 14, 27 (PL 34, 133).
[35] *Ibid* (PL 34, 134).

praising God the Father, God the Son, and God the Holy Spirit. Just think: the Almighty, who through his Providence rules the whole universe, does not want the forced service of slaves; he prefers to have children who are free. Although we are born *proni ad peccatum* ("inclined to sin"), due to the fall of our first parents, he has placed in the soul of each and everyone of us a spark of his infinite intelligence, an attraction towards the good, a yearning for everlasting peace. And he brings us to understand that we will attain truth, happiness, and freedom if we strive to make this seed of eternal life grow in our hearts.

But we can still say "no" to God, rejecting **34**
this source of new and permanent happiness. Anyone who does so stops being a son and becomes a slave. "Each thing is that which it is fitted to be according to its nature; hence, when it goes in search of something alien to its nature, it is not acting according to its own manner of being, but under an alien impulse; and this is to act in a servile manner. Man is rational by nature. When he acts according to reason, he proceeds by his own movement, according to what he is: and this is proper to freedom. When he sins, he works against

reason, and then he is allowing himself to be led by the impulse of another, he is subject to limitations imposed by another and so anyone who commits sin is a slave to sin (John 8:34)."[36]

Allow me to insist on this point. It is quite evident, as we can see in ourselves and in others, that everybody is a slave in some form or other. Some stoop before riches; others worship power; some, the relative tranquillity of scepticism, and there are those who discover in sensuality their golden calf. The same happens in noble things. We put effort into a job of work, into an undertaking, large or small, into scientific, artistic, literary, or spiritual activities. Wherever there is commitment and real passion, the person involved lives enslaved, joyfully devoting himself to fulfilling his task.

35 We will be slaves either way. Since we must serve anyway, for whether we like it or not this is our lot as men, then there is nothing better than recognizing that Love has made us slaves of God. From the moment we recognize this, we cease being slaves and become friends, sons. Then we see the difference: we find ourselves

[36] St Thomas Aquinas, *Super Evangelium S. Ioannis lectura,* Chap. VIII, lect. IV, Sec. 3, no. 1204 (Marietti, Turin 1952).

tackling the honest occupations of the world just as passionately and just as enthusiastically as others do, but with peace in the depth of our hearts. We are happy and calm, even in the midst of difficulties, for we are not putting our trust in passing things, but in what lasts forever. "We are not children of the slave but of the free woman."[37]

Where does our freedom come from? It comes from Christ our Lord. This is the freedom with which he has ransomed us.[38] That is why he teaches, "if the Son makes you free, you will be free indeed."[39] We Christians do not have to ask anyone to tell us the true meaning of this gift, because the only freedom that can save man is Christian freedom.

I like to speak of the adventure of freedom, because that is how your lives and mine unfold. I insist that it is freely, as children and not as slaves, that we follow the path which our Lord has marked out for each one of us. We relish our freedom of action as a gift from God.

I opt for God because I want to, freely, without compulsion of any kind. And I under-

[37] Gal 4:31.
[38] Cf. *Ibid*.
[39] Jn 8:36.

take to serve, to convert my whole life into a means of serving others, out of love for my Lord Jesus. It is this freedom which moves me to cry out that nothing on earth can separate me from the love of Christ.[40]

Answerable to God

36 " 'God created man in the beginning and he left him in the power of his own free will' (Ecclesiasticus 15:14). This could not be so unless man had freedom of choice."[41] We are answerable to God for all the actions we freely perform. There is no room here for anonymity. Each one finds himself face to face with his Lord, and he can decide to live as God's friend or as his enemy. This is the beginning of the path of the interior struggle which is a lifelong undertaking because, as long as we are on this earth, we will never achieve complete freedom.

Moreover, our Christian faith tells us to ensure, that everyone enjoys a climate of freedom, the first step for this being to remove any

[40] Cf. Rom 8:39.

[41] St Thomas Aquinas, *Quaestiones disputatae De malo*, q.6, sed contra.

element of insidious compulsion in the manner of presenting the faith. "If we are brought to Christ by force, we believe without wanting to; this is violence, not freedom. We can enter the Church unwillingly. We can approach the altar unwillingly. We can even receive the sacrament unwillingly. But we can only believe if we want to."[42] It is clear also that, when one reaches the use of reason, personal freedom is required to enter the Church, and to correspond to the continual calls which our Lord makes to us.

In the parable of the wedding feast, when **37**
the master of the house finds out that some guests have declined his invitation with poor excuses, he tells his servant, "Go out into the highways and hedgerows and compel—*compelle intrare*—people to come in."[43] Surely this is coercion, an act of violence against the legitimate freedom of each individual conscience?

If we meditate on the Gospel and reflect on the teachings of Jesus, we will not mistake these commands for coercion. See how gently Christ invites: "If you have a mind to be perfect...If any man would come after me..." His *compelle*

[42] St Augustine, *In Ioannis Evangelium tractatus*, 26, 2 (PL 35, 1607).

[43] Lk 14:23.

intrare implies no violence, either physical or moral. Rather, it reflects the power of attraction of Christian example, which shows in its way of acting the power of God: "See how the Father attracts. He delights in teaching, and not in imposing necessity on men. That is how he attracts men towards himself."[44]

When we breathe this air of freedom, we see clearly that evil is an enslavement, not a liberation. "He who sins against God keeps the freedom of his will to the extent that he is free from coercion, but he has lost it in that he is no longer free from blame."[45] Such a person may show that he has acted according to his preferences, but he does not speak with the voice of true freedom, because he has become the slave of his decision and he has decided for the worst, for the absence of God, where there is no freedom to be found.

38 I tell you once again: I accept no slavery other than that of God's Love. This is because, as I have told you on other occasions, religion is the greatest rebellion of men, who refuse to live like animals, who are dissatisfied and

[44] St Augustine, *In Ioannis Evangelium tractatus*, 26, 7 (PL 35, 1610).

[45] *Quaestiones disputatae De malo, q.6, ad 23.*

restless until they know their Creator and are on intimate terms with him. I want you to be rebels, free and unfettered, because I want you—it is Christ who wants us!—to be children of God. Slavery or divine sonship, this is the dilemma we face. Children of God or slaves to pride, to sensuality, to the fretful selfishness which seems to afflict so many souls.

Love of God marks out the way of truth, justice, and goodness. When we make up our minds to tell our Lord, "I put my freedom in your hands," we find ourselves loosed from the many chains that were binding us to insignificant things, ridiculous cares, or petty ambitions. Then our freedom, which is a treasure beyond price, a wonderful pearl that it would be a tragedy to cast before swine,[46] will be used by us entirely to learn how to do good.[47]

This is the glorious freedom of the children of God. Christians who let themselves be browbeaten or become inhibited or envious in the face of the licentious behavior of those who have not accepted the Word of God, show that they have a very poor idea of the faith. If we truly fulfill the law of Christ—that is, if we

[46] Cf. Mt 7:6.
[47] Cf. Is 1:17.

make the effort to do so, because we will not always fully succeed—we will find ourselves endowed with a wonderful gallantry of spirit that does not need to look elsewhere to discover the full meaning of human dignity.

Our faith is not in any way a burden or a limitation. What a poor idea of Christianity one would have if one thought that way! When we decide for God we lose nothing, and we gain everything. He who at the expense of his soul "secures his own life, will lose it; it is the man who loses his life for my sake that will secure it."[48]

We have drawn the winning card, the first prize. If anything prevents us from seeing this clearly, let us look inside our own souls. We may find that our faith is weak, that we have little personal contact with God, that our life of prayer is impoverished. We must beg our Lord, through his Mother who is our Mother too, to increase his love in us, to grant us a taste of the sweetness of his presence. Only when we love do we attain the fullest freedom: the freedom of not wanting ever to abandon, for all eternity, the object of our love.

[48] Mt 10:39.

TIME IS A TREASURE*

As I talk to you, and we make conversation together with God, our Lord, I am simply voicing aloud my personal prayer. I like to remind myself of this very often. You for your part must also make an effort to nourish your own prayer within your souls, even in situations, such as the one we are in today, when we find ourselves having to deal with a topic which, at first sight, does not seem very conducive to a loving dialogue, which is what our conversation with God should aim to be. I say "at first sight," because, of course, everything that happens to us, everything that goes on around us, can and indeed should form a theme for our meditation.

I want to talk to you about time, that passes so swiftly. I am not going to repeat to you the

* A homily given on January 9, 1956.

well-known phrase about one year more being one year less...Nor am I going to suggest that you ask around what others think of the passage of time. If you were to do so, you would probably hear something like, "Oh divine treasure of youth that slips away, never more to return...," though I admit you may come across other views with a deeper and more supernatural content.

Nor is it my purpose to dwell nostalgically on the brevity of human life. For us Christians the fleetingness of our journey through life should instead be a spur to help us make better use of our time. It should never be a motive for fearing our Lord, and much less for looking upon death as a disastrous and final end. It had been said in countless ways, some more poetical than others that, by the grace and mercy of God, each year that ends is a step that takes us nearer to Heaven, our final home.

When I reflect on this, how well I understand St Paul's exclamation when he writes to the Corinthians, *tempus breve est.*[1] How short indeed is the time of our passing through this

[1] 1 Cor 7:29.

world! For the true Christian these words ring deep down in his heart as a reproach to his lack of generosity, and as a constant invitation to be loyal. Brief indeed is our time for loving, for giving, for making atonement. It would be very wrong, therefore, for us to waste it, or to cast this treasure irresponsibly overboard. We mustn't squander this period of the world's history which God has entrusted to each one of us.

Let us open the Gospel of St Matthew at **40**
chapter twenty-five. We read, "The Kingdom of Heaven will be like ten virgins, who went to bring the bridegroom and his bride home, taking their lamps with them. Five of these were foolish, and five were wise."[2] The evangelist tells us that the wise virgins had made good use of their time. They had prudently gone and provided themselves with the necessary amount of oil, and were ready when they were told: "See, it's time. Behold, the bridegroom is on his way; go out to meet him!"[3] They turned up their lamps and went out joyfully to welcome him.

[2] Mt 25:1-2.
[3] Cf. *Ibid* 25:6.

That day will come for us. It will be our last day, but we're not afraid of it. Trusting firmly in God's grace, we are ready from this very moment to be generous and courageous, and take loving care of little things: we are ready to go and meet our Lord, with our lamps burning brightly. For the feast of feasts awaits us in Heaven. "Dearly beloved brethren, it is we who are called to take part in the wedding feast of the Word, we who already have faith in the Church, who are nourished on Sacred Scripture, and who rejoice because the Church is united to God. Ask yourselves now, I pray you, whether you have come to the feast wearing your wedding garment: examine your thoughts attentively."[4] I assure you, and I say the same to myself, that our wedding garment has to be woven with our love of God, a love we will have learnt to reap even in the most trivial things we do. It is precisely those who are in love who pay attention to details, even when they're doing apparently unimportant things.

41 But let us follow the thread of the parable. What happens to the foolish virgins? As soon

[4] St Gregory the great, *Homiliae in Evangelia*, 38, 11 (PL 76, 1289).

as the cry is raised, they do their best to get ready to receive the Bridegroom. They go off to buy oil. But their decision had come too late, and while they were away, "the bridegroom came; those who stood ready escorted him to the wedding, and the door was shut. Afterwards those other virgins came, with the cry, 'Lord, Lord, open to us.' "[5] It's not that they hadn't done anything. They had tried to do something...But in the end they were to hear his stern reply: "I do not recognize you."[6] Either they didn't know how to get ready properly or they didn't want to and they forgot to take the sensible precaution of buying oil in due time. They were not generous enough to carry out properly the little that had been entrusted to them. They had been told with many hours to spare, but they had wasted their time.

Let us take a good honest look at our own lives. How is it that sometimes we just can't find those few minutes it would take to finish lovingly the work we have to do, which is the very means of our sanctification? Why do we neglect our family duties? Why that tendency

[5] Mt 25:10-11.
[6] *Ibid* 25:12.

to rush through our prayers, or through the Holy Sacrifice of the Mass? How are we so lacking in calm and serenity when it comes to fulfilling the duties of our state, and yet so unhurried as we indulge in our own whims? You might say these are trifling matters. You're right, they are, but these trifles are the oil, the fuel we need to keep our flame alive and our light shining.

From the first hour

42 "Here is an image of the Kingdom of Heaven; a rich man went out at daybreak to hire laborers for his vineyard."[7] You know how the story continues. The man goes back several times to the marketplace to hire workers. Some were called at dawn, others almost at nightfall.

All receive a silver piece, "the wages that I promised you, in other words, my own image and likeness. For the image of the King is engraved on each silver piece."[8] Such is the mercy of God. He calls each one bearing in

[7] *Ibid* 20:1.

[8] St Jerome, *Commentariorum in Matthaeum libri*, 3, 20 (PL 26, 147).

mind his personal circumstances, because he wants "all men to be saved."[9] In our case, we were born Christians, brought up in the faith, and then we received a clear calling from our Lord. The facts are undeniable. Therefore, when you sense he's beckoning you, even if it is at the last hour, how can you think of lingering in the marketplace, basking in the sun as so many of those workers did, because they had time on their hands?

We should never have time on our hands, not even a second—and I am not exaggerating. There is work to be done. The world is a big place and there are millions of souls who have not yet heard the doctrine of Christ in all its clarity. I am addressing each one of you individually. If you have time on your hands, think again a little. It's quite likely that you have become lukewarm; that, supernaturally speaking, you have become a cripple. You are not moving, you are at a standstill. You are barren, you are not doing all the good you should be doing to the people around you, in your environment, in your work, and in your family.

[9] 1 Tim 2:4.

43 You might tell me, "Why should I make an effort?" It is not I who answer you, but St Paul: "Christ's love is urging us."[10] A whole lifetime would be little, if it was spent expanding the frontiers of your charity. From the very beginnings of Opus Dei I have repeated tirelessly that cry of our Lord: "By this shall men know that you are my disciples, if you love one another."[11] I did this to encourage generous souls to put it into practice in their own lives. This is precisely how we shall be recognized as Christians, if we make charity the starting point of everything we do.

He, who is purity personified, does not assert that his disciples will be known by the purity of their lives. He, who so lived sobriety that he didn't even have a stone upon which to lay his head,[12] and spent so many days in prayer and fasting,[13] did not declare to his apostles: "you will be known as my chosen ones because you are not gluttons or drunkards."

The purity of Christ's life was—and will be in every generation—a slap in the face to the

[10] 2 Cor 5:14.
[11] Jn 13:35.
[12] Cf. Mt 8:20.
[13] Cf. *Ibid* 4:2.

society of his day, a society which then as now was often so corrupt. His temperance also stung those whose lives were one long banquet, interrupted only by self-induced vomiting so that they could then get back to eating, thus fulfilling to the letter the words of Saul: their stomachs have become their god.[14]

Our Lord's humility was yet another blow 44
for those who spent their lives only looking after themselves. Here in Rome I have often commented—perhaps you yourselves have heard me say it—that, under its now ruined arches, there used to march in triumph victorious emperors and generals, all vain and haughty and full of pride. And as they passed under these monuments they may have had to lower their heads for fear of striking the great archways with their majestic brows. Yet again, Christ, who is so humble, does not state: "you will be known as my disciples by your modesty and humility."

I would like to help you realize that, even after twenty centuries, the Master's commandment is still as strikingly new as ever. It is, as it were, a letter of introduction proving that

[14] Cf. Phil 3:19.

one is truly a son of God. Ever since I became a priest I have very often preached that, for so many people alas, this commandment continues to be new, because they have never, or hardly ever, made an effort to put it into practice. It is sad to have to say this, but it is true. Nevertheless, the Messiah's words are quite clear. He stresses, once and for all, "by this you will be known, by the love you have for one another!" This is why I feel I must remind people constantly about these words of our Lord. St Paul adds, "bear one another's burdens; then you will be fulfilling the law of Christ."[15] Think of the amount of time you have wasted, perhaps with the false excuse that you could easily afford it, and yet you have so many brothers, your friends about you, who are overworked! Help them unobtrusively, kindly, with a smile on your lips, in such a way that it will be practically impossible for them to notice what you are doing for them. Thus, they will not even be able to express their gratitude, because the discreet refinement of your charity will have made your help pass undetected.

[15] Gal 6:2.

The foolish virgins, poor things, with their empty lamps, might argue that they hadn't had a free moment. The workers at the marketplace end up wasting most of the day, because they don't feel duty bound to render any useful service, even though our Lord was seeking them constantly, urgently, from the very first hour. When he calls us to his service, let us say "Yes" and bear "the day's burden and the heat"[16] for love's sake, in which case it will be no burden.

Being profitable in God's service

Let us now consider the parable of the man **45**
who "went on his travels; he summoned his servants and entrusted his goods to them."[17] Each one is given a different amount to administer in his master's absence. I think it is appropriate here to consider how the man who accepted the one talent behaved. He acted in a way which in my part of the world we'd call "playing the cuckoo." His petty mind thinks

[16] Mt 20:12.
[17] *Ibid* 25:14.

and wonders, then is made up: "he went off and made a hole in the ground, and there hid his master's money."[18]

What kind of work can our man undertake henceforth, now that he has given up the very tools of his trade? He has opted irresponsibly for the easy way out. He will simply give back what he has received. From now on he will just kill time, minutes, hours, days, months, years, his whole life! The others meanwhile are busy trading. They are noble fellows and keen to give back more than they have received, for the master has a right to expect a profit. His instructions had been very clear: *negotiamini dum venio;*[19] look after the business and make it yield a profit, until the owner returns. Not so our man, and thus, his whole life becomes useless.

46 What a shame it would be to have as one's occupation in life that of killing time which is a God-given treasure! No excuse could justify such behavior. "Let no one say, 'I only have one talent, I can't do anything.' Even with just one talent you can act in a meritorious

[18] *Ibid* 25:18.
[19] Lk 19:13.

way."[20] How sad not to turn to good account and obtain a real profit from the few or many talents that God has given to each man so that he may dedicate himself to the task of serving other souls and the whole of society!

When a Christian kills time on this earth, he is putting himself in danger of "killing Heaven" for himself, that is, if through selfishness, he backs out of things and hides away and doesn't care. A person who loves God not only hands over to the service of Christ, what he has and what he is in life. He gives his very self. He is not small-minded. He does not see himself in his health, in his good name, or in his career.

"Mine, mine, mine," is the way many people **47**
think and talk and act. How unpleasant an attitude this is! St Jerome comments that, "truly the words of Scripture, 'to seek excuses for sins' (Ps 140:4) are fulfilled by those people who, apart from having the sin of pride, are also lazy and careless."[21]

It is pride that constantly makes people think: "mine, mine, mine." It is a vice that

[20] St John Chrysostom, *In Matthaeum homiliae*, 78, 3 (PG 58, 714).

[21] St Jerome, *Commentariorum in Matthaeum libri*, 4, 25 (PL 26, 195).

makes men sterile and fruitless. It destroys their keenness to work for God and leads them to waste their time. As for you, don't lose your effectiveness; instead, trample on your selfishness. You think your life is for yourself? Your life is for God, for the good of all men, through your love for our Lord. Your buried talent, dig it up again! Make it yield, and you will taste the joy of knowing that in this supernatural business it does not matter if in this world the results are not wonders that men can admire. What really matters is to hand over all that we are and all that we have, striving to make our talent yield, and constantly exerting ourselves in order to produce good fruit.

God may have given us just one more year in which to serve him. Don't think of five, or even two. Just concentrate on this one year, that has just started. Give it to God, don't bury it! This is the resolution we ought to make.

At the foot of the vine

48 "There was a rich man who planted a vineyard; he walled it in, and dug a winepress and built a tower in it, and then let it out to some vinedressers, while he went on his travels."[22]

I would like you to meditate with me on what this parable teaches, bearing in mind the points we are interested in now. This story has traditionally been seen to refer to the destiny of God's chosen people, above all pointing out how we human beings respond with unfaithfulness and ingratitude to so much love on God's part.

In particular I should like to concentrate on the phrase "he went on his travels." I come immediately to the conclusion that we Christians must not abandon the vineyard where God has placed us. We must direct our energies to the work before us, within these walls, toiling in the winepress. And then taking our rest in the tower when our day's work is over. If we were to give in to comfort, it would be like telling Jesus, "Look, my time is mine, not yours. I don't want to tie myself down to looking after your vineyard."

Our Lord has given us as a present our very 49
lives, our senses, our faculties, and countless graces. We have no right to forget that each of

[22] Mt 21:33.

us is a worker, one among many, on this plantation where he has placed us to cooperate in the task of providing food for others. This is our place, here within the boundaries of this plantation. Here is where we have to toil away each day with Jesus, helping him in his work of redemption.[23]

Allow me to insist. You think your time is for yourself? Your time is for God! It may well be that, by God's mercy, such selfish thoughts have never entered into your mind. I'm telling you these things in case you ever find your heart wavering in its faith in Christ. Should that happen, I ask you—God asks you—to be true to your commitments, to conquer your pride, to control your imagination, not to be superficial and run away, not to desert.

The workers in the marketplace had all day to spare. The one who buried his talent wanted to kill the passing hours. The one who should have been looking after the vineyard went off elsewhere. They all prove insensitive to the great task the Master has entrusted to each and every Christian, that of seeing ourselves as his

[23] Cf. Col 1:24.

instruments, and acting accordingly, so that we may co-redeem with him, and of offering up our entire lives in the joyful sacrifice of surrendering ourselves for the good of souls.

The barren fig tree

Again it is St Matthew who tells us that Jesus 50
felt hungry one day on his way back from Bethany.[24] I am always deeply moved by the example of our Lord, and especially when I see that as well as being perfect God he is true and perfect Man, and as such teaches us to make use even of our frailty and our own natural weaknesses, and to offer ourselves completely, just as we are, to the Father, who will gladly accept our holocaust.

He was hungry. The Maker of the universe, the Lord of all creation, experiences hunger! Thank you, Lord, for inspiring the sacred author to include this small touch here, a detail that makes me love you more and which encourages me to desire ardently to contemplate your sacred Humanity! *Perfectus Deus, perfectus*

[24] Cf. Mt 21:18.

homo,[25] perfect God and perfect Man, of flesh and bone, just like you and I.

51 Jesus had worked hard the previous day, so when he set off once more on his way he felt hungry. Moved by his need, he goes up to a fig tree which, from a distance, boasts a magnificent foliage. St Mark tells us that "it was not the season for figs,"[26] but our Lord comes to pick them, knowing full well that he won't find any at this time of year. However, when the tree proves to be barren in spite of its apparent fertility and luxuriant leaves, Jesus commands, "Let no man ever eat fruit of yours hereafter."[27]

Hard words, indeed! May you never more bear fruit! How must the disciples have felt, especially if they considered that it was the Wisdom of God who had thus spoken? Jesus curses the fig tree because in it he has found only the appearance of fruitfulness—many leaves. Let this be a lesson to us. There is no excuse for being unproductive. Some might say "I don't know enough..." But that is no excuse. Or else, "I am unwell, I haven't much talent,

[25] Symbol, *Quicumque.*
[26] Mk 11:13.
[27] *Ibid* 11:14.

the conditions are not right, my surroundings..." These aren't excuses either. How pitiful the man who adorns himself with the foliage of a false apostolate, who has all the outward appearance of leading a fruitful life, but is not sincerely attempting to yield fruit! It looks as though he is using his time well. He seems to get around, to organize things, to be inventing new ways of solving all kinds of problems...but he has nothing to show for his efforts. No one will benefit from his works if they have no supernatural content.

Let us ask our Lord that we may be souls who are ready to work with a heroism that proves fruitful. For there is no lack of people here on earth who, on being approached, turn out to be nothing but large, shiny, glossy leaves. Foliage, just foliage and nothing more. Meanwhile, many souls are looking to us hoping to satisfy their hunger, which is a hunger for God. We must not forget that we have all the means we need. We have sufficient doctrine and the grace of God, in spite of our wretchedness.

I'd like to remind you once more that we **52**
don't have much time left, *tempus breve est*,[28]

[28] 1 Cor 7:29.

because life on earth is short, and also that, since we have the means, all that's needed is our goodwill to make use of the opportunities that God grants us. From the moment that our Lord came into this world, "the acceptable time, the day of salvation"[29] commenced for us and for all men. May our Father God never have to cast upon us the reproach he spoke through the prophet Jeremiah, "the kite, circling in the air, knows its time; turtledove can guess, and swallow, and stork, when they should return; only for my people the divine appointment passes unobserved."[30]

There are no bad or inopportune days. All days are good, for serving God. Days become bad only when men spoil them with their lack of faith, their laziness and their indolence, which turns them away from working with God and for God. "At all times I will bless the Lord."[31] Time is a treasure that melts away. It escapes from us, slipping through our fingers like water through the mountain rocks. Tomorrow will soon be another yesterday. Our lives

[29] 2 Cor 6:2.
[30] Jer 8:7.
[31] Ps 33:2.

are so very short. Yesterday has gone and today is passing by. But what a great deal can be done for the love of God in this short space of time!

No excuses will do us any good. Our Lord has been very generous with us. He has instructed us patiently. He has explained his precepts to us through parables. He has insisted tirelessly. As with Philip, he could ask us, "here am I, who have been all this while in your company; have you not learned to recognize me yet?"[32] The time has now come for us to get down to hard work, filling each moment of the day and bearing, willingly and joyfully, "the day's burden and the heat."[33]

Going about our Father's business

There's a passage in St Luke's Gospel, **53**
chapter two, which I think will help us to finish off well what we have been reflecting on today. In this passage Christ is a child. How his Mother and St Joseph must have suffered when, on their way back from Jerusalem, they could not find him among their relatives and friends.

[32] Jn 14:9.
[33] Mt 20:12.

And then what joy when they recognize him from afar, as he instructs the teachers of Israel. But notice the words that issue from his lips. Don't they seem hard? The Son says in reply to his Mother, "How is it that you sought me?"[34]

Surely they were right to have looked for him? Souls who know what it is to lose Jesus Christ and to find him again, are able to understand this..."How is it that you sought me? Didn't you know that I must be about by my Father's business?"[35] Didn't you know that I must devote my time entirely to my heavenly Father?

54 The fruit of our prayer today should be the conviction that our journey on earth, at all times and whatever the circumstances, is for God; that it is a treasure of glory, a foretaste of Heaven, something marvellous, which has been entrusted to us to administer, with a sense of responsibility, being answerable both to men and to God. But it is not necessary for us to change our situation in life. Right in the middle of the world we can sanctify our profession or job, our home life, and social relations—in fact

[34] Lk 2:49.
[35] *Ibid.*

all those things that seem to have only a worldly significance.

When at the age of twenty-six I perceived the full depth of what it meant to serve our Lord in Opus Dei, I asked with all my heart to be granted the maturity of an eighty-year-old man. I asked my God, with the childlike simplicity of a beginner, to make me older, so that I would know how to use my time well and learn how to make the best use of every minute, in order to serve him. Our Lord knows how to grant these riches. Perhaps the time will come when you and I will be able to say, "I have understood more than the elders, because I have fulfilled your commandments."[36] Youth need not imply thoughtlessness, just as having grey hair does not necessarily mean that a person is prudent and wise.

Come with me to Mary, the Mother of Christ. You, who are our Mother and have seen Jesus grow up and make good use of the time he spent among men, teach me how to spend my days serving the Church and all mankind. My good Mother, teach me, whenever necessary, to hear in the depths of my heart, as a

[36] Ps 118:100.

gentle reproach, that my time is not my own, because it belongs to our Father who is in Heaven.

WORKING FOR GOD*

Many people begin, but few finish. And we, 55
who are trying to behave as God's children, have to be among those few. Remember that only work that is well done and lovingly completed deserves the praise of the Lord which is to be found in Holy Scripture: "better is the end of a task than its beginning."[1]

You may already have heard me tell this story on other occasions; but even so, I would like to bring it up again because it contains a very striking lesson. I was once looking through the Roman Ritual in search of the prayers for blessing the last stone of a building, obviously the most important stone, since it symbolically represents the hard and enter-

* A homily given on February 6, 1960.

[1] Eccles 7:8.

prising work of many people, who have persevered in the task throughout the long years of construction. To my surprise, I found that no such prayers existed, and I had to be satisfied with a *benedictio ad omnia,* that is, an all-purpose blessing. I must say that at first I just couldn't believe that there was such an omission in the Ritual, and I spent quite a while going over the index without finding what I wanted.

Many Christians are no longer convinced that the fullness of Life that God rightly expects from his children means that they have to have a careful concern for the quality of their everyday work, because it is this work, even in its most minor aspects, which they have to sanctify.

It is no good offering to God something that is less perfect than our poor human limitations permit. The work that we offer must be without blemish and it must be done as carefully as possible, even in its smallest details, for God will not accept shoddy workmanship. "Thou shalt not offer anything that is faulty," Holy Scripture warns us, "because it would not be worthy of him."[2] For that reason, the work of each one

[2] Lev 22:20.

of us, the activities that take up our time and energy, must be an offering worthy of our Creator. It must be *operatio Dei,* a work of God that is done *for* God: in short, a task that is complete and faultless.

If you consider the many compliments paid to Jesus by those who witnessed his life, you will find one which in a way embraces all of them. I am thinking of the spontaneous exclamation of wonder and enthusiasm which arose from the crowd at the astonishing sight of his miracles: *bene omnia fecit,*[3] he has done everything exceedingly well: not only the great miracles, but also the little everyday things that didn't dazzle anyone, but which Christ performed with the accomplishment of one who is *perfectus Deus, perfectus homo,*[4] ("perfect God and perfect Man"). 56

Our Lord's whole life fills me with love for him, but I have a special weakness for his thirty hidden years spent in Bethlehem, Egypt, and Nazareth. That period, so long in comparison with his public life and which the Gospels hardly mention, might seem empty of any

[3] Mk 7:37.
[4] Symbol *Quicumque.*

special meaning to a person who views it superficially. And yet, I have always maintained that this silence about our Lord's early life speaks eloquently for itself, and contains a wonderful lesson for us Christians. They were years of intense work and prayer, years during which Jesus led an ordinary life, a life like ours, we might say, which was both divine and human at the same time. In his simple workshop, unnoticed, he did everything to perfection, just as he was later to do before the multitudes.

Work as a participation in God's creative power

57 From the beginning of creation man has had to work. This is not something that I have invented. It is enough to turn to the opening pages of the Bible. There you can read that, before sin entered the world, and in its wake death, punishment, and misery,[5] God made Adam from the clay of the earth, and created for him and his descendants this beautiful world we live in, *ut operaretur et custodiret illum*[6]

[5] Cf. Rom 5:12.

("so that we might cultivate it and look after it").

We must be convinced, therefore, that work is a magnificent reality, and that it has been imposed on us as an inexorable law which, one way or another, binds everyone, even though some may try to seek exemption from it. Make no mistake about it. Man's duty to work is not a consequence of original sin, nor is it just a discovery of modern times. It is an indispensable means which God has entrusted to us here on this earth. It is meant to fill out our days and make us sharers in God's creative power. It enables us to earn our living and, at the same time, to reap "the fruits of eternal life,"[7] for "man is born to work as the birds are born to fly."[8]

To this you might reply that many centuries have gone by and very few people think along these lines; that most people, when they work, do so for very different reasons: some for money, some to support their families, others to get on in society, to develop their capabilities,

[6] Gen 2:15.
[7] Jn 4:36.
[8] Job 5:7.

or perhaps to give free play to their disordered desires, or to contribute to social progress. In other words, most people regard their work as something that has to be done and cannot be avoided.

This is a stunted, selfish, and earthbound outlook, which neither you nor I can accept. For we have to remember and remind people around us that we are children of God, who have received the same invitation from our Father as the two brothers in the parable: "Son, go and work in my vineyard."[9] I give you my word that if we make a daily effort to see our personal duties in this light, that is, as a divine summons, we will learn to carry them through to completion with the greatest human and supernatural perfection of which we are capable. Occasionally we may rebel, like the elder of the two sons, who replied to his father, "I will not,"[10] but we will learn how to turn back repentant and will redouble our efforts to do our duty.

58 "If the mere presence of an important person who is worthy of respect is enough to improve

[9] Mt 21:28.
[10] *Ibid* 21:29.

the behavior of the people before him, how is it that the continual presence of God, which reaches out to every corner and is acknowledged by our faculties and gratefully loved, does not increasingly better us in our speech, actions, and feelings?"[11] Indeed, if the fact that God sees us were fully impressed on our consciences, and if we realized that all our work, absolutely all of it is done in his presence—for nothing escapes his eyes—how carefully we would finish things and how differently we would react! This is the secret of the holiness which I have now been preaching for so many years. God has called on all of us to imitate him. He has called you and me so that, living as we do in the midst of the world—and continuing to be ordinary everyday people!—we may put Christ at the top of all honest human activities.

Now you will understand even better that if anyone among you didn't love work, his own particular job; if he didn't feel sincerely committed to some noble occupation in this world so as to sanctify it, or if he were to lack a professional vocation, then that person would

[11] Clement of Alexandria, *Stromata*, 7, 7 (PG 9, 450-451).

never be able to understand the supernatural substance of what this priest is saying to you, for the very good reason that he would be lacking an indispensable condition for doing so: that of being a worker.

59 I should tell you (and I don't think I am being presumptuous in saying this) that I realize immediately when I am speaking with someone if my words are going in one ear and out the other or making no impression. Let me open my heart to you so that you can help me give thanks to God. When I saw in 1928 what our Lord wanted of me, I immediately set to work. At the time (thank you, my God, for there was much to suffer and much to love!) I was taken for a madman. Some people indeed, in an excess of understanding, called me a *dreamer*, but a dreamer of impossible dreams. In spite of all this and of my own shortcomings, I went ahead without getting discouraged. And since the project was not of my doing, it found its way through the difficulties. Today it is a reality spread throughout the world from pole to pole, and it seems so natural to most people, because our Lord made sure that it was recognized as something of his own doing.

I was saying that I only need exchange a couple of words with someone and I can tell whether or not he understands me. I am not like the hen who was sitting on her nest when an unknown hand slipped a duck's egg under her. The days passed and it wasn't until the chickens hatched and she saw the fluffy creature waddling about awkwardly, one leg this way, the other that way, that she realized that it wasn't one of hers and that it would never learn to chirp no matter how hard it tried. I have never ill treated anyone who turned his back on me, not even when my offer of help was repaid with insolence. That is why, back in 1939, my attention was arrested by an inscription on a building where I was preaching a retreat to some university students. It read: "Let each wayfarer follow his own way."* It was very useful advice.

Forgive this digression and, though we **60**
haven't really gone off the track, let us return to the central idea. Be convinced that our professional vocation is an essential and inseparable part of our condition as Christians. Our Lord wants you to be holy in the place where

* *Cada caminante siga su camino.*

you are, in the job you have chosen for whatever reason. To me, every job that is not opposed to the divine law is good and noble, and capable of being raised to the supernatural plane, that is, inserted into the constant flow of Love which defines the life of a child of God.

I cannot avoid getting a little uneasy when someone, in speaking about his job, plays the role of a victim. He talks about how his work takes up so many hours each day, when the truth is that he isn't doing half as much as many of his professional colleagues are and they quite likely are only driven by selfish or, at best, by merely human motives. All of us who are here engaged in a personal dialogue with Jesus have very definite occupations: doctors, lawyers, economists...Think a moment about those of your colleagues who are outstanding for their professional prestige, their integrity or their spirit of service and self-sacrifice. Isn't it true that they devote many hours of the day, and even of the night, to their jobs? Isn't there anything we can learn from them?

While I speak, I too am examining the way I have behaved and I confess that, in putting the question to myself, I feel a little ashamed and wish immediately to ask God's forgiveness, thinking how weak my response has been and how far short it has fallen of the mission that God has given us to carry out in the world. One of the Fathers of the Church writes: "Christ has appointed us to be like lamps, so as to be teachers to others; to act as leaven; to live like angels among men, like adults among children, like spiritual beings among the merely rational; to be seed and to yield fruit. There would be no need of speaking if our lives shone in this way. Words would be superfluous if we had deeds to show for them. There would not be a single pagan left if we were truly Christian."[12]

The exemplary value of professional life

We must avoid the error of thinking we can 61
reduce the apostolate to the performance of a few pious practices. You and I are Christians but at the same time, and without any break in continuity, we are citizens and workers with clear obligations, which we have to fulfill in an exemplary manner if we really want to become saints. Jesus himself is urging us: "You are the

[12] St John Chrysostom, *In Epistolam I ad Timotheum homiliae*, 10, 3 (PG 62, 551).

light of the world. A city set on a mountain cannot be hidden. Neither do men light a lamp and put it under a measure, but upon the lampstand, so as to give light to all in the house. Even so, let your light shine before men, in order that they may see your good works and give glory to your Father in Heaven."[13]

Professional work, whatever it is, becomes a lamp to enlighten your colleagues and friends. That is why I usually tell those who become members of Opus Dei, and the same applies to all of you now listening to me: "What use is it telling me that so and so is a good son of mine—a good Christian—but a bad shoemaker?" If he doesn't try to learn his trade well, or doesn't give his full attention to it, he won't be able to sanctify it or offer it to our Lord. The sanctification of ordinary work is, as it were, the hinge of true spirituality for people who, like us, have decided to come close to God while being at the same time fully involved in temporal affairs.

62 You must fight against the tendency to be too lenient with yourselves. Everyone has this difficulty. Be demanding with yourselves!

[13] Mt 5:14-16.

Sometimes we worry too much about our health, or about getting enough rest. Certainly it is necessary to rest, because we have to tackle our work each day with renewed vigor. But, as I wrote many years ago, "to rest is not to do nothing. It is to turn our attention to other activities that require less effort."

At other times, relying on flimsy excuses, we become too easygoing and forget about the marvellous responsibility that rests upon our shoulders. We are content with doing just enough to get by. We let ourselves get carried away by false rationalizations and waste our time, whereas Satan and his allies never take a holiday. Listen carefully to St Paul and reflect on what he said to those Christians who were slaves. He urged them to obey their masters, "not serving to the eye as pleasers of men, but as slaves of Christ, doing the will of God from your heart, giving your service with good will as to the Lord and not to men."[14] What good advice for you and me to follow!

Let us ask our Lord Jesus for light, and beg him to help us discover, at every moment, the divine meaning which transforms our profes-

[14] Eph 6:6-7.

sional work into the hinge on which our calling to sanctity rests and turns. In the Gospel you will find that Jesus was known as *faber, filius Mariae*[15] ("the workman, the Son of Mary"). Well, we too, with a holy pride, have to prove with deeds that we *are* workers, men and women who really work!

Since we should behave at all times as God's envoys, we must be very much aware that we are not serving him loyally if we leave a job unfinished; if we don't put as much effort and self-sacrifice as others do into the fulfillment of professional commitments; if we can be called careless, unreliable, frivolous, disorganized, lazy, or useless...Because people who neglect obligations that seem less important will hardly succeed in other obligations that pertain to the spiritual life and are undoubtedly harder to fulfill. "He who is faithful in very little is faithful also in much; and he who is dishonest in very little is dishonest also in much."[16]

63 I am not speaking of imaginary ideals. I confine myself to a very definite reality which is of paramount importance, and which is

[15] Mk 6:3.
[16] Lk 16:10.

capable of transforming an environment that is utterly pagan and hostile to God's designs, as indeed happened at the beginning of the era of our salvation. Savor these words of an anonymous author of those times, who sums up the grandeur of our vocation as follows: Christians, he writes, "are to the world what the soul is to the body. They live in the world but are not worldly, as the soul is in the body but is not corporeal. They live in every town and city, as the soul is in every part of the body. They work from within and pass unnoticed, as the soul does of its essence...They live as pilgrims among perishable things with their eyes set on the immortality of Heaven, as the immortal soul now dwells in a perishable house. Their numbers increase daily amid persecutions, as the soul is made beautiful through mortifications...And Christians have no right to abandon their mission in the world, in the same way that the soul may not voluntarily separate itself from the body."[17]

We would, therefore, be on the wrong path if we were to disregard temporal affairs, for our Lord awaits us there as well. You can be sure

[17] *Epistola ad Diognetum*, 6 (PG 2, 1175).

that it is through the circumstances of ordinary life, ordained or permitted by the infinite wisdom of divine Providence, that we come close to God. But we shall not attain our goal if we do not strive to finish our work well; if we do not sustain the effort we put in when we began our work with human and supernatural zeal; if we do not carry out our work as well as the best do and, if possible, even better than the best. And I think that if you and I really want to, we *will* work better than the best, because we will use all the honest human means as well as the supernatural ones which are required in order to offer our Lord a perfect job of work, finished like filigree and pleasing in every way.

Turning work into prayer

64 I have often said that we must not allow these periods of conversation with Jesus, who sees us and hears us from the Tabernacle, to degenerate into an impersonal type of prayer. If we want our meditation to develop right away into a personal dialogue with our Lord (for which the sound of words is not necessary),

we must shed the cloak of anonymity and put ourselves in his presence, just as we are. We must avoid hiding ourselves in the crowd that fills the church, or diluting our prayer into a meaningless patter that does not come from the heart and is little better than a reflex habit, empty of any real content.

To this I now add that your work too must become a personal prayer, that it must become a real conversation with our Father in Heaven. If you seek sanctity in and through your work, you will necessarily have to strive to turn it into personal prayer. You cannot allow your cares and concerns to become impersonal and routine, because if you were to do so, the divine incentive that inspires your daily tasks will straightaway wither and die.

As I say these things, my memory goes back to the journeys I made to the battlefronts during the Spanish civil war. I had no material resources but I went wherever there was anyone who needed my services as a priest. In the very special circumstances we were in, which might well have given a number of people cause to justify their moral negligence and slackness, I did not limit myself to giving purely ascetical advice. I was concerned then, as now, with the one thing which I would like our Lord to awaken in each one of you. I was interested in the welfare of their souls, and also in their happiness here on earth. I encouraged them to make good use of their time by doing something worthwhile, and not to look upon the war as something of a closed parenthesis in their lives. I asked them not to give in to laziness, but to do all they could to avoid letting their trenches and sentry posts become like the station waiting rooms of the period where people killed time waiting for trains that seemed never to arrive...

I suggested specific occupations (for example, study or learning a language), occupations that were compatible with their military duties. I advised them never to cease being men of God, and to try turning everything they did into *operatio Dei* ("God's work"). I was greatly moved when I saw how wonderfully those boys responded, for their situation was far from easy. The solidity of their interior spirit was remarkable.

65 I also remember my stay in Burgos around that time. A lot of young men on leave, as well as many who were stationed in the city, came to spend a few days with me. The living quarters that I shared with a few of my "sons" consisted of a single room in a dilapidated hotel and, though we lacked even the most basic amenities, we organized things in such a way that the men who came—there were hundreds of them—had whatever they needed to rest and recover their strength.

We used to go for walks along the banks of the River Arlanzón. There we would talk and, while they opened their hearts, I tried to guide them with suitable advice to confirm their decisions or open up new horizons in their interior lives. And always, with God's help, I would do all I could to encourage them and stir up in their hearts the desire to live genuinely Christian lives. Our walks would sometimes take us as far as the monastery of Las Huelgas. On other occasions we would find our way to the cathedral.

I used to enjoy climbing up the cathedral towers to get a close view of the ornamentation at the top, a veritable lacework of stone that must have been the result of very patient and laborious craftsmanship. As I chatted with the young men who accompanied me, I used to point out that none of the beauty of this work could be seen from below. To give them a material lesson in what I had been previously explaining to them, I would say: "This is God's work, this is working for God! To finish your personal work perfectly, with all the beauty and exquisite refinement of this tracery stonework." Seeing it, my companions would understand that all the work we had seen was a prayer, a loving dialogue with God. The men who spent their energies there were quite aware that no one at street level could appreciate their efforts. Their work was for God alone. Now do you see how our professional work can bring us close to our Lord? Do your job as those medieval stonemasons did theirs, and your work too will be *operatio Dei*, a human work with a divine substance and finish.

66 "Since we are convinced that God is to be found everywhere, we plough our fields praising the Lord, we sail the seas and ply all our other trades singing his mercies."[18] Doing things this way, we are united to God at every moment. Even when you find yourselves isolated and away from your normal surroundings, like those boys in the trenches, you will

[18] Clement of Alexandria, *Stromata*, 7, 7 (PG 9, 451).

be living in our Lord by means of your continual hard work, which you will have learned to turn into prayer, because you will have started it and finished it in the presence of God the Father, of God the Son, and of God the Holy Spirit.

But don't forget that you are also in the presence of men, and that they expect from you, from you personally, a Christian witness. Thus, as regards the human aspect of our job, we must work in such a way that we will not feel ashamed when those who know us and love us see us at our work, nor give them cause to feel embarrassed. If you work in the spirit that I am trying to teach you, you will not embarrass those who rely on you, nor will you have any cause to blush. You will not be like the man in the parable who set out to build a tower: "When he had laid the foundations and was unable to finish, all who beheld him began to mock him, saying, 'This man began to build and was not able to finish.' "[19]

Believe me. If you don't lose your supernatural outlook, you will crown your work. You will finish your cathedral to the very last stone.

[19] Lk 14:29-30.

67 *Possumus!*[20] With God's help, we too can be victorious in this battle. Rest assured that it is not difficult to convert work into a prayerful dialogue. As soon as you offer it up and then set to work, God is already listening and giving encouragement. We acquire the style of contemplative souls, in the midst of our daily work! Because we become certain that he is watching us, while he asks us to conquer ourselves anew: a little sacrifice here, a smile there for someone who bothers us, beginning the least pleasant but most urgent job first, carefulness in little details of order, perseverance in the fulfillment of our duty when it would be so easy to abandon it, not leaving for tomorrow what should be finished today: and all this, to please him, our Father God! On your desk or in some inconspicuous place that nobody notices, you perhaps place your crucifix to awaken in you a contemplative spirit and to act as a textbook for your mind and soul where you learn the lessons of service.

If you make up your mind to follow these ways of contemplation, in the midst of your ordinary work, without doing anything odd or

[20] Mt 20:22.

withdrawing from the world, you will immediately feel that you are a friend of the Master, with the God-given task of opening up the divine ways of the earth to the whole of mankind. Yes. With your work you will help to spread Christ's kingdom in every continent. You will offer up hour after hour of work for far-off lands which are being born to the faith, for the peoples of the East who are being cruelly forbidden to profess their faith, and for the traditionally Christian nations where it seems that the light of the Gospel has grown dim and souls are struggling in the obscurity of ignorance...Then, how valuable your hour of work becomes as you persevere with the same effort a little longer, a few minutes more, until the job is finished! In a simple and practical way you are converting contemplation into apostolate, seeing it as an imperative necessity of your heart, which beats in unison with the most sweet and merciful Heart of Jesus, our Lord.

Do everything for Love's sake

How shall I manage, you seem to ask, to act always in a spirit that leads me to finish all my **68** professional work perfectly? The answer comes not from me, but from St Paul: "Work courageously, be strong. And let everything you do be done in a spirit of charity."[21] Do everything for Love's sake and do it freely. Never give to fear or routine. Serve God our Father.

Having put them very much to the test, I am very fond of repeating these artless but very expressive verses:

My life consists in loving,
And if with loving I'm familiar,
'Tis because I've sorrowed much;
For there's no finer lover,
Than one who's suffered much.*

Go about your professional duties for Love's sake. Do everything for the sake of Love and (precisely because you are in love, even though you may taste the bitterness of misunderstand-

[21] 1 Cor 16:13-14.
*"*Mi vida es toda de amor*
y, si en amor estoy ducho,
es por fuerza del dolor,
que no hay amante mejor
que aquel que ha sufrido mucho."

ing, of injustice, of ingratitude, and even of failure in men's eyes) you will see the result in the wonders that your work produces—rich, abundant fruit, the promise of eternity!

It happens, however, that some people (who 69
are good, or should we rather say "goodish") pay lip service to the beautiful ideal of spreading our faith, but in practice they make do with a superficial and careless professional output. They seem scatter-brained. If we happen to come across such Christians, we should do our best to help them, affectionately but uncompromisingly, having recourse where necessary to the gospel remedy of fraternal correction: "Brethren, if a man is found guilty of some fault, you who are spiritually minded ought to show a spirit of gentleness in correcting him. Have an eye upon thyself, lest thou too be tempted. Bear one another's burdens and so you will be fulfilling the law of Christ."[22] If besides the fact that they claim to be Catholics there are other factors involved, because, for instance, those at fault are older, or have more experience or responsibility, then there is all the more reason to talk to them. We should try to

[22] Gal 6:1-2.

get them to react, helping them take their work more seriously, trying to guide them, like a good parent does or a teacher, but without humiliating them.

It is very moving to pause and meditate on the way St Paul behaved. "You know well enough what you have to do to imitate us. We were no vagabonds among you. We would not even be indebted to you for our daily bread, but we worked night and day in labor and toil, so that we might not burden any of you...The charge we gave you on our visit was this: if any man will not work, neither let him eat."[23]

70 For the love of God, for the love of souls, and to live up to our Christian vocation, we must give good example. So as not to give scandal, or to provoke even the faintest suspicion that the children of God are soft and useless, so as not to disedify...,you must strive to show an example of balanced justice, to behave properly as responsible men. The farmer who ploughs his field while constantly raising his heart to God, just as much as the carpenter, the blacksmith, the office worker, the academic—all Christians in fact—have to be an

[23] 2 Thess 3:7-10.

example for their colleagues at work. And this without conceit, since we realize very clearly in our hearts that only with God's help can we secure the victory, for by ourselves *alone* we could not even lift a piece of straw from the ground.[24] Therefore, everyone, in his job, in whatever place he has in society, must feel obliged to make his work God's work, sowing everywhere the peace and joy of the Lord. "The perfect Christian is always a bearer of peace and joy. Peace, because he realizes he is in the presence of God; joy, because he sees himself surrounded by God's blessings. Such a Christian is truly a royal personage, a holy priest of God."[25]

To achieve this goal, we must act like souls **71**
urged on by Love and never as people under punishment or a curse. "Whatever you do, in word or deed, do all in the name of the Lord Jesus, giving thanks to God the Father through him."[26] Thus, we shall complete our tasks perfectly, using our time to the full, for we shall be instruments who are in love with God. We shall be conscious of all the responsibility and

[24] Cf. Jn 15:5.
[25] Clement of Alexandria, *Stromata*, 7, 7 (PG 9, 451).
[26] Col 3:17.

trust that God has placed on our shoulders in spite of our own weaknesses. In all your actions, because you are relying on God's strength, you must behave as one motivated solely by Love.

But let's not close our eyes to reality and content ourselves with a naive and superficial outlook that could lead us to think that the road ahead is an easy one, and that to follow it we only need to make a few sincere resolutions and have an ardent desire to serve God. Make no mistake about it. As the years go by, you will have to face (perhaps sooner than you think) situations that are especially difficult and which will call for a great spirit of sacrifice and an even greater forgetfulness of self. Foster then the virtue of hope and boldly make your own that cry of the Apostle: "For I reckon that the sufferings of the present time are not worthy to be compared with the glory to come that will be revealed in us."[27] Reflect in peace and security on what it will be like to have the infinite Love of God poured out on this poor creature that we are. The time has come, amid your ordinary occupations, to exercise your faith,

[27] Rom 8:18.

awaken your hope, and revive your love; that is, to activate the three theological virtues, which help us to banish immediately (without dissimulation, deceit, or evasion) any ambiguities in our professional conduct or in our interior life.

Again we hear the voice of St Paul: "There- **72**
fore, my beloved brethren, be steadfast and immovable in your resolve, doing your full share continually in the Lord's work, since you know that your labor in the Lord's service cannot be spent in vain."[28] Don't you see? A complete range of virtues is called into play when we set about our work with the purpose of sanctifying it: fortitude, to persevere in our work despite the difficulties that naturally arise and to ensure that we never let ourselves be overwhelmed by anxiety; temperance, in order to spend ourselves unsparingly and to overcome our love of comfort and our selfishness; justice, so as to fulfill our duties towards God, society, our family, and our fellow workers; prudence, to know in each case what course to take, and then to set about it without hesitation...And all this, I emphasize, is for the

[28] 1 Cor 15:58.

sake of Love, with a keen and immediate sense of responsibility for the results of our work and its apostolic impact.

"Love is deeds, not sweet words," says the proverb, and I don't think there is anything else to add.

Lord, give us your grace. Open the door to the workshop in Nazareth so that we may learn to contemplate you, together with your holy Mother Mary and the holy Patriarch St Joseph, whom I love and revere so dearly, the three of you dedicated to a life of work made holy. Then, Lord, our poor hearts will be enkindled, we shall seek you and find you in our daily work, which you want us to convert into a work of God, a labor of Love.

HUMAN VIRTUES[*]

In the seventh chapter of his Gospel, St Luke 73
writes: "One of the Pharisees invited him to a meal; so he went into the Pharisee's house and took his place at the table."[1] At this point a woman, who is known publicly in the city as a sinner, arrives and comes up to wash the feet of Jesus who, in keeping with the customs of the time, is eating in a reclined position. The woman's tears are the water for this washing of feet which is so moving; her hair, the towel for drying them. With ointment poured from a fine alabaster jar, she anoints the Master's feet, and she kisses them.

The Pharisee thinks badly of this. He cannot imagine that Jesus could have so much mercy

[*] A homily given on September 6, 1941.

[1] Lk 7:36.

in his heart. "If this man were a prophet," he thinks himself, "he would know who and what manner of woman this is."[2] Jesus reads his thoughts and explains to him: "Do you see this woman? I came into your house and you gave me no water for my feet; she has washed my feet with her tears, and wiped them with her hair. You gave me no kiss of greeting; she, from the moment she entered, has never ceased to kiss my feet. You did not pour oil on my head; she has anointed my feet, and with ointment. And so I tell you, great sins have been forgiven her, for she has greatly loved."[3]

We cannot pause now to consider the divine marvels of our Lord's most merciful Heart. Instead let us turn our attention to another aspect of the scene, to the way Jesus notices the omission of the expression of human courtesy and refinement which the Pharisee failed to show him. Christ is *perfectus Deus, perfectus homo.*[4] He is perfect God, the Second Person of the Blessed Trinity, and perfect man. He comes to save, not to destroy nature. It is from him

[2] *Ibid* 7:39.
[3] *Ibid* 7:44-47.
[4] Symbol, *Quicumque.*

that we learn that it is unchristian to treat our fellowmen badly, for they are creatures of God, made to his image and likeness.[5]

Human virtues

There is a certain type of secularist outlook that one comes across, and also another approach which one might call "pietistic," both of which share the view that Christians somehow are not fully and entirely human. According to the former, the demands of the Gospel are such as to stifle our human qualities; whereas for the latter, human nature is so fallen that it threatens and endangers the purity of the faith. The result, either way, is the same. They both fail to grasp the full significance of Christ's Incarnation, they do not see that "the Word was made flesh," became man, "and dwelt amongst us."[6] 74

My experience as a man, as a Christian, and as a priest teaches me just the opposite. There is no human heart, no matter how deeply

[5] Cf. Gen 1:26.
[6] Jn 1:14.

immersed in sin, which does not conceal, like embers among the ashes, a flicker of nobility. Whenever I have sounded out such hearts, talking to them individually with the words of Christ, they have always responded.

In this world of ours there are many people who neglect God. It may be that they have not had an opportunity to listen to his words, or that they have forgotten them. Yet their human dispositions are honest, loyal, compassionate, and sincere. I would go so far as to say that anyone possessing such qualities is ready to be generous with God, because human virtues constitute the foundation for the supernatural virtues.

75 It is true that in themselves such personal qualities are not enough, for no one is saved without the grace of Christ. But if a man fosters and cultivates the seeds of virtue within him, God will smooth out his path, and such a person will be able to become holy because he has known how to live as a man of goodwill.

You may perhaps have noticed other cases which are in a certain sense just the opposite; so many people who call themselves Christians because they have been baptized and have received other sacraments, but then prove to be disloyal and deceitful, insincere and proud, and...they fail to achieve anything. They are like shooting stars, lighting up the sky for an instant and then falling away to nothing.

If we accept the responsibility of being children of God, we will realize that God wants us to be very human. Our heads should indeed be touching Heaven, but our feet should be firmly on the ground. The price of living as Christians is not that of ceasing to be human or of abandoning the effort to acquire those virtues which some have even without knowing Christ. The price paid for each Christian is the redeeming Blood of our Lord and he, I insist, wants us to be both very human and very divine, struggling each day to imitate him who is *perfectus Deus, perfectus homo*.

I don't know if I could say which is the most **76**
important human virtue. It depends on the point of view from which they are considered. In any case, this question doesn't really get us anywhere, for it is not a matter of practising one or even a number of virtues. We have to try to acquire and to practise all of them. Each individual virtue is interwoven with the others and, thus, our effort to be sincere will also make us upright, cheerful, prudent, and composed.

I am not convinced either when I hear people making a great distinction between personal and social virtues. No virtue worthy of its name can foster selfishness. Every virtue necessarily works to the good both of our own soul and to the good of those around us. We are all of us men and all likewise children of God, and we cannot think that life consists in building up a brilliant *curriculum vitae* or an outstanding career. Ties of solidarity should bind us all and, besides, in the order of grace we are united by the supernatural bond of the Communion of Saints.

At the same time, we must bear in mind that decision making and responsibility derive from the personal freedom of each individual. Virtues are, therefore, also radically personal, they pertain *to the person.* Nevertheless, in this great battle of love no one fights alone. None of us, I like to say, is a floating line of verse. In some way we are always either helping or hindering each other. We are all links in the same chain. Join with me now in asking our Lord to grant that this chain may anchor us to his Heart until that day comes when we shall contemplate him face to face forever in Heaven.

Fortitude, composure, patience, magnanimity

Let us now consider some of these human virtues. While I am talking I would like you, on your own, to keep up a conversation with our Lord. Ask him to help us all, to encourage us to penetrate more deeply today into the mystery of his Incarnation, so that we too, in our own flesh, may learn how to give living witness to our fellowmen of him who has come to save us. 77

No man, whether he be a Christian or not, has an easy life. To be sure, at certain times it seems as though everything goes as we had planned. But this generally lasts for only a short time. Life is a matter of facing up to difficulties and of experiencing in our hearts both joy and sorrow. It is in this forge that man can acquire fortitude, patience, magnanimity, and composure.

The person with fortitude is one who perseveres in doing what his conscience tells him he ought to do. He does not measure the value of a task exclusively by the benefit he receives from it, but rather by the service he renders to others. The strong man will at times suffer, but he stands firm; he may be driven to tears, but he will brush them aside. When difficulties come thick and fast, he does not bend before them. Remember the example given us in the book of the Machabees: an old man, Eleazar, prefers to die rather than break God's law. "By manfully giving up my life now, I will show myself worthy of my old age and leave to the young a noble example of how to die a good death willingly and nobly for the revered and holy laws."[7]

78 The man who knows how to be strong will not be in a hurry to receive the reward of his virtue. He is patient. Indeed it is fortitude that teaches us to appreciate the human and divine virtue of patience. " 'By your patience you will gain possession of your souls.' (Lk 21:19) The possession of the soul is attributed to patience, which in effect is the root and guardian of all the virtues. We secure possession of our souls through patience, for, by learning to have dominion over ourselves, we begin to possess that which we are."[8] And it is this very patience that moves us to be understanding with others, for we are convinced that souls, like good wine, improve with time.

[7] 2 Mac 6:27-28.

[8] St Gregory the Great, *Homiliae in Evangelia*, 35, 4 (PL 76, 1261).

We have to be strong and patient and, therefore, calm and composed, but not with the composure of the man who buys his own tranquility at the expense of ignoring his brothers or neglecting the great task (which falls to us all) of tirelessly spreading good throughout the world. We can keep calm because there is always forgiveness and because there is a solution for everything, except death; and for the children of God, death is life. We must try to keep our peace, even if only so as to act intelligently, since the man who remains calm is able to think, to study the pros and cons, to examine judiciously the outcome of the actions he is about to undertake. He then plays his part calmly and decisively. 79

I have been briefly reviewing some of the human virtues. I have no doubt that, as you pray to our Lord, many others will spring to mind. I would like to pause now for a few moments to consider that wonderful quality which is magnanimity. 80

Magnanimity means greatness of spirit, a largeness of heart wherein many can find refuge. Magnanimity gives us the energy to break out of ourselves and be prepared to undertake generous tasks which will be of benefit to all. Small-mindedness has no home in the magnanimous heart, nor has meanness, nor egoistic calculation, nor self-interested trickery. The magnanimous person devotes all his strength, unstintingly, to what is worthwhile. As a result he is capable of giving himself. He is not content with merely giving. He gives *his very self*. He, thus, comes to understand that the greatest expression of magnanimity consists in giving oneself to God.

Industriousness, diligence

81 There are two human virtues, industriousness and diligence, which merge into one, for they both help us in our efforts to make good use of the talents we have each received from God. They are virtues because they lead us to finish things properly. As I have been preaching since 1928, work is not a curse; nor is it a punishment for sin. Genesis had already spoken about the fact of work before ever Adam rebelled against God.[9] According to our Lord's

[9] Cf. Gen 2:15.

plans, work was to be a permanent feature of man who, through work, would cooperate in the immense task of creation.

A hardworking person makes good use of time, for time is not only money, it is glory, God's glory! He does as he ought and concentrates on what he is doing, not out of routine nor to while away the passing hours, but as the result of attentive and pondered reflection. This is what makes a man diligent. Our everyday usage of this word "diligent" already gives us some idea of its Latin origin. "Diligent" comes from the verb *diligo*, which means to love, to appreciate, to choose something after careful consideration and attention. The diligent man does not rush into things. He does his work thoughtfully and lovingly.

Our Lord, perfect man in every way, chose a manual trade and carried it out attentively and lovingly for almost the entirety of the years he spent on this earth. He worked as a craftsman among the other people in his village. This human and divine activity of his shows us clearly that our ordinary activities are not an insignificant matter. Rather they are the very hinge on which our sanctity turns, and they offer us constant opportunities of meeting God, and of praising him and glorifying him through our intellectual or manual work.

Truthfulness and justice

82 In order to practise the human virtues, we need to make a sustained effort, since it is not easy to maintain a spirit of honesty and integrity for any length of time when faced with situations that seem to put our own safety at risk. Take truthfulness, a virtue so clean and pure. Can it be true that it has fallen into disuse? Has the practice of compromise, of "gilding the pill" and "putting on a show" finally triumphed? People are afraid of the truth and to justify their attitude they make the shabby excuse that no one practises or tells the truth anymore, that everyone has to resort to pretense and lies.

Fortunately this is not so. There are many people, Christians or not, who are ready to sacrifice honor and reputation for the sake of the truth, people who aren't always feverishly turning this way and that in search of "the warmest place in the sun." These are the very people who, because they love the truth, are happy to put things right when they discover they have made a mistake; whereas those who begin by lying, those for whom the truth has become merely a high-sounding word to cover up their baseness, such people refuse to make amends.

If we are truthful, we will practise justice. 83
I could go on talking about justice and never tire, but here we can only outline a few of its characteristics, bearing in mind that the purpose of the considerations I have been making is to build a real and genuine interior life upon the deep foundations of the human virtues. Justice means giving to each his due. I would, however, go further and say that this is not enough. However much a particular person is due, we must be ready to give him more, because each single soul is a masterpiece of God's making.

The best way of living charity lies in generously outstripping the demands made on us by justice. Such charity will generally go unnoticed, but it is very fruitful in Heaven and indeed also on earth. It would be a mistake to think that when expressions such as "the happy mean" or "a just mean" are used regarding the moral virtues, they imply mediocrity, or somehow aiming at doing half of what we could do. The mean we are asked to aim at lies midway between excess and defect, and is in fact a summit, a peak: the best course of action, as indicated to us by prudence. Though when it comes to the theological virtues, there is no middle course. We cannot believe, or hope, or love too much. We are called to love God without limit, with a love that overflows to those around us in an abundance of generosity, understanding, and charity.

The rewards of temperance

84 Temperance is self-mastery. Not everything we experience in our bodies and souls should be given free rein. Nor ought we to do everything we can do. It is easier to let ourselves be carried away by so-called natural impulses; but this road ends up in sadness and isolation in our own misery.

Some people don't want to deny anything to their stomach, eyes, or hands. They refuse to listen when they are advised to lead clean lives. As for the faculty of generating new life—a great and noble faculty, a participation in God's creative power—they misuse it and make it a tool for their own selfish ends.

But I never did like talking about impurity. I would rather consider the rich rewards that temperance brings. I want to see men who are really men, and not slaves to cheap glitter, as worthless as the trinkets that magpies gather. A manly person knows how to do without those things that may harm his soul and he also comes to realize that his sacrifice is more apparent than real; for living this way, with a spirit of sacrifice, means freeing oneself from many kinds of slavery and savoring instead, in the depths of one's heart, the fullness of God's love.

Life then takes on again shades and tones which intemperance had tended to blur. We find ourselves able to care for the needs of others, to share what is ours with everyone, to devote our energies to great causes. Temperance makes the soul sober, modest, understanding. It fosters a natural sense of reserve which everyone finds attractive because it denotes intelligent self-control. Temperance does not imply narrowness, but greatness of soul. There is much more deprivation in the intemperate heart which abdicates from self-dominion only to become enslaved to the first caller who comes along ringing some pathetic, tinny cow bell.

Wisdom of the heart

85 "The wise heart will be reckoned prudent,"[10] we read in the book of Proverbs. We would have a mistaken idea of prudence if we thought it fainthearted or lacking in daring. Prudence expresses itself as a habit which inclines us to act well, by shedding light on the end and by helping us to seek the most suitable means of achieving it.

But prudence does not stand highest in the scale of values. We should ask ourselves always: prudence, for what? For there is a false kind of prudence ("cunning" would be a better name for it) which is at the service of selfishness and is expert in using the best means to achieve warped ends. In such circumstances, cleverness and perspicacity only serve to worsen one's dispositions and to bring upon oneself the re-

[10] Prov 16:21.

proach St Augustine made in one of his sermons: "Are you trying to bend the heart of God, which is always upright, so that it may fall in with the perversity of yours?"[11] This is the false prudence of the person who thinks his own efforts are quite sufficient to save him. "Do not seek to consider yourselves prudent,"[12] says St Paul, "for it is written, 'I will destroy the wisdom of the wise and the prudence of the prudent.' "[13]

St Thomas points out three aspects of this good habit of the intellect. They are: to seek advice, to judge correctly, and to decide.[14] To be prudent the first step is to acknowledge our own limitations. This is the virtue of humility. Through it, we admit that in certain matters we cannot cover everything, that in so many cases we cannot take in all the circumstances that have to be borne in mind in order to make a fair judgment. So, we look for advice; but not from just anyone. We go to a person with the right qualities, to someone **86**

[11] St Augustine, *Enarrationes in Psalmos*, 63, 18 (PL 36, 771).
[12] Rom 12:16.
[13] 1 Cor 1:19.
[14] Cf. St Thomas Aquinas, *Summa theologiae*, II-II, q.47, a.8.

who wants to love God as sincerely as we do and who tries to follow him faithfully. It is not enough to ask just anyone for his opinion. We must go to a person who can give us sound and disinterested advice.

Next we have to judge, because as a rule, prudence demands that we come to a suitable decision, and promptly. Though at times it is prudent to delay a decision until all the factors that should influence our judgment have been brought together, on other occasions it would be very imprudent not to begin to carry out immediately what we see needs to be done. This is specially true when the good of others is at stake.

87 Such wisdom of the heart, such prudence will never become the prudence of the flesh that St Paul speaks of,[15] the prudence of those who are intelligent but try not to use their intelligence to seek and love our Lord. A truly prudent person is ever attentive to God's promptings and, through this vigilant listening, he receives in his soul the promise and reality of salvation: " 'I glorify thee, Father, Lord of Heaven and earth, for having hidden these

[15] Cf. Rom 8:6.

things from the wise and prudent and revealed them to little ones.' "[16]

Wisdom of the heart guides and governs many other virtues. Through prudence, a man learns to be daring without being rash. He will not make excuses (based on hidden motives of indolence) to avoid the effort involved in living wholeheartedly according to God's plans. The temperance of the prudent man is not insensitive or misanthropic; his justice is not harsh nor is his patience servile.

A person is prudent not because he never **88**
makes a mistake, but because he corrects his errors. He shows his prudence in preferring to miss the mark twenty times rather than give in to an easygoing "do nothing" attitude. He won't rush into things foolishly or behave with absurd rashness. He will run the risk of his decisions. Fear of failure will not make him give up in his effort to do good. As we go through life we find ourselves coming across people who are objective and know how to weigh things up, who don't get heated or try to tip the balance towards that which favors them. Almost instinctively, we find ourselves trusting

[16] Mt 11:25.

such people, because, unassumingly and quietly, they always act in a good and upright manner.

This openhearted virtue is indispensable for Christian living. But the highest goal of prudence is not social harmony or the peace which results from not creating friction. The fundamental motive behind prudence is to fulfill the will of God who wants us to be straightforward without being childish, friends of truth but never bewildered or superficial. "The prudent heart shall possess knowledge,"[17] the knowledge given by God's Love, that ultimate knowledge which can save us and bring to all creation the reward of peace and understanding and, to each soul, eternal life.

An ordinary way

89 We have been speaking about human virtues. Now perhaps some of you might wonder: if I behave in this way, will it not involve cutting myself off from my normal environment? Isn't it something alien to the everyday

[17] Prov 18:15.

world? No. Nowhere is it written that Christians should be strangers to the world. Our Lord Jesus, by his deeds and by his teaching, has bestowed praise on another human virtue which is particularly dear to me, the virtue of naturalness or simplicity.

Remember how our Lord comes into the world, just like every other human being. He spends his childhood and adolescence in a village in Palestine, where he is no different from his fellow villagers. Time and again in his public life we hear echoes of his everyday existence in Nazareth. He speaks about work. He is concerned to see that his disciples rest.[18] He makes a point of meeting people of every sort and never refuses to talk with anyone. To his followers he expressly indicates that they should not hinder children from coming to him.[19] Recalling perhaps memories of his own childhood, he uses the example of the children playing in the marketplace.[20]

Surely all this is quite normal, natural, and straightforward? Surely it can be lived in ordinary life? What happens is that people tend

[18] Cf. Mk 6:31.
[19] Cf. Lk 18:16.
[20] Cf. *Ibid* 7:32.

to get used to what is plain and ordinary and, without realizing it, they begin to look for what is showy and artificial. You will have come across examples of this, as I have, as when for instance you remark on the beauty of some freshly cut roses, with delicately fragrant petals, and someone comments "They look so perfect, they must be artificial!"

90 Naturalness and simplicity are two marvellous human virtues which enable men to take in the message of Christ. On the other hand, all that is tangled and complicated, the twisting and turning about one's own problems, all this builds up a barrier which often prevents people from hearing our Lord's voice. Remember Christ's reproach to the Pharisees: they had enmeshed themselves in a maze-ridden world which made them pay tithes of mint, dill, and cumin, while neglecting the most essential duties of the law, of justice, and of faith. They were careful to strain everything they drank so as not to let even a mosquito pass, and they ended up swallowing a camel.[21]

No. Neither the decent human lives of those who, through no fault of their own, do not

[21] Cf. Mt 23:23-24.

know Christ, nor the lives of Christians, should be odd or strange. The human virtues which we are considering today lead us, each and everyone of them, to the same conclusion. That man is truly human who strives to be truthful, loyal, sincere, courageous, temperate, generous, serene, just, hardworking, patient. Such behavior may be difficult to achieve, but it can never be strange. If some people find it surprising, it is because their eyes have grown dim and they are clouded by a hidden cowardice and a lack of determination.

Human virtues and supernatural virtues

Once a person is striving to improve in the human virtues, his heart is already very close to Christ. If he is a Christian, he will realize that the theological virtues (faith, hope, and charity) and all the other virtues which God's grace brings with it are an encouragement never to neglect the good qualities he shares with so many of his fellowmen. **91**

The human virtues are, I insist, the foundation for the supernatural ones. These in turn provide us with constant encouragement to behave as good human beings. In either case, it is not sufficient merely to want to have these virtues. We have to learn how to practise them. *Discite benefacere*[22] ("learn to do good"). We need to make a habit of exercising each virtue, by actually being sincere, truthful, balanced, calm, and patient...for love is proved by deeds and we cannot love God only by word, but "with deeds and in truth."[23]

92 When a Christian fights to acquire these virtues, his soul is preparing to receive the grace of the Holy Spirit fruitfully. In this way his good human qualities are strengthened by the motions of the Paraclete in his soul. The Third Person of the Blessed Trinity, the soul's sweet guest,[24] pours out his gifts: wisdom, understanding, counsel, fortitude, knowledge, piety, and the fear of the Lord.[25]

Then one experiences joy and peace,[26] a joyous peace, an interior rejoicing that goes hand in hand with the human virtue of cheerfulness. At the very moment when everything

[22] Is 1:17.
[23] 1 Jn 3:18.
[24] Sequence, *Veni, Sancte Spiritus*.
[25] Cf Is 11:2.
[26] Gal 5:22.

seems to be collapsing before our eyes, we realize that quite the opposite is true, "because you, Lord, are my strength."[27] If God is dwelling in our soul, everything else, no matter how important it may seem, is accidental and transitory, whereas we, in God, stand permanent and firm.

Through the gift of piety, the Holy Spirit helps us to realize with certainty that we are children of God. And, being children of God, how can we be sad? Sadness is the end product of selfishness. If we truly want to live for God, we will never lack cheerfulness, even when we discover our errors and wretchedness. Cheerfulness finds its way into our life of prayer, so much so that we cannot help singing for joy. For we are in love, and singing is a thing that lovers do.

If we live our lives in this way, we shall be **93**
bringing peace to the world. We shall be making God's service attractive to others, because "God loves a cheerful giver."[28] Christians are ordinary people, but their hearts overflow with the joy that comes when we set

[27] Ps 42:2.
[28] 2 Cor 9:7.

out to fulfill, with the constant help of grace, the will of the Father. Christians don't see themselves as victims, underrated, or restricted in their behavior. They walk head on high, because they are men and children of God.

Our faith brings out the full meaning of these human virtues, which no one should ever neglect. Christians should be second to none as human beings. Those who follow Christ are able (not by their own merit but by the grace of God) to communicate to those around them what they at times suspect but cannot quite grasp: that true happiness, a genuine spirit of serving our neighbor, can only come by passing through the Heart of our Redeemer, *perfectus Deus, perfectus homo.*

Let us turn to Mary, our Mother, and the most excellent creature ever fashioned by God's hands. Let us ask her to make us humanly good so that our human virtues, woven into the life of grace, may become our best way of helping those who, with us, are working in the world to bring peace and happiness to all men.

HUMILITY*

Let us consider for a moment the texts of today's Mass, Tuesday in Passion Week, for they will help us to distinguish "true godliness" from "false godliness."** We shall be speaking about humility, for this is the virtue which helps us to recognize, at one and the same time, both our wretchedness and our greatness. 94

Our wretchedness is all too evident. I am not here referring to our natural limitations, to those great ambitions that people dream of, but in fact, never achieve, if only for lack of time.

* A homily given on April 6, 1965.

** The author writes *endiosamiento bueno* and *endiosamiento malo*. *Endiosamiento* is a rich concept. In the good sense, it expresses the soul's becoming clothed by, filled with, totally immersed in God, "divinized," "deified." In the bad sense, it refers to pride, a false deification, in defiance of God, and in complicity with the tempter's words, "You will be like God" (Gen 3:5). (Translator's note).

I am thinking rather of the things we do badly, of our falls, of the mistakes that could have been avoided and were not. We are continually experiencing our personal inadequacies. Moreover, there are times when it seems as if all our failings come together, as if wanting to show themselves more clearly, to make us realize just how little we are worth. When that happens, what are we to do?

Expecta Dominum[1] ("Hope in the Lord"). Live by hope, full of faith and love, the Church says to us. *Viriliter age*[2] ("be of good heart"). What does it matter that we are made of clay, if all our hope is placed in God? And if at a certain moment you should fall or suffer some setback (not that it has to happen), all you have to do is to apply the remedy, just as, in the normal course of events, you would do for the sake of your bodily health. And then: off to a fresh start!

95 Haven't you noticed the way families look after valuable ornaments or decorative pieces, a vase for example; how they take care lest it get broken? Until one day the baby happens to

[1] Ps 26:14 (Introit of the Mass).
[2] *Ibid.*

be playing nearby and knocks it over. The precious souvenir is dashed to pieces, and all the family are very upset. But they immediately set about repairing it. The pieces are gathered up and carefully glued together, and in the end it is restored to its former beauty.

However, when the broken object is a simple piece of crockery or just a piece of earthenware, it is usually enough to get some simple rivets, clips of iron, or other metal to bind the fragments together. The pot or vessel thus repaired takes on an original charm of its own.

We can apply this lesson to our own interior life. When we are faced with weaknesses and sins, with our mistakes—even though, by God's grace, they be of little account—let us turn to God our Father in prayer and say to him, "Lord, here I am in my wretchedness and frailty, a broken vessel of clay. Bind me together again, Lord, and then, helped by my sorrow and by your forgiveness, I shall be stronger and more attractive than before!" What a consoling prayer, which we can say every time something fractures this miserable clay of which we are made.

Let us not be surprised to discover our frailty. Let it not come as a shock to see how easily our good behavior breaks down, for little or no reason. Have confidence in the Lord, whose help is always at hand. "The Lord is my light and my salvation. Whom shall I fear?"[3] No one. If we approach our heavenly Father in this way, we will have no grounds for fearing anyone or anything.

Listening to God

96 If we turn to Sacred Scripture we will see that humility is absolutely necessary when we are making ready to listen to God. "Where there is humility, there is wisdom,"[4] says the book of Proverbs. Humility means looking at ourselves as we really are, honestly and without excuses. And when we realize that we are worth hardly anything, we can then open ourselves to God's greatness: it is there our greatness lies.

How well our Lady, Jesus' Holy Mother, understood this! She, the most exalted of all God's creatures that have existed or ever will exist upon this earth! Mary glorifies the power

[3] *Ibid* 26:1 (Introit of the Mass).
[4] Prov 11:2.

of our Lord, who "has put down the mighty from their thrones and has exalted the lowly."[5] And she sings of how his divine providence has once again been fulfilled in her: " 'because he has regarded the lowliness of his handmaid, behold henceforth all generations shall call me blessed.' "[6]

Mary becomes transformed in holiness in the depths of her most pure heart on seeing the humility of God: " 'the Holy Spirit shall come upon you, and the power of the Most High shall overshadow you; and, therefore, the Holy One to be born of you shall be called the Son of God.' "[7] The Blessed Virgin's humility is a consequence of that unfathomable depth of grace which comes into operation with the Incarnation of the Second Person of the Blessed Trinity in the womb of his ever Immaculate Mother.

When St Paul considers this mystery, he too **97**
breaks into a joyful hymn which we can savor today word by word: "Yours is to be the same mind which Christ Jesus showed. Though being by nature God, he did not consider being equal

[5] Lk 1:52.
[6] *Ibid* 1:48.
[7] *Ibid* 1:35.

to God a thing to be coveted," (for he was God by essence) "but emptied himself, and took the nature of a slave, fashioned in the likeness of men, presenting himself to us in human form; and then he humbled himself, becoming obedient unto death, even to death on a cross."[8]

In his preaching, our Lord Jesus Christ very often sets before our eyes the example of his own humility. "Learn from me, for I am meek and humble of heart,"[9] so that you and I may know that there is no other way, and that only our sincere recognition of our nothingness is powerful enough to draw divine grace towards us. St Augustine says: "It was for us that Jesus came to suffer hunger and to be our food, to suffer thirst and to be our drink, to be clothed with our mortality and to clothe us with immortality, to be poor so as to make us rich."[10]

98 "God resists the proud, but gives his grace to the humble,"[11] the Apostle St Peter teaches. In any age, in any human setting, there is no other way, to live a godly life, than that of humility. Does this mean that God takes pleas-

[8] Phil 2:5-8.
[9] Mt 11:29.
[10] St Augustine, *Enarrationes in Psalmos*, 49, 19 (PL 36, 577).
[11] 1 Pt 5:5.

ure in our humiliation? Not at all. What would he, who created all things and governs them and maintains them in existence, gain from our prostration? God only wants us to be humble and to empty ourselves, so that he can fill us. He wants us not to put obstacles in his way so that—humanly speaking—there will be more room for his grace in our poor hearts. For the God who inspires us to be humble is the same God who "will refashion the body of our lowliness, conforming it to the body of his glory, by exerting the power by which he is able also to subject all things to himself."[12] Our Lord makes us his own, he makes us divine with a "true godliness."

The enemy is pride

What is it that impedes this humility, this 99
"true godliness?" It is pride. Pride is the capital sin that leads to "false godliness." Pride encourages one, even perhaps in very trivial matters, to follow the subtle prompting which Satan made to our first parents: "your eyes will be

[12] Phil 3:21.

opened and you will be like God, knowing good and evil."[13] Elsewhere in the Scriptures we read that "the beginning of the pride of man is to draw away from God."[14] Indeed this vice, once it has taken root, infects a man's entire way of life, until it becomes what St John calls *superbia vitae*[15] ("the pride of life").

Proud? About what? Sacred Scripture finds both tragic and comic expressions to stigmatize pride: Why are you so proud, you who are but dust and ashes? Even in life, you are vomiting your entrails. A slight illness: the doctor smiles. The king that reigns today will be dead tomorrow.[16]

100 When pride takes hold of a soul, it is no surprise to find it bringing along with it a whole string of other vices: greed, self-indulgence, envy, injustice. The proud man is always vainly striving to dethrone God, who is merciful to all his creatures, so as to make room for himself and his ever cruel ways.

We should beg God not to let us fall into this temptation. Pride is the worst sin of all, and

[13] Gen 3:5.
[14] Ecclus 10:14.
[15] 1 Jn 2:16.
[16] Cf. Ecclus 10:9, 11-12.

the most ridiculous. If, with its multiple delusions, it manages to get a hold, the unfortunate victim begins to build up a facade, to fill himself with emptiness, and becomes conceited like the toad in the fable which, in order to show off, puffed itself up until it burst. Pride is unpleasant, even from a human point of view. The person who rates himself better than everyone and everything is constantly studying himself and looking down on other people, who in turn react by ridiculing his foolish vanity.

When we hear pride spoken of, perhaps we 101
imagine it as despotic, domineering behavior. We associate it with the clamor of the mob acclaiming the passing victor, who, like a Roman emperor, bows his head lest his glorious brow graze the white marble of the high triumphal arches.

But let us be realistic. This type of pride is found only in people with crazy imaginations. We have to fight against other forms of pride that are more subtle, and more frequent: against the pride of preferring our own excellence to that of our neighbor; against vanity in our conversations, thoughts, and gestures; against an almost sickly touchiness that takes offense at words and actions that are in no way meant to be insulting.

All this can be, and is, a common temptation. A person can come to see himself as the sun and center of all those around him. Everything must center round himself. And to satisfy this unhealthy urge, the proud person will sometimes even fake pain, sadness, or illness to attract attention so that others will make a fuss of him.

Most of the conflicts arising in the interior life of many people are products of their own imagination: "the things people have said, what they are thinking, whether I am appreciated...". The poor soul suffers, through his pathetic foolishness, harboring suspicions that are unfounded. In this miserable mood everything makes him bitter and he tries to upset others also. All this because he doesn't wish to be humble, because he hasn't learned to forget himself in order to give himself generously in the service of others for the love of God.

A donkey for his throne

102 Let us turn once again to the Gospels, and look at ourselves in our model, in Jesus Christ.

James and John, through their mother, have asked Jesus for places at his right and at his left. The other disciples are angry with them. What is our Lord's answer to all this? " 'Whoever has a mind to be great among you, must be your servant; and whoever has a mind to be first among you, must be the slave of all; for the Son of Man has not come to be served but to serve, and to give his life as a ransom for many.' "[17]

On another occasion they were going to Capharnaum. Jesus may have been walking ahead of them as he did on other days. "And there, when they were in the house, he asked them, 'What were you arguing about on the way?' But they kept silence, for on the way they had" once more "been disputing among themselves which of them was the greatest. Then he sat down, and called the twelve to him, and said, 'If anyone has a mind to be the first, he must be the last of all, and the servant of all.' And he took a little child, and set him in the midst of them; and taking him into his arms, he said to them, 'Whoever welcomes such a child as this in my name, welcomes me; and

[17] Mk 10:43-45.

whoever welcomes me, welcomes, not me, but him who sent me.' "[18]

Doesn't this way Jesus has of doing things move us to love him? He teaches them the doctrine and then, to enable them to understand it, he gives them a living example. He calls a little child, one of the children running around the house, and he lovingly embraces him. How eloquent our Lord's silence is! With it he has already said everything. He loves those who become as little children. He then adds that the reward for this simplicity, for this humility of spirit, is the joy of being able to embrace him and his Father who is in Heaven.

When the time for his Passion draws near
103 and Jesus wants to illustrate his kingship in a very vivid way, he makes a triumphant entry into Jerusalem, mounted on a donkey! It had been written that the Messiah was to be a king of humility: " 'Tell the daughter of Sion: Behold your king comes to you, meek and seated on an ass, on a colt, the foal of a beast of burden.' "[19]

[18] *Ibid* 9:32-36.
[19] Mt 21:5; Zach 9:9.

Now it is the Last Supper. Christ has prepared everything to bid farewell to his disciples, while they, for the umpteenth time, have become embroiled in an argument about which one of the chosen group is to be considered the greatest. Jesus then "rising from supper, laid his garments aside, took a towel and put it about him. Then he poured water into a basin and began to wash the feet of his disciples, wiping them with the towel that girded him."[20]

Once again he preaches by example, by his deeds. In the presence of the disciples, who are arguing out of pride and vanity, Jesus bows down and gladly carries out the task of a servant. Afterwards, when he returns to the table, he explains to them: "Do you understand what it is I have done to you? You call me Master and Lord, and you are right, it is what I am. Why then, if I have washed your feet, I who am the Master and the Lord, you in your turn ought to wash each other's feet."[21] This tactfulness of our Lord moves me deeply. He does not say: "If I do this, how much more ought you to?" He puts himself at their level,

[20] Jn 13:4-5.
[21] *Ibid* 13:12-14.

and he lovingly chides those men for their lack of generosity.

As he did with the first twelve, so also, with us, our Lord can and does whisper in our ear, time and again, *exemplum dedi vobis*[22] ("I have given you an example of humility. I have become a slave, so that you too may learn to serve all men with a meek and humble heart").

The fruits of humility

104 "The greater you are, the more in all things abase yourself, and you shall find favor with God."[23] If we are humble, God will never abandon us. He humbles the arrogance of the proud, but he saves the humble. He frees the innocent man, who is rescued because his hands are clean.[24] The infinite mercy of our Lord is not slow in coming to the aid of those who humbly call upon him. And then he acts as he truly is, as God Almighty. Although there may be many dangers, though the soul may feel harassed and find itself surrounded on all sides

[22] *Ibid* 13:15.
[23] Ecclus 3:20.
[24] Cf. Job 22:29-30.

by the enemies of its salvation, it will not perish. This is not merely something that was true in days gone by. It continues to happen now.

As I read today's Epistle, I pictured Daniel 105
there surrounded by hungry lions and, without wishing to be pessimistic, for I cannot say that "old times were better" since every age has its good and bad aspects, I was thinking that at the present time there are also many lions running loose, and that we have to live in this environment. They are lions looking for someone to devour: *tamquam leo rugiens, circuit quaerens quem devoret.*[25] ("He goes about like a roaring lion, to find his prey").

What can we do to avoid these wild beasts? Perhaps our lot won't be the same as Daniel's. While I am not one for miraculous solutions, I love the wondrous greatness of God when he performs them, and I realize that it would have been easier for God to allay the prophet's hunger, or to place food in front of him. Yet God did not do it that way. Rather he arranged for another prophet, Habacuc, to be transported miraculously from Judea to bring him food.

[25] 1 Pt 5:8.

God did not mind working a great miracle here, because Daniel was in the lions' den not through any fault of his own, but on account of the injustice of the devil's hirelings, because he was a servant of God and a destroyer of idols.

We ourselves are also called to destroy many idols, not by doing anything spectacular but by living with the naturalness of an ordinary Christian, sowing peace and joy around us. In this way we will topple the idols of misunderstanding, of injustice, of ignorance, and of those who claim to be self-sufficient and arrogantly turn their backs on God.

Don't be frightened; don't fear any harm, even though the circumstances in which you work are terrible, worse even than those of Daniel in the pit with all those ferocious beasts. God's hand is as powerful as ever and, if necessary, he will work miracles. Be faithful! With a loving, responsible, and cheerful faithfulness to the teaching of Christ. Be convinced that our times are no worse than those of other centuries, and that our Lord is always the same.

I knew an elderly priest who used to say with a smile: "As for me, I'm always calm and peaceful." That is how we should always be, immersed in the world, with hungry lions all around, yet never losing our peace, our calm. Always loving, believing and hoping, and never forgetting that our Lord will work all the miracles we need, if and when we need them.

Let me remind you that if you are sincere, 106
if you show yourselves as you really are, if you acquire that "true godliness" by being humble and not proud, then you and I will be safe in any environment. We will always be able to talk of battles won and call ourselves the victors. Ours will be the intimate victories of God's love, which bring peace, understanding, and happiness to the soul.

Humility will spur us on to carry out great tasks, but only on condition that we never lose sight of our inadequacy, and that we are convinced, and more so each day, of our own helplessness. St Ambrose says: "Admit without hesitation that you are a servant obliged to carry out a great number of tasks. Do not swagger about because you are called a child of God. Let us acknowledge the grace, but not forget our nature. Do not become swollen-headed if you have served well, because you have done what you were supposed to do. The sun carries out its task and the moon obeys; the angels perform their duties. The instrument chosen by God for the Gentiles says: 'I do not deserve the name of Apostle, because I have persecuted the Church of God' (1 Cor 15:9) ...May we also refrain from seeking praise for ourselves,"[26] for our own merits, which are always pitiful and small.

Humility and joy

107 "Rescue me from what is deceitful and impious in man."[27] Once again the text of the Mass brings us to "true godliness." It sets before our eyes the poor material of which we are made and all our evil inclinations. And then it begs God: *emitte lucem tuam,*[28] send forth your light and your truth, which have led me and brought me to your holy mountain. I don't mind telling you that I have been deeply moved while praying these words of the Gradual.

How then are we to behave in order to acquire this "true godliness"? In the Gospel we

[26] St Ambrose, *Expositio Evangelii secundum Lucam*, 8, 32 (PL 15, 1774).

[27] Cf. Ps 42:1 (Gradual of the Mass).

[28] *Ibid* 42:3 (Gradual of the Mass).

read that Jesus "did not wish to go about in Judea because the Jews were seeking to put him to death."[29] He, who could have eliminated his enemies with a simple desire of his will, also used human means. He, who was God and could change circumstances with a mere wish, has left us a marvellous lesson here: he did not go to Judea. "His brethren said to him, 'Leave here and go to Judea that your disciples also may see the works that you do.' "[30] They would have him do something spectacular. Do you see? Do you see that this is a lesson in "true godliness" and "false godliness"?

"True godliness." Today's Offertory prayer proclaims: "all who know thy name, O Lord, hope in thee, for you forsake not those who seek thee."[31] And we who are but mended vessels of clay rejoice, "for he has not forgotten the prayers of the poor in spirit,"[32] the prayers of the humble.

Put not the slightest trust in those who **108**
present the virtue of humility as something degrading, or as a virtue condemning us to a

[29] Jn 7:1.
[30] *Ibid* 7:3.
[31] Ps 9:11.
[32] *Ibid* 9:13.

permanent state of dejection. To know we are made of clay, riveted together again, is a continual source of joy. It means acknowledging our littleness in the eyes of God: a little child, a son. Can there be any joy to compare with that of the person who, knowing himself to be poor and weak, knows also that he is a son of God? Why do we men become dejected? It is because life on earth does not go the way we had hoped, or because obstacles arise which prevent us from satisfying our personal ambitions.

Nothing like this happens when a person lives the supernatural reality of his divine filiation. "If God is for us, who can be against us?"[33] As I never tire of repeating: let them be sad who are determined not to recognize that they are children of God!

Finally, we find in today's liturgy two petitions which should spring like arrows from our lips and hearts: "O almighty God, may our ceaseless celebration of these divine mysteries help us to merit the gifts of Heaven."[34] And "O Lord, grant that we may constantly serve you

[33] Rom 8:31.
[34] Postcommunion of the Mass.

in accordance with your will."[35] Service, my children, service: that is our role; to be "servants to all, so that in our days the faithful people may grow in merit and in number."[36]

Let us turn our eyes towards Mary. No **109**
creature ever surrendered herself to the plans of God more humbly than she. The humility of the *ancilla Domini*[37] ("the handmaid of the Lord"), is the reason we invoke her as *causa nostrae laetitiae* ("cause of our joy"). After Eve had sinned through her foolish desire to be equal to God, she hid herself from the Lord and was ashamed: she was sad. Mary, in confessing herself the handmaid of the Lord, becomes the Mother of the Divine Word, and is filled with joy. May the rejoicing that is hers, the joy of our good Mother, spread to all of us, so that with it we may go out to greet her, our Holy Mother Mary, and thus become more like Christ, her Son.

[35] Prayer *Super populum.*
[36] *Ibid.*
[37] Lk 1:38.

DETACHMENT*

Now that we are at the beginning of Holy Week, and so very close to the moment when the Redemption of the whole human race was accomplished on Calvary, it seems to be an especially appropriate time for you and me to reflect on how our Lord Jesus Christ saved us, and to contemplate this love of his—this truly inexpressible love—for poor creatures like us, who have been made from the clay of the earth. 110

Memento homo, quia pulvis es, et in pulverem reverteris.[1] ("Remember man that thou art dust, and unto dust thou shalt return," from the Rite of the Imposition of Ashes). Thus did our Mother the Church admonish us at the beginning of Lent so that we might never forget how

* A homily given on April 4, 1955, Monday in Holy Week.
[1] Cf. Gen 3:19.

very little we are, and that some day our bodies, now so full of life, will dissolve like a cloud of dust kicked up by our footsteps on a country road and will pass away "like a mist dispersed by the rays of the sun."[2]

The example of Christ

But after this stark reminder of our personal insignificance, I would also like to put before you another splendid truth: the magnificence of God who sustains and divinizes us. Listen to the words of the Apostle: "You know the graciousness of our Lord Jesus Christ, how, being rich, he became poor for our sake, that by his poverty you might become rich."[3] Reflect calmly on this example of our Lord, and you will see at once that here we have abundant material on which we could meditate a whole lifetime and from which to draw specific and sincere resolutions to be more generous. We should never lose sight of the goal which we have to reach, namely, that each one of us must become identified with Jesus Christ, who, as

[2] Wis 2:4.
[3] 2 Cor 8:9.

you have just heard, became poor for you and for me, and suffered, that we might have an example of how to follow in his footsteps.[4]

Have you never wondered, out of a holy curiosity, just how Jesus carried through to its conclusion this outpouring of his love? Once again it is St Paul who gives us the answer: "though being by nature God, (...) he emptied himself, and took the nature of a slave, fashioned in the likeness of men."[5] My children, fill yourselves with wonder and gratitude at such a mystery and learn from it. All the power, all the majesty, all the beauty, all the infinite harmony of God, all his great and immeasurable riches, God whole and entire was hidden for our benefit in the Humanity of Christ. The Almighty appears determined to eclipse his glory for a time, so as to make it easy for his creatures to approach their Redeemer. 111

"No man," St John writes, "has ever seen God; but now his only begotten Son, who abides in the bosom of the Father, has himself revealed him,"[6] appearing to the astonished gaze of men: first, as a newborn babe, in

[4] Cf. 1 Pt 2:21.
[5] Phil 2:6-7.
[6] Jn 1:18.

Bethlehem; then, as a child just like other children; later on, in the temple, as a bright and alert 12-year-old; and finally in the lovable and attractive image of the Teacher who stirred the hearts of the enthusiastic crowds that accompanied him.

112 We have only to consider a few traits of God's Love made flesh and our souls are touched by his generosity; they are set on fire and feel gently impelled to contrition for having been petty and selfish on so many occasions. Jesus does not mind lowering himself in order to raise us from our destitution to the dignity of being children of God and brothers of his. You and I, unlike him, often pride ourselves stupidly on the gifts and talents we have received, to the point of making them a pedestal from which to impose our will on others, as if the merits of our few relatively successful efforts derived from ourselves alone. "What do you have that you have not received from God? And if what you have, you have received, why do you boast as if you had not received it?"[7]

When we think of God's self-giving and the way he humbled himself—I am saying this so

[7] 1 Cor 4:7.

that each one of us can meditate on it and apply it to himself—then the vainglory and presumption of the proud man stands out as a truly hideous sin, for the very reason that such conduct is poles apart from the model given us by Jesus Christ. Think about it slowly: He, being God, humiliated himself; man, puffed up with self-love, tries to build himself up at any cost, without recognizing that he is but a creature of clay, and poor clay at that.

When you were children, you may have **113**
heard the fable of the farmer who was given a golden pheasant. When the initial delight and surprise were over, the new owner began looking for a place where he could keep the pheasant. After several hours of doubting and changing his mind, he decided to put the pheasant in the hen house. The hens greatly admired the handsome newcomer and flocked round him with all the astonishment that might accompany the discovery of a demigod. While all this commotion was going on, feeding time came round and, as the farmer threw in the first handfuls of grain, our pheasant, who was starving after all the waiting, jumped greedily at the chance of filling his empty stomach. When they saw such vulgarity, their handsome

hero gobbling down his food as hungrily as the commonest of birds, his disillusioned barnyard companions fell to pecking their fallen idol until they had plucked out all his feathers. Such is the sorry collapse of self-worship, which is made all the more disastrous the more presumptuously it is built upon the foundation of one's own unaided ability.

As the trustees of certain talents, both supernatural and human, which you have to make good use of, draw your own practical conclusions for your daily life. And, at the same time, get rid of the ridiculous delusion that you have something that belongs to you alone as if it were the fruit of your own efforts. Remember there is an ever present factor, God, which no one can ignore.

114 Bearing in mind what I have just said, I want you to be completely convinced that, if we really want to follow our Lord closely and be of real service to God and the whole of mankind, then we must be thoroughly detached from ourselves, our intellectual talents, our health, our good name, our noble ambitions, our triumphs and successes.

I would also include—because your decision ought to go that far—the high ideals which lead us to seek only to give all the glory to God and to praise him. We can ensure our detachment by tailoring our will to this clear and precise rule: "Lord, I want this or that only if it pleases you, because, if not, I'm not the slightest bit interested." By acting in this way, we are dealing a mortal blow to the selfishness and vanity that lurk in every conscience. At the same time, we will find true peace of soul through this selfless conduct that leads to an ever more intimate and intense possession of God.

If we are to imitate Jesus Christ, our hearts need to be entirely free from attachments. " 'If anyone wishes to come after me, let him deny himself, take up his cross, and follow me. For he who would save his life shall lose it; but he who loses his life for my sake shall find it. For what does it profit a man, if he gains the whole world at the cost of losing his own soul?' "[8] St Gregory makes the following comments: "It would not be enough to live detached from things, if we were not to renounce ourselves as well. But...where shall we go outside of ourselves? Who is the one who renounces, if he leaves himself?

[8] Mt 16:24-26.

"You must know that we find ourselves in two situations: in the one, we have fallen through sin; in the other, we have been formed by God. We have been created in one mode of existence but we find ourselves in another because of ourselves. So let us renounce ourselves as regards what we have become through sin, but let us stand firm in that which we have been constituted by grace. Thus, if the man who was proud is converted to Christ and becomes humble, then he has already renounced self; if a lustful man changes to a life of continence, he too has renounced self as regards what he was before; if a miser ceases to covet and, instead of seizing other people's property, begins to be generous with his own, he has most surely denied himself."[9]

Christian self-control

115 Our Lord asks for generous hearts that are truly detached. We will achieve this if we resolutely cut the thick bonds or the subtle threads that tie us to ourselves. I won't hide from you the fact that this entails a constant

[9] St Gregory the Great, *Homiliae in Evangelia*, 32, 2 (PL 76, 1233).

struggle, overriding our own intelligence and will, a renunciation which, frankly, is more difficult than the giving up of the most prized material possessions.

The detachment which our Lord preached, and which he expects from every Christian, necessarily brings with it external manifestations. Jesus *coepit facere et docere.*[10] ("He began to do and to teach"). Before teaching with words he proclaimed his doctrine with deeds. You have seen that he was born in a stable, in the most abject poverty, and that the first time he slept on this earth was on straw in a manger. Later, in the years of his apostolic journeyings, you will recall, among many other examples, the clear warning he gave to a man who offered to become one of his disciples: "Foxes have holes, and the birds of the air their resting places; but the Son of Man has nowhere to lay his head."[11] Nor should you forget to contemplate the Gospel scene which shows the Apostles staving off their hunger on the Sabbath day by plucking some ears of corn that were growing by the wayside.[12]

[10] Acts 1:1.
[11] Lk 9:58.
[12] Cf. Mk 2:23.

116 You might say that our Lord's approach to the mission he received from his Father was to live from day to day, just as he advised his hearers in one of the most divinely challenging statements of his teaching: "Therefore, I say to you, do not be anxious for your life, what you shall eat; nor for your body, what you shall clothe it with. Life is a greater thing than food, the body than clothing. See how the ravens never sow nor reap, have neither storehouse nor barn, and yet God feeds them; have you not an excellence far beyond theirs?...See how the lilies grow; they do not toil, or spin, and yet I tell you that even Solomon in all his glory was not arrayed like one of these. If God, then, so clothes the grasses which live today in the fields and will feed the oven tomorrow, will he not be much more ready to clothe you, men of little faith?"[13]

If only we could live with more trust in divine Providence, strong in faith, in the certainty of God's daily protection which never fails, how many worries and anxieties we would be spared! Then that fretfulness which, as Jesus said, is typical of pagans, of "the

[13] Lk 12:22-24, 27-28.

heathen world,"[14] that is, of people who lack a supernatural outlook on life, would disappear. Now that I am confiding in you as a friend, as a priest, and as a father, I would like to remind you that in every circumstance of our lives we are, by God's mercy, children of our almighty Father, who is in Heaven but who also dwells in the intimacy of our hearts. I would like to engrave upon your minds the conviction that since "your Father well knows what you need,"[15] we have every reason to be optimistic on our journey through this life, with our souls completely detached from those earthly things that seem so very necessary. God will provide. Believe me, this is the only way to be lords of creation[16] and to avoid the pitiful slavery into which so many people fall because they forget that they are children of God and spend their time worrying about tomorrow or a future that they may never see.

Once again, let me share with you a *tiny bit* **117**
of my own experience. I open my heart to you in the presence of God, utterly convinced that

[14] *Ibid* 12:30.
[15] *Ibid.*
[16] Cf. Gen 1:26-31.

I am not a model for anyone, that I am but a piece of old rag, a poor instrument—a deaf and clumsy instrument—which our Lord has used to show conclusively that he can and does write perfectly, even with the leg of a table. So, when I am talking about myself, it never occurs to me—in no way whatsoever—to think that there is any merit of mine in what I have done. Even less would I try to press you into following the paths where our Lord has led me, since it may well be that the Master will not ask you for that which has helped me so much to work unhindered in this Work of God, to which I have dedicated my entire life.

Let me assure you, it's something which I have touched with my own hands and seen with my own eyes, that, if you trust in God's Providence, if you abandon yourselves in his all-powerful arms, you will never lack the means to serve God, his Holy Church, and the souls of men; and this without having to neglect any of your duties. You will then rejoice in the joy and peace which *mundus dare non potest* ("the world cannot give")[17] which possessing all the goods of the world cannot give.

[17] Cf. Jn 14:27.

From the very beginning of Opus Dei in 1928, apart from the fact that I had no human resources whatever, I have never personally controlled even a penny. Nor have I intervened directly in the financial aspects which naturally arise in any project that involves people—men of flesh and blood, not angels—who need material instruments to do their work efficiently.

Opus Dei has needed, and I think it's safe to assume that to the end of time it will always need the generous cooperation of many people in order to maintain its apostolic works. One reason for this is that such activities never show a profit. Another reason is that, even though the number of helpers increases and the work done by my children expands, if there is love of God the apostolate grows and the requests multiply. And so, more than once I have made my children laugh for, while strongly urging them to respond faithfully to God's grace, I was encouraging them to go to our Lord and fearlessly ask him for more grace *and* for the money, the ready cash, that we needed so badly.

In the early years we were short of everything, even the most basic necessities. Attracted by the fire of God, there came to my side workers, clerks, university students, etc., who had no idea of the straits we were in, because in Opus Dei we have always managed, with God's help, to work in such a way that both our sacrifices and our prayers have been both abundant and unnoticed. When I now look back on those times my heart overflows in humble thanksgiving. What certainty we felt in our souls! We knew that in seeking first the Kingdom of God and his justice, we would be given all the rest as well.[18] And I can assure you that not a single apostolic initiative had to be abandoned for lack of material resources. Wherever it was necessary our Father God, through his ordinary providence, would ensure in one way or another that we got what we required so that we could see that He is always a "generous paymaster."

118 If you want to be your own masters at all times, I advise you to make a very real effort to be detached from everything, and to do so without fear or hesitation. Then, when you go about your various duties, whether personal, family, or otherwise, make honest use of

[18] Cf. Mt 6:33.

upright human means with a view to serving God, his Church, your family, your profession, your country, and the whole of mankind. Remember that what really matters is not whether you have this or lack that, but whether you are living according to the truth taught us by our Christian faith, which tells us that created goods are only a means, nothing more. So, do not be beguiled into imagining that they are in any way definitive: "Do not lay up for yourselves treasures on earth, where there is rust and moth to consume it, and where there are thieves to break in and steal it. Lay up treasure for yourselves in Heaven, where there is no moth or rust to consume it, no thieves to break in, and steal. For where your treasure is, there your heart is too."[19]

When a man tries to build his happiness exclusively around the things of this world, and in this I have witnessed some real tragedies, he perverts their proper use and destroys the order so wisely established by the Creator. As a consequence the heart is left sad and unsatisfied. It starts following paths which lead to everlasting unhappiness and it ends up, even

[19] *Ibid* 6:19-21.

in this world, a slave, the victim of the very same goods which had perhaps been gained at the cost of countless efforts and renunciations. But, above all, I recommend you never to forget that God cannot find a place, that he cannot dwell in a heart which is bogged down by a coarse, disorderly, and empty love. "No man can serve two masters; either he will hate the one and love the other, or else he will devote himself to the one and despise the other. You cannot serve God and money."[20] "Let us then anchor our hearts in a love that can make us happy...Let us desire the treasures of Heaven."[21]

119 I am not, of course, encouraging you to give up fulfilling your duties or claiming your rights. On the contrary, for any of us in normal circumstances to retreat on this front would be tantamount to a cowardly desertion from the battle for sanctity to which God has called us. You should, therefore, with a sure conscience, endeavor (above all through your work) to ensure that neither you nor your family lack what is necessary to live with Christian dignity. If at times you feel the pinch of poverty, don't

[20] *Ibid* 6:24.
[21] *In Matthaeum homiliae*, 63, 3 (PG 58, 607).

get dejected and don't rebel against it. I do, however, insist that you should try to use all the upright means available to get over such a situation, because to do otherwise would be to tempt God's providence. But while you are so fighting, remember too the *omnia in bonum*: all things, even scarcity and poverty, work together unto the good of those who love God.[22] Get into the habit, from now on, of facing up cheerfully to little shortcomings and discomforts, to cold and heat, to the lack of things you feel you can't do without, to being unable to rest as and when you would like to, to hunger, loneliness, ingratitude, lack of appreciation, disgrace...

Father...do not take them out of the world

It is we, men walking in the street, ordinary **120**
Christians immersed in the bloodstream of society, whom our Lord wants to be saints and apostles, in the very midst of our professional work; that is, sanctifying our job in life, sanctifying ourselves in it and, through it, helping

[22] Cf. Rom 8:28.

others to sanctify themselves as well. Be convinced that it is there that God awaits you, with all the love of a Father and Friend. Consider too that, by doing your daily work well and responsibly, not only will you be supporting yourselves financially, you will also be contributing in a very direct way to the development of society. You will be relieving the burdens of others and maintaining countless welfare projects, both local and international, on behalf of less privileged individuals and countries.

121 When we behave this way, acting quite normally (just the same as our fellowmen do) and with a supernatural outlook, we are simply following the example set by Jesus Christ who is true God and true Man. See how full of naturalness his life is. For thirty years he passes unnoticed as just another workman, without calling attention to himself, and he is known in his village as the son of the carpenter. The same is true of his public life. There is nothing off-key about it, nothing odd or eccentric. He had his group of friends like any one of his compatriots. There was nothing distinctive in his bearing: so much so, in fact, that Judas had to arrange a sign in order to single him out:

"Whomever I kiss, that is he."[23] There was nothing peculiar about Jesus and I must say that I am greatly touched by this rule of behavior of our Lord who passed through life as just one more among men.

John the Baptist, who had a special vocation, wore a garment of camel's hair and ate locusts and wild honey. Our Savior wore a seamless tunic, ate and drank as the others did, rejoiced at their happiness, was moved by the sorrows of his neighbors, and did not refuse the rest and shelter that his friends offered him. He made no secret of the fact that he had earned his living for many years working alongside Joseph the craftsman. This is the way we should behave in this world: as our Lord did. I could sum up my advice very briefly as follows: we ought to go about in clean clothes, with a clean appearance and, most important of all, with a clean soul.

It is worth noting that even our Lord, who preached such marvellous detachment from worldly goods, at the same time went to great lengths not to waste them. After the miracle of the multiplication of the loaves, whereby he

[23] Mt 26:48.

had so generously satisfied the hunger of over five thousand men, "he said to his disciples, 'Gather the fragments that are left over, lest they be wasted.' They, therefore, gathered them up; and they filled twelve baskets."[24] If you reflect carefully on this whole scene, you will learn never to be mean or miserly, but rather how to be good administrators of the talents and the material resources God has given you.

122 Following this example we see in our Lord, who is our model, I preach that detachment is self-dominion. It is not a noisy and showy beggarliness, nor is it a mask for laziness and neglect. You should dress in accordance with the demands of your social standing, your family background, your work...as your companions do, but to please God: eager to present a genuine and attractive image of true Christian living. Do everything with naturalness, without being extravagant. I can assure you that in this matter it is better to err on the side of excess than to fall short. How do you think our Lord dressed? Haven't you pictured to yourself the dignity with which he wore his seamless cloak which had probably been woven for him by our

[24] Jn 6:12-13.

Lady? Don't you remember how, in Simon's house, he was grieved because he had not been offered water to wash his hands before taking his place at the table?[25] No doubt he drew attention to this example of bad manners to underline his teaching that love is shown in little details. But he also wants to make it clear that he stands by the social customs of his time, and, therefore, you and I must make an effort to be detached from the goods and comforts of the world, but without doing anything that looks odd or peculiar.

As far as I am concerned, one of the signs that we're aware of being lords of the earth and God's faithful administrators is the care we take of the things we use: keeping them in good condition, making them last and getting the best out of them so that they serve their purpose for as long a time as possible and don't go to waste. In the centers of Opus Dei you will find the decoration simple, attractive and, above all, clean, because poverty in a home is not to be confused with bad taste or with dirt. Nevertheless, it seems quite natural to me that, in keeping with your means and your social

[25] Cf. Lk 7:36-50.

and family commitments, you should possess some objects of value which you take care of with a spirit of mortification and detachment.

123 Many years ago, twenty-five and more, I used to visit an eating place run by a charitable group for the benefit of beggars who were so poor that their only food each day was the meal they were given there. There was a large canteen looked after by a number of kind women. After the first meal was served, more beggars would come in to finish off the left-overs. Among this second group of beggars one man in particular attracted my attention. He was the proud owner of...a pewter spoon! He would take it carefully out of his pocket, look at it covetously and, after he had downed his meager ration, he would look at the spoon again with eyes that seemed to exclaim: "It's mine!" Next he would lick it a couple of times to clean it and then, with deep satisfaction, would hide it away again in the folds of his tattered garment. True enough, the spoon was *his*! Here was a wretchedly poor beggar who, among his companions in misfortune, thought himself to be rich.

Around that same time I knew a titled lady who belonged to the Spanish aristocracy. In the eyes of God such a thing counts for nothing. We are all equal, all of us are children of Adam and Eve, weak creatures with virtues and defects, and capable, all of us, if our Lord abandons us, of committing the worst crimes imaginable. Ever since Christ redeemed us, there are no distinctions of race, language, color, birth, or wealth: *we are all children of God.* This lady, of whom I have just been speaking, lived in an ancestral mansion. But she spent next to nothing on herself. On the other hand, she paid her servants very well and gave the rest of her money to the needy, while depriving herself of almost everything. This lady had many of the goods which so many people are anxious to obtain but she personally was poor, given to mortification and completely detached from everything. Am I making myself clear? In any event, all we need to do is listen to the words of our Lord: " 'Blessed are the poor in spirit, for theirs is the Kingdom of Heaven.' "[26]

If you want to achieve this spirit, I would advise you to be sparing with yourself while being very generous towards others. Avoid unnecessary expenditure on luxuries and

[26] Mt 5:3.

comforts, whether out of caprice, or vanity, etc. Don't create needs for yourself. In other words, learn from St Paul "to live in poverty and to live in abundance, to be filled and to be hungry, to live in plenty and to live in want: I can do all things in him who comforts me."[27] Like the Apostle, we too will come out winners in this spiritual combat if we keep our hearts unattached and free from ties.

"All of us who enter the arena of the faith," says St Gregory the Great, "are committed to fight against evil spirits. The devils possess nothing in this world and, therefore, since they enter the lists naked, we too must fight naked. Because, if someone who is clothed fights against someone who goes naked, he will soon be dragged down, since his enemy has something to get a grip on. And what are the things of this world if not a kind of apparel?"[28]

God loves the cheerful giver

124 Within the general framework of total detachment which our Lord asks of us, I would

[27] Phil 4:12-13.

[28] St Gregory the Great, *Homiliae in Evangelia*, 32, 2 (PL 76, 1233).

like to point out to you another particularly important aspect: our health. Most of you here are young. You are passing through that splendid period of being full of life, brimming over with energy. But time passes and inexorably we begin to notice a physical decline; then come the limitations of maturity and finally the infirmities of old age. Moreover, any one of us, at any moment, can fall ill or suffer some bodily disorder.

Only if we have a truly Christian appreciation of our periods of physical well-being, of "our good times," will we be able to accept with supernatural cheerfulness such happenings as people mistakenly call bad. Without going into too many details, I would like to pass on to you my own personal experience in this area. When we are sick we can get very tiresome: "they aren't looking after me properly, nobody cares about me, I'm not getting the attention I deserve, nobody understands me..." The devil, who is always on the lookout, can attack from any angle. When people are ill, his tactics consist in stirring up a kind of psychosis in them so as to draw them away from God and fill the atmosphere with bitterness, or destroy that treasure of merits earned (on behalf of souls everywhere) by pain, that is when it is borne with supernatural optimism, when it is loved! Therefore, if God wills that we be struck down by some affliction, take it as a sign that he considers us mature enough to be associated even more closely with his redeeming Cross.

What we need, therefore, is a long-term preparation, by practising daily a holy detachment from self, so that we are prepared to bear sickness or misfortune gracefully if our Lord permits them. Begin now to make use of everyday opportunities: something you may have to do without, small recurring pains, voluntary mortifications, and also put into practice the Christian virtues.

125 We have to make demands on ourselves in our daily lives. In this way we will not go about inventing false problems and ingenious needs which, in the last analysis, are prompted by conceit, capriciousness, and a comfort-loving and lazy approach to life. We ought to be striding towards God at a fast pace, carrying no deadweights or impediments which might hinder our progress. Since poverty of the spirit does not consist in not having things but rather in being truly detached from what we have, we need to be vigilant so as not to be deceived by

our imagination into thinking we can't survive unless we have certain things. As St Augustine puts it: "Seek what suffices, seek what is enough, and don't desire more. Whatever goes beyond that, produces anxiety not relief: it will weigh you down, instead of lifting you up."[29]

In giving you this advice I am not thinking of exceptional or complicated situations. I know a person who used some slips of paper as book marks on which he wrote out some ejaculatory prayers to help him keep in the presence of God. One day he found himself wanting to keep those *treasures* and he suddenly realized that he was getting attached to the silly bits of paper. Now you see what a model of virtue we have here! I wouldn't mind telling you about every one of my weaknesses, if it were of any use to you. I have merely drawn the cloak aside a little because something similar might be happening to you: your books, your clothes, your desk, your...tin can idols?

In such cases, my recommendation is that you consult your spiritual director. Don't be childish or scrupulous about it. At times the best remedy will be the small mortification of

[29] St Augustine, *Sermo* LXXXV, 6 (PL 38, 523).

doing without something for a short space of time. Or, to take a different example, it would probably do you no harm to give up your normal means of transport occasionally and to give to charity the money you thereby save, no matter how small the amount may be. In any case, if you really have a true spirit of detachment from things, you will not fail to find all kinds of effective and unobtrusive ways of putting it into practice.

Having opened my heart to you, I must also confess to one attachment which I have no intention of ever giving up; it is my deep love for each and every one of you. I have learned it from the best Teacher there is, and I would like to follow his example most faithfully, by loving all men with all my heart, starting with those about me. Are you not moved when you think of Jesus' ardent charity—his tenderness!—which lead the Evangelist to describe one of his disciples as the one *quem diligebat Iesus*[30] ("the one whom Jesus loved")?

126 We will finish with a quotation which the Gospel of today's Mass offers for our consideration: "Six days before the Paschal feast, Jesus

[30] Jn 13:23.

went to Bethany where Lazarus, whom Jesus raised to life, had died. And a feast was made for him there, at which Martha was waiting at table, while Lazarus was one of his fellow guests. And now Mary brought in a pound of pure spikenard ointment, which was very precious, and poured it over the feet of Jesus, wiping his feet with her hair. And the house was filled with the scent of the ointment."[31] What a shining proof of magnanimity is this *extravagance* on Mary's part! Judas, on the other hand, laments this *waste* of so valuable a perfume; in his greed he had been calculating the price: it would have fetched at least "three hundred silver pieces."[32]

True detachment leads us to be very generous with God and with our fellowmen. It makes us actively resourceful and ready to spend ourselves in helping the needy. A Christian cannot be content with a job that only allows him to earn enough for himself and his family. He will be big-hearted enough to give others a helping hand, both out of charity and as a matter of justice, in the manner described by

[31] *Ibid* 12:1-3.
[32] *Ibid* 12:5.

St Paul when writing to the Romans: "Macedonia and Achaia have thought fit to make a contribution for the poor among the saints at Jerusalem. They have thought fit to do it, I say, and indeed they are in their debt. For if the Gentiles have shared in their spiritual blessings, they should also contribute to their temporal needs in return."[33]

Don't be mean and grudging with people who, without counting the cost, have given of their all, everything they have, for your sake. Just ask yourselves, How much does it cost you—in financial terms as well—to be Christians? Above all, don't forget that "God loves a cheerful giver. And God has the power to supply you abundantly with every kind of blessing, so that, with all your needs well supplied at all times, you may have something to spare for every work of mercy."[34]

As we draw closer during this Holy Week to the suffering of Jesus Christ, let us ask the Blessed Virgin Mary to enable us, like her,[35] to keep all these things in our minds and ponder over them in our hearts.

[33] Rom 15:26-27.
[34] 2 Cor 9:7-8.
[35] Cf. Lk 2:19.

IN THE FOOTSTEPS OF CHRIST*

Ego sum via, veritas et vita.[1] I am the way, the truth, and the life. In these clear and unmistakable words our Lord traces out for us the true path that leads to everlasting happiness. *Ego sum via*: ("He is the only road linking Heaven and earth"). He is speaking to all men, but in a very special way he is thinking of people who, like you and me, are determined to take our Christian vocation seriously, so that God may always be present in our thoughts, on our lips, and in everything we do, including our most ordinary and routine actions. 127

Jesus is the way. Behind him on this earth of ours he had left the clear outlines of his

* A homily given on April 3, 1955.

[1] Jn 14:6.

footprints. They are indelible signs which neither the erosion of time nor the treachery of the evil one have been able to erase. *Iesus Christus heri, et hodie; ipse et in saecula*[2] ("Jesus Christ is the same, yesterday, today, and forever"). How I love to recall these words! Jesus Christ, the very Jesus who was alive yesterday for his Apostles and the people who sought him out; this same Jesus lives today for us, and will live forever. Yet, at times, we poor men fail to recognize his ever-present features, because our eyes are tired and our vision clouded. Now, as we begin this time of prayer close to the tabernacle, ask him, like the blind man in the Gospel did, *Domine, ut videam*[3] ("Lord, that I may see")! Enlighten my intelligence and let Christ's words penetrate deep into my mind. Strengthen his Life in my soul so that I may be transformed in readiness for eternal Glory.

The Christian's way

128 How crystal clear Christ's teaching is. As usual, let us turn to the New Testament, this

[2] Heb 13:8.
[3] Lk 18:41.

time to St Matthew, chapter eleven: "Learn from me, for I am meek and humble of heart."[4] Don't you see? We have to learn from him, from Jesus who is our only model. If you want to go forward without stumbling or wandering off the path, then all you have to do is walk the road he walked, placing your feet in his footprints and entering into his humble and patient Heart, there to drink from the wellsprings of his commandments and of his love. In a word, you must identify yourself with Jesus Christ and try to become really and truly another Christ among your fellowmen.

To make sure there is no mistake here, let us read another quotation from St Matthew. In chapter sixteen, our Lord makes his doctrine even clearer: "If anyone wishes to come my way, let him deny himself, take up his cross, and follow me."[5] God's way is one of renunciation, of mortification, and of self-surrender, but it is not one of sadness or faintheartedness.

Reflect on the example that Christ gave us, from the crib in Bethlehem to his throne on Calvary. Think of his self-denial and of all he went

[4] Mt 11:29.
[5] *Ibid* 16:24.

through: hunger, thirst, weariness, heat, tiredness, ill-treatment, misunderstandings, tears...[6] But at the same time think of his joy in being able to save the whole of mankind. And now I would like you to engrave deeply in your mind and upon your heart—so that you can meditate on it often and draw your own practical conclusions—the summary St Paul made to the Ephesians when he invited them to follow resolutely in our Lord's footsteps: "Be imitators of God, as very dear children, and walk in love, as Christ has loved us and delivered himself up for us, a sacrifice breathing out fragrance as he offered it to God."[7]

129 Jesus gave himself up for us in a holocaust of love. What about you, who are a disciple of Christ? You, a favored son of God; you, who have been ransomed at the price of the Cross; you too should be ready to deny yourself. So, no matter what situation we may find ourselves in, neither you nor I can ever allow ourselves to behave in a way that is selfish, materialistic, comfort-loving, dissipated or—forgive me if I

[6] Cf. *Ibid* 4:1-11; 8:20; 8:24; 12:1; 21:18-19. Lk 2:6-7; 4:16-30; 11:53-54. Jn 4:6; 11:33-35, etc.

[7] Eph 5:1-2.

speak too candidly—just plain stupid! "If all you want is the esteem of your fellowmen, and you long to be respected and appreciated, and you only seek a pleasant life, then you have strayed from the path...Only those who travel the rugged, narrow, and austere path of tribulation are allowed to enter the city of the saints, there to rest and reign with the King for eternity."[8]

You yourself must decide of your own free will to take up the cross; otherwise, your tongue may say that you are imitating Christ, but your actions will belie your words. That way, you will never get to know the Master intimately, or love him truly. It is really important that we Christians convince ourselves of this. We are not walking with our Lord unless we are spontaneously depriving ourselves of many things that our whims, vanity, pleasure, or self-interest clamor for. Not a single day should pass that has not been seasoned with the salt and grace of mortification; and, please get rid of the idea that you would then be miserable. What a sad little happiness you will have if you don't learn to overcome yourself, if you

[8] Pseudo-Macarius, *Homiliae*, 12, 5 (PG 34, 559).

let your passions and fancies dominate and crush you, instead of courageously taking up your cross!

130 As I speak of these things, there comes to mind the dream of that author of the golden age of Spanish literature—I am sure some of you have heard me mention it in other meditations. The writer sees two roads opening up before him. One of them is broad and smooth, easy to travel, with many comfortable inns, taverns, and other places of beauty and delight. Along this road go great crowds of people on horseback or in carriages, in a hubbub of music and mindless laughter. One sees a multitude intoxicated by a joy which is simply ephemeral and superficial, for this road leads to a bottomless precipice. It is the road taken by the world-minded, ever seeking material pleasure, boasting a happiness that they do not really possess, and craving insatiably for comfort and pleasure...They are terrified at the thought of suffering, self-denial, or sacrifice. They have no wish to know anything about the Cross of Christ. They think it is sheer madness. But then it is they who are insane, for they are slaves of envy, gluttony, and sensuality. They end up suffering far more, and only too late do they

realize that they have squandered both their earthly and their eternal happiness in exchange for meaningless trifles. Our Lord has warned us about this. "The man who tries to save his life shall lose it; it is the man who loses his life for my sake who will secure it. How is a man the better for it if he gains the whole world at the cost of losing his own soul?"[9]

In that dream there is another path which goes in a different direction. It is so steep and narrow that the travellers who take it cannot go on horseback. All who take it must go on foot, perhaps having to zigzag from side to side, but they move steadily on, treading on thorns and briars, picking their way round rocks and boulders. At times their clothing gets torn, and even their flesh. But at the end of this road a garden of paradise awaits them, eternal happiness, Heaven. This is the way taken by holy people, who humble themselves and who, out of love for Jesus, gladly sacrifice themselves for others. It is the path of those who are not afraid of an uphill climb, who bear the cross lovingly, no matter how heavy it may be, because they know that if they fall under its weight they can

[9] Mt 16:25-26.

still get up and continue their ascent. Christ is the strength of these travellers.

131 What does it matter that we stumble on the way, if we find in the pain of our fall the energy to pick ourselves up and go on with renewed vigor? Don't forget that the saint is not the person who never falls, but rather the one who never fails to get up again, humbly and with a holy stubbornness. If the book of Proverbs says that the just man falls seven times a day,[10] who are we poor creatures, you and I, to be surprised or discouraged by our own weaknesses and falls! We will be able to keep going ahead, if only we seek our fortitude in him who says: "Come to me all you who labor and are burdened and I will give you rest."[11] Thank you, Lord, *quia tu es, Deus, fortitudo mea*[12] ("because you, and you alone, my God, have always been my strength, my refuge, and my support").

If you really want to make progress in the interior life, be humble. Turn constantly and confidently to the help of our Lord and of his Blessed Mother, who is your Mother too. No

[10] Cf. Prov 24:16.
[11] Mt 11:28.
[12] Ps 42:2.

matter how much the still open wound of your latest fall may hurt, embrace the cross once more and calmly, without getting upset, say: "With your help, Lord, I'll fight so as not to be held back. I'll respond faithfully to your invitations. I won't be afraid of steep climbs, nor of the apparent monotony of my daily work, nor of the thistles and loose stones on the way. I know that I am aided by your mercy and that, at the end of the road, I will find eternal happiness, full of joy and love forever and ever."

Later, in the same dream, our writer discovers a third path. It too is narrow and, like the second, it is both steep and rugged. Those who travel it walk solemnly and regally in the midst of countless hardships. Yet they end up falling over the same terrible precipice that the first road leads to. This is the path of the hypocrites, people who lack a right intention, who are motivated by a false zeal and pervert divine works by mixing them with their own selfish and temporal ambitions. "It is folly to undertake a hard and difficult task just to be admired; to put great effort into keeping God's commandments with but an earthly reward in mind. Whoever practises virtue for the sake of some human benefit is like a person who sells off a priceless heirloom for just a few coins. He could have won Heaven, but he is content instead with fleeting praise...That is why they say that the hopes of hypocrites are like a spider's web: so much effort goes into weaving it, and in the end it is blown away by a puff of the wind of death."[13]

Keeping the end in sight

132 My purpose in reminding you of these hard realities is to stimulate you to examine carefully the motives that inspire your behavior, so that you can put right what needs to be corrected and direct everything to the service of God and your fellowmen. Don't forget that God has passed by our side, that he has cast his loving glance upon us, and "has called us to a vocation of holiness, not because of anything we have done, but out of his own good pleasure and the grace he has lavished on us since the world began."[14]

[13] St Gregory the Great, *Moralia*, 2, 8, 43-44 (PL 75, 844-845).
[14] 2 Tim 1:9.

Purify your intentions then. Do everything for the love of God and embrace your daily cross joyfully. This is something I have repeated thousands of times because I believe that these ideas should be engraved on every Christian heart. When we advance beyond the stage of simply tolerating difficulties or sufferings (whether physical or moral) and, instead, love them and offer them to God in reparation for our sins and the sins of all mankind, then, I assure you, they do not distress us.

It is no longer just any cross we are carrying. We discover that it is the Cross of Christ, and with it the consolation of knowing that our Redeemer has taken it upon himself to bear its weight. We cooperate as Simon of Cyrene did, who, when he was returning from work on his farm intending to take a well-earned rest, was forced to lend his shoulders to help Jesus.[15] For a soul in love, it is no misfortune to become voluntarily Christ's Simon of Cyrene and, in this way, to give such close company to his suffering Humanity, reduced to a state of rags and tatters. For if we do this we can be certain of our closeness

[15] Cf. Mk 15:21.

to God, who blesses us by choosing us for this task.

Many people have spoken to me in amazement of the joy which, thanks be to God, my children in Opus Dei have and which they spread to others. Faced with this evident truth, I always give the same reply, because I know no other. Their happiness has its foundation in the fact that they fear neither life nor death; that they are not overwhelmed when they meet with misfortune; that they strive daily to live with a spirit of sacrifice, in spite of their own defects and weaknesses, and they are constantly ready to deny themselves in order to make the Christian path easier and more pleasant for others.

Like the beating of our heart

133 While I am speaking I know that you are trying, in the presence of God, to take a close look at your past behavior. Isn't it true that most of the annoyances which have made your soul restless and have taken your peace away, are due to your failure to live up to the calls of divine grace? Or rather, that you were

perhaps following the path of the hypocrites by thinking only of yourselves? With the sorry idea of keeping up the mere appearance of a Christian attitude for the sake of those around you, you were inwardly refusing to renounce self, to mortify your unruly passions, and to give yourself unconditionally, in complete surrender, as Jesus did.

You see, in these periods of meditation in front of the tabernacle you can't confine yourselves simply to listening to the priest's words, as if he were giving voice to the intimate prayer of each individual present. I am making some suggestions, giving some indications, but it is for you to make the effort to take them in and reflect on them, so as to convert them into the theme of a very personal inner conversation between yourselves and God, in such a way that you can apply them to your present situation and then, in the light that our Lord offers you, distinguish what is going well from what is going badly and, with the help of his grace, correct your course.

Thank our Lord for the great number of good works which you have disinterestedly carried out, for with the psalmist you too can sing: "He drew me out of the deadly pit, where the mire had settled deep. He gave me a foothold on rock and gave strength to my steps."[16] Also ask him to forgive your omissions, or the false steps you took when you entered the wretched maze of hypocrisy, saying that you desired only the glory of God and the good of your neighbor, while in fact you were really honoring yourselves...Be daring, be generous, and say "No:" you don't want to deceive our Lord and mankind anymore.

134 It is the moment to turn to your Blessed Mother in Heaven, so that she may take you into her arms and win for you a glance of mercy from her Son. And try at once to make some practical resolutions: put a stop once and for all, even though it hurts, to that little defect that holds you back, as God and you yourself know so well. Pride, sensuality, and a lack of supernatural spirit will combine forces to suggest to you: "That? But what a small and insignificant little thing it is!" Don't play with the temptation. Instead, answer: "Yes, in this too I will surrender myself to the divine call." And you will be right, for love is shown especially in little things. Normally the sacri-

[16] Ps 39:3.

fices that our Lord asks of us, even the most difficult ones, refer to tiny details, but they are as continuous and invaluable as the beating of our hearts.

How many mothers have you known who have been the heroines of some epic or extraordinary event? Few, very few. Yet you and I know many mothers who are indeed heroic, truly heroic, who have never figured in anything spectacular, who will never hit the headlines, as they say. They lead lives of constant self-denial, happy to curtail their own likes and preferences, their time, their opportunities for self-expression or success, so that they can carpet their children's lives with happiness.

Let's take other examples, again from eve- 135
ryday life. St Paul refers to some: "Anyone who has to compete in the arena must keep all his appetites under control; and he does it to win a perishable crown, whereas ours is imperishable."[17] All you have to do is look around you. See how many sacrifices men and women make, willingly or less willingly, to take care of their bodies, protect their health, or gain the

[17] 1 Cor 9:25.

respect of others...Are we unable to stir ourselves at the thought of the immensity of God's love, so poorly requited by men, and mortify what needs to be mortified so that our hearts and minds may be more attentive to our Lord?

In the consciences of many, the meaning of Christianity has been so distorted that when they speak of mortification and penance they think only of the rigorous fasts and hair shirts mentioned in the awe-inspiring tales that are found in some lives of saints. At the start of this meditation we took as a self-evident premise the fact that we must imitate Jesus, taking him as the model for our behavior. It is true that he made ready for his preaching by retiring into the wilderness to fast for forty days and forty nights.[18] But, before this, and afterwards, he practised the virtue of temperance with such naturalness that his enemies took advantage of it to slander him as a "glutton and a drunkard, the friend of publicans and sinners."[19]

136 I would like you to discover the full depth of this simplicity of our Lord, who lived a life of penance without any special fuss, for it is

[18] Cf. Mt 4:1-11.
[19] Lk 7:34.

the type of life he is asking of you: " 'When you fast, do not show it by gloomy looks, as the hypocrites do. They make their faces unsightly, so that men can see they are fasting; believe me they have their reward already. But do you, at the times of fasting, anoint your head and wash your face, so that your fast may not be known to men, but to your Father who dwells in secret; and then your Father, who sees what is done in secret, will reward you.' "[20]

That is how you ought to practise the spirit of penance: looking towards God and behaving like a son, like a little child who shows his father how much he loves him by giving up the few treasures he has: a spool of thread, a tin soldier with no head, a bottle top...Their value is slight, yet he finds it hard to make up his mind. But in the end love wins, and he happily hands them over.

Let me insist again and again that this is the **137**
road that God wants us to follow when he calls us to his service in the midst of the world to sanctify others and to sanctify ourselves by means of our daily occupations. With that enormous common sense of his, combined with

[20] Mt 6:16-18.

his great faith, St Paul preached that "in the law of Moses it is written: 'thou shalt not muzzle the ox that treads out the corn,' "[21] and then he asks: "Is God here concerned about oxen? Or does he not rather say it for us? Yes, truly for your sake it was laid down; for hope makes the ploughman plough, and the thresher to thresh, in the anticipation of sharing in the crop."[22]

Christian life can never be reduced to an oppressive set of rules which leave the soul in a state of exasperation and tension. Rather, it accommodates itself to individual circumstances as a glove fits the hand, and it says that, as well as praying and sacrificing ourselves constantly, we should never lose our supernatural outlook as we go about our everyday tasks, be they big or small. Remember that God loves his creatures to distraction. How can a donkey work if it is not fed or given enough rest, or if its spirit is broken by too many beatings? Well, your body is like a little donkey, and it was a donkey that was God's chosen throne in Jerusalem, and it carries you along the divine

[21] Dt 25:4.
[22] 1 Cor 9:9-10.

pathways of this earth of ours. But it has to be controlled so that it doesn't stray away from God's paths. And it has to be encouraged so that it can trot along with all the briskness and cheerfulness that you would expect from a poor beast of burden.

A spirit of penance

Are you trying to make sincere resolutions? **138**
Ask our Lord to help you to take a tough line with yourself, for love of him; to help you apply, with all naturalness, the purifying touch of mortification to everything you do. Ask him to help you to spend yourselves in his service, silently and unnoticed, like the flickering lamp that burns beside the tabernacle. And if you can't think of anything by way of a definite answer to the divine guest who knocks at the door of your heart, listen well to what I have to tell you.

Penance is fulfilling exactly the timetable you have fixed for yourselves, even though your body resists or your mind tries to avoid it by dreaming up useless fantasies. Penance is getting up on time and also not leaving for later, without any real reason, that particular job that you find harder or most difficult to do.

Penance is knowing how to reconcile your duties to God, to others and to yourself, by making demands on yourself so that you find enough time for each of your tasks. You are practising penance when you lovingly keep to your schedule of prayer, despite feeling worn out, listless, or cold.

Penance means being very charitable at all times towards those around you, starting with the members of your own family. It is to be full of tenderness and kindness towards the suffering, the sick and the infirm. It is to give patient answers to people who are boring and annoying. It means interrupting our work or changing our plans, when circumstances make this necessary, above all when the just and rightful needs of others are involved.

Penance consists in putting up good-humoredly with the thousand and one little pinpricks of each day; in not abandoning your job, although you have momentarily lost the enthusiasm with which you started it; in eating gladly whatever is served, without being fussy.

For parents and, in general, for those whose work involves supervision or teaching, penance is to correct whenever it is necessary. This should be done bearing in mind the type of fault committed and the situation of the person who needs to be so helped, not letting oneself be swayed by subjective viewpoints, which are often cowardly and sentimental.

A spirit of penance keeps us from becoming too attached to the vast imaginative blueprints we have made for our future projects, where we have already foreseen our master strokes and brilliant successes. What joy we give to God when we are happy to lay aside our third-rate painting efforts and let *him* put in the features and colors of his choice!

I could continue pointing out a multitude of **139**
details (I have just mentioned those that came immediately to mind) which you can take advantage of during the course of the day to come closer to God and to your neighbor. But here let me emphasize that, in giving you these examples, I am not in any way disparaging great penances. On the contrary, they may prove to be very good and holy, and even necessary, when our Lord leads you by that road, always assuming that they have been approved by the person who directs your soul. But I warn you that great penances are also

compatible with great falls, which are brought about by pride. On the other hand, if you continually wish to please God in the little battles that go on inside you—a smile, for example, when you don't feel like smiling; and I assure you that a smile is sometimes more difficult than an hour's worth of cilice—then there is little room left for pride, or for the ridiculous notion of thinking we are great heroes. Instead, we will see ourselves as a little child, who is hardly able to offer even the merest trifles to his father, but who then sees them received most joyfully.

139 So, does a Christian have to be mortified always? Yes, but for love. For this treasure of our vocation "we carry it in vessels of clay, to show that the abundance of the power is God's and not ours. In all things we suffer tribulation, but we are not distressed; we are sore pressed, but we are not destitute; we endure persecution, but we are not forsaken; we are cast down, but we do not perish; always bearing about in our body the dying of Jesus, so that the life of Jesus may be made manifest in our bodily frame."[23]

[23] 2 Cor 4:7-10.

Perhaps up to this moment we had not felt urged to follow so closely in the footsteps of Christ. Perhaps we did not realize that we could unite our little renunciations to his redeeming sacrifice: to make up for our own sins, for the sins of men of all ages, and for the evil work of Lucifer who continues to oppose God with his *non serviam* ("I will not serve")! How can we dare to cry out without hypocrisy, "Lord, I am hurt by the offenses that wound your most loving Heart," if we don't make up our minds to deprive ourselves of this or that triviality, or to offer up some small sacrifice in praise of his Love? Penance, genuine reparation, sets us on the path of self-giving, of charity. We give ourselves to make reparation, and we live charity to help others, as Christ has helped us. 140

From now on, be in a hurry to fall in love. Love itself will prevent us from complaining and protesting. For we put up with setbacks often enough, but then we feel sorry for ourselves, so that not only do we waste God's grace, but we also tie his hands and make it harder for him to ask us for things in the future: *Hilarem enim datorem diligit Deus*[24] ("God loves

[24] *Ibid* 9:7.

the cheerful giver, the person who gives with the spontaneity of a loving heart, without all the fuss and bother of one who gives himself as if he were doing God a favor").

141 Take another look over your life and ask forgiveness for this or that fault which you notice immediately with the eyes of your conscience: for using your tongue badly; for thoughts that revolve continually around yourselves; for those critical judgments you made and consented to and which now cause you to worry foolishly, leaving you restless and fretful. Believe me, you can be very happy! Our Lord wants us to be glad, to be drunk with joy, stepping out along the same roads of happiness that he himself walked! We only become miserable when we persist in straying off those roads, and take the path of selfishness and sensuality or, much worse, when we take the path of the hypocrites.

The Christian must prove himself to be genuine, truthful, and sincere in all that he undertakes. His conduct should reflect a spirit—the spirit of Christ. If anyone in this world has a duty to be consistent with his beliefs it is the Christian, for he has been entrusted with a gift that he must make fruitful,[25] and that gift is the truth which liberates and saves.[26] "But Father," you might ask me, "how am I to achieve this sincerity of life?" Jesus Christ has given his Church all the means necessary. He has shown us how to pray, how to get to know his heavenly Father. He has sent us his spirit, the Great Unknown, who acts within our souls. And he has left us those visible signs of his grace that we call the Sacraments. Use them. Intensify your life of piety. Pray every day. And never refuse to shoulder the sweet burden of Christ's Cross.

It is Jesus who has invited you to follow him like a good disciple so that you can journey through this earthly life, sowing the peace and joy which the world cannot give. Therefore—and let me emphasize this once more—we have to walk without fear of life and without fear of death, without shrinking at any cost from pain and sorrow which, for a Christian, are always a means of purification and a chance for showing that we really love our fellowmen, through the thousand and one circumstances of ordinary life.

[25] Cf. Lk 19:13.
[26] Cf. Jn 8:32.

Our time is up and I have to bring these considerations to a close. With them I have tried to stir your soul so that you might respond by making a few specific resolutions—not many, but definite ones. You should realize that God wants you to be glad and that, if you do all you can, you will be happy, very, very happy, although you will never be a moment without the Cross. But that Cross is no longer a gallows. It is the throne from which Christ reigns. And at his side, his Mother, our Mother too. The Blessed Virgin will obtain for you the strength that you need to walk decisively in the footsteps of her Son.

of men!, carrying huge burning candles. Strong and robust men they were, accompanying our Lord in the Holy Eucharist, with a faith that was greater than those candles that weighed so much.

Last night when I found myself awake several times I repeated, as an aspiration, the words, *quasi modo geniti infantes*[2] ("as newborn babes"). It occurred to me that the Church's invitation today is very well suited to all of us who feel the reality of our divine filiation. It is certainly right that we be very strong, very solid, men of mettle who can influence our environment; and yet, before God, how good it is to see ourselves as little children!

We are children of God

Quasi modo geniti infantes, rationabile, sine dolo lac concupiscite[3] ("Like children just born into the world, cry out for the clean and pure milk of the spirit"). How marvellous this verse from St Peter is and how appropriate that the liturgy

[2] *Ibid.*
[3] *Ibid.*

GETTING TO KNOW GOD*

Low Sunday brings to my memory a pious tradition of my own country. On this day, in which the liturgy invites us to hunger for spiritual food—*rationabile, sine dolo lac concupiscite*,[1] to desire the spiritual milk, that is free from guile—it was customary to take Holy Communion to the sick (they did not have to be seriously ill) so that they could fulfill their Easter duties. 142

In some large cities, each parish would organize its own eucharistic procession. From my days as a university student in Saragossa, I remember frequently seeing thousands of people crossing the Coso in three separate contingents made up entirely of men, thousands

* A homily given on April 5, 1964, Low Sunday.

[1] 1 Pt 2:2 (Introit of the Mass).

should then add: *exsultate Deo adiutori nostro: iubilate Deo Iacob*[4] ("leap with joy in honor of God; acclaim the God of Jacob, who is also our Lord and Father"). But today I would like us, you and I, to meditate not so much on the Holy Sacrament of the Altar, which draws from our hearts the greatest possible praise for Jesus, but on the certainty of our divine filiation and on some of the consequences deriving from it for all who want to live their Christian faith nobly and earnestly.

For reasons that I need not go into now **143**
(but which Jesus, who is presiding over us here from the Tabernacle, knows full well,) my life has led me to realize in a special way that I am a son of God and I have experienced the joy of getting inside the heart of my Father, to rectify, to purify myself, to serve him, to understand others and find excuses for them, on the strength of his love and my own lowliness.

This is why I want to insist now that you and I need to be made anew, we need to wake up from the slumber of feebleness by which we are so easily lulled and to become aware once

[4] Ps 80:2 (Introit of the Mass).

again, in a deeper and more immediate way, of our condition as children of God.

The example of Jesus, every detail of his life in those Eastern lands, will help us to fill ourselves with this truth. "If we admit the testimony of men," we read in today's Epistle, "the testimony of God is greater."[5] And what does God's testimony consist of? Again St John tells us: "See how God has shown his love towards us; that we should be counted as his sons, should be his sons...Beloved, we are sons of God even now."[6]

Over the years, I have sought to rely unfalteringly for my support on this joyous reality. No matter what the situation, my prayer, while varying in tone, has always been the same. I have said to him: "Lord, you put me here. You entrusted me with this or that, and I put my trust in you. I know you are my Father, and I have seen that tiny children are always absolutely sure of their parents." My priestly experience tells me that abandonment such as this in the hands of God stimulates souls to acquire a strong, deep, and serene piety, which

[5] 1 Jn 5:9.
[6] *Ibid* 3:1-2.

drives them to work constantly and with an upright intention.

The example of Jesus Christ

Quasi modo geniti infantes...It has made me **144**
very happy to spread everywhere this attitude of being children, little children of God, an attitude which enables us to savor those other words we find in the liturgy of today's Mass: "all that is born of God overcomes the world;"[7] it conquers difficulties and achieves victory in this great battle for the peace of souls and of society.

Our wisdom and our strength lie precisely in our being convinced of our littleness, of our nothingness in the eyes of God. But at the same time he himself is prompting us to get moving, to proclaim confidently his only begotten Son, Jesus Christ, even though we have errors and miseries, provided, that is, that, as well as being weak, we are fighting to overcome our weaknesses.

[7] Ibid 5:4.

You must have often heard me repeat the following advice contained in Scripture: *discite benefacere*[8] ("learn to do good"), for there can be no doubt that we need to learn how to do good and to teach others to do the same. In this, we have to begin with ourselves, by striving to discover which particular good we should be aiming at, for each one of us, for each of our friends, for each and every man. I know no better way of considering the greatness of God than to start from this inexpressible and simple fact that he is our Father and we are his children.

145 Let us take another look at the Master. You too may find yourself now hearing his gentle reproach to Thomas: "Let me have your finger; see, here are my hands. Let me have your hand; put it into my side. Cease your doubting, and believe;"[9] and, with the Apostle, a sincere cry of contrition will rise from your soul: "My Lord, and my God!"[10] I acknowledge you once and for all as the Master. From now on, with your help, I shall always treasure your teachings and I shall strive to follow them loyally.

[8] Is 1:17.
[9] Jn 20:27.
[10] *Ibid* 20:28.

If we go back a few pages in the Gospel we can relive the scene in which Jesus retires to pray and his disciples are nearby, probably watching him. When Jesus has finished, one of them boldly asks him: " 'Lord, teach us how to pray, as John did for his disciples.' And he told them, 'When you pray, you are to say, Father, hallowed be thy name.' "[11]

Note the surprising thing about this reply. The disciples share their daily lives with Jesus and there, in the course of their ordinary conversations, our Lord tells them how they should pray. He reveals to them the great secret of God's mercy: that we are children of God and we can talk things over with him and spend time with him, just as trustingly as a son does with his father.

When I see how some people set about the life of piety, which is the way a Christian should approach his Lord, and I find them presenting such an unattractive picture, all theory and formulas, plagued with soulless chanting, better suited to anonimity than to a personal, one to One conversation with God our Father (genuine vocal prayer is never anony-

[11] Lk 11:1-2.

mous), then I am reminded of our Lord's words: " 'When you are at prayer, do not use many phrases, like the heathens, who think to make themselves heard by their eloquence. You are not to be like them; your heavenly Father knows well what your needs are before you ask him.' "[12] A Father of the Church comments on this passage as follows: "I understand from this that Christ is telling us to avoid long prayers, not long as regards time but as regards the endless multiplicity of words...For our Lord himself set us the example of the widow who, by dint of supplication, conquered the resistance of the unjust judge; and the other example of the inconsiderate individual who arrives late at night and who, through insistence more than friendship, gets his friend out of bed (cf. Luke 11:5-8; 18:1-8). With these two examples, he is telling us to ask constantly, not by composing endless prayers, but rather telling him of our needs with simplicity."[13]

In any case, if on beginning your meditation you don't succeed in concentrating your attention so as to be able to talk with God; if you

[12] Mt 6:7-8.

[13] St John Chrysostom, *In Matthaeum homiliae*, 19, 4 (PG 57, 278).

feel dry and your mind seems incapable of expressing a single idea, or your affections remain dull, my advice is that you try to do what I have always tried to do on such occasions: put yourselves in the presence of your Father and tell him this much at least: "Lord, I don't know how to pray. I can't think of anything to tell you." You can be sure that at that very moment you have already begun to pray.

Piety, a childlike attitude towards God

The piety which is born of divine filiation 146
is a profound attitude of the soul which eventually permeates one's entire existence. It is there in every thought, every desire, every affection. Haven't you noticed in families how children, even without realizing it, imitate their parents? They imitate their gestures, their habits; much of their behavior is the same as that of their parents.

Well, the same kind of thing happens to a good son of God. One finds oneself acquiring—without knowing how, or by what means—a marvellous godliness, which enables us to focus events from the supernatural viewpoint of faith; we come to love all men as our Father in Heaven loves them and, what is more important, we become more fervent in our daily efforts to come closer to God. Our wretchedness, I insist, doesn't matter, because we have the loving arms of our Father God to lift us up.

Have you noticed what a great difference there is between a child falling and a fall by an adult? In the case of children, most falls are unimportant; they are always falling over! If they do start crying, their fathers tell them: "Look here now, men don't cry." And the incident ends with the children trying earnestly to please their fathers.

But what happens if an adult loses his balance and falls awkwardly to the ground? If it weren't so pitiful, his misfortune would provoke merriment and laughter. Besides, the fall may have serious consequences and, if it's an old man, it might even give rise to a fracture that will never heal. In our interior life, it does all of us good to be *quasi modo geniti infantes*, like those tiny tots who seem to be made of rubber and who even enjoy falling over because they get up again right away and are once more running around, and also because they know their parents will always be there to console them, whenever they are needed.

If we try to act like them, our stumbling and failures in the interior life (which, moreover, are inevitable) will never result in bitterness. Our reaction will be one of sorrow but not discouragement, and we'll smile with a smile that gushes up like fresh water out of the joyous awareness that we are children of that Love, that grandeur, that infinite wisdom, that mercy, that is our Father. During the years I have been serving our Lord, I have learned to become like a little child of God. I would ask you to do likewise, to be *quasi modo geniti infantes,* children who long for God's word, his bread, his food, his strength, to enable us to behave henceforth as Christian men and women.

Be very childlike! The more childlike, the **147**
better. I speak from my experience as a priest, who has had to pick himself up many times in these past thirty-six years (how long and yet how short they now seem to me!) which have been spent striving to fulfill a very precise requirement of God's Will. There's one thing that has helped me always, the fact that I am still a child, and I am always climbing onto my

Mother's lap and finding refuge in the Heart of Christ, my Lord.

Serious falls, of the kind that can do great damage to the soul, at times almost irreparable damage, can always be traced back to the pride of thinking oneself to be grown up and self-sufficient. In such cases, people seem almost incapable of asking for help from those who can give it: not only from God, but also from a friend, or from a priest. And the poor soul, alone in its misfortune, sinks into confusion and loses its way.

Let us beseech God, right now, never to let us feel self-satisfied, but rather to make us grow ever more desirous of his help, his word, his Bread, his consolation, and his strength: *rationabile, sine dolo lac concupiscite,* foster your hunger, your ambition to be like children. Believe me, it is the best way to conquer pride; and it's the only way to make our conduct good, great hearted, divine. "Believe me, unless you become like little children again, you shall not enter the kingdom of Heaven."[14]

148 The scenes of my student days come back to me again. What a demonstration of faith it

[14] Mt 18:3.

was! I can almost hear the liturgical singing, breathe the smell of incense, see those thousands and thousands of men, each with his own misery—but each with a childlike heart; a little child who may perhaps be unable to lift up his eyes to meet those of his father. "Know and see that it is an evil and bitter thing for you, to have forsaken the Lord your God."[15] Let us renew our firm decision never to forsake our Lord for the cares of this world. Let us increase our thirst for God, making specific resolutions for our daily conduct, like little ones who recognize how needy they are and who therefore, keep looking and calling for their Father.

But let me go back to what I was telling you before: we have to learn to behave like children, we have to learn how to be God's sons. At the same time, we have to pass on to others this outlook which in the midst of our natural weaknesses, will make us "strong in the faith,"[16] fruitful in good works, and certain of our way, so that no matter what kind of mistakes we may make, even the most embarrassing, we will never hesitate to react and return to the

[15] Jer 2:19.
[16] 1 Pt 5:9.

sure path of divine filiation which ends up in the open and welcoming arms of our Father God.

Which of you here does not remember the arms of his father? They probably weren't as caressing, as gentle and tender as those of his mother. But our fathers' strong and powerful arms held us tight and safe and warm. Lord, I thank you for those tough arms. Thank you for those strong hands. Thank you for that sturdy and tender heart. I was going to thank you also for my errors! No, you don't want them! But you understand them, and excuse them and forgive them.

This is the wisdom God wants us to practise in our dealings with him. This indeed is a good mathematical lesson to learn to recognize that we are really a zero, but that our Father God loves each one of us just as we are; yes, indeed, just as we are! I—who am nothing but a poor man—love each one of you as he is, so just imagine what God's Love will be like! That is, provided we struggle, provided we are determined to bring our life into line with our conscience, a well-formed conscience.

Plan of life

When we examine how our piety is and what it should be like, that is, what specific points of our personal relationship with God need improving, if you have understood me right, you will reject the temptation of imagining fantastic feats, because you will have discovered that our Lord is quite happy if we offer him little tokens of love any moment of the day. 149

Try to commit yourself to a plan of life and to keep to it: a few minutes of mental prayer, Holy Mass—daily, if you can manage it—and frequent Communion; regular recourse to the Holy Sacrament of Forgiveness—even though your consciences do not accuse you of mortal sin; visiting Jesus in the tabernacle; praying and contemplating the mysteries of the Holy Rosary, and so many other marvellous devotions you know or can learn.

You should not let them become rigid rules, or water-tight compartments. They should be flexible, to help you on your journey, you who live in the middle of the world, with a life of hard professional work and social ties and obligations which you should not neglect, because in them your conversation with God still continues. Your plan of life ought to be like a rubber glove which fits the hand perfectly.

Please don't forget that the important thing does not lie in doing many things; limit yourself, generously, to those you can fulfill each day, whether or not you happen to feel like doing them. These pious practices will lead you, almost without your realizing it, to contemplative prayer. Your soul will pour forth more acts of love, aspirations, acts of thanksgiving, acts of atonement, spiritual communions. And this will happen while you go about your ordinary duties, when you answer the telephone, get on to a bus, open or close a door, pass in front of a church, when you begin a new task, during it and when you have finished it: you will find yourself referring everything you do to your Father God.

150 Rest and repose in the fact of being children of God. God is a Father who is full of tenderness, of infinite love. Call him "Father" many times a day and tell him—alone, in your hearts —that you love him, that you adore him, that you feel proud and strong because you are his son. All this implies a genuine program of interior life, which needs to be channelled through your relationship of piety with God, through these acts (which should be few, I insist, but constant) which will enable you to develop the attitudes and manner of a good son.

I must also warn you against the danger of routine—the real sepulcher of piety. Routine is often disguised as an ambition to do or to embark upon great feats, while daily duties are lazily neglected. When you see this beginning to happen, look at yourselves sincerely before our Lord: ask yourself if the reason why you may have become tired of always struggling on the same thing, is not simply that you were not seeking God; check if your faithful perseverance in work has not fallen off, due to lack of generosity and a spirit of sacrifice. It is then that your norms of piety, your little mortifications, your apostolic efforts that are not reaping an immediate harvest, all seem to be terribly sterile. We find ourselves empty and perhaps we start dreaming up new plans merely to still the voice of our Heavenly Father who asks us to be totally loyal to him. And with this dream, or rather nightmare, of mighty wonders in our soul, we become oblivious to reality, forgetting the way that will lead us most certainly straight towards sanctity. It is a clear sign that we have lost our supernatural outlook, our conviction that we are tiny children and our confidence that our Father will work wonders in us, if we begin again with humility.

Signposts painted red

151 One of my most vivid childhood memories is of seeing, up in the mountains near my home, those signposts they planted alongside the hill paths. I was struck by those tall posts usually painted red. It was explained to me then that when the snow fell, covering up everything, paths, seeded fields and pasture thickets, boulders and ravines, the poles stood out as sure reference points, so that everyone would always know where the road went.

Something similar happens in the interior life. There are times of spring and summer, but there are also winters, days without sun, and nights bereft of moonlight. We can't afford to let our friendship with Jesus depend on our moods, on our ups and downs. To do so would imply selfishness and laziness, and is certainly incompatible with love.

Therefore, in times of wind and snow, a few solid practices of piety, which are not sentimental but firmly rooted and adjusted to one's special circumstances, will serve as the red posts always marking out the way for us, until the time comes when our Lord decides to make the sun shine again. Then the snows melt and our hearts beat fast once more, burning with a fire that never really went out. It was merely hidden in the embers, beneath the ashes produced by a time of trial, or by our own poor efforts or lack of sacrifice.

I do not deny that over the years people **152**
have come to me and have told me with real sorrow: "Father, I don't know what's come over me, but I find I am tired and cold. My piety used to be so solid and straightforward, but now it feels like play acting..." Well, for those who are going through such a phase, and for all of you, I answer: "Play acting? Wonderful! The Lord is playing with us as a father does with his children."

We read in Scripture: *ludens in orbe terrarum*[17] ("that God plays over the whole face of the earth"). But he does not abandon us because

[17] Prov 8:31.

he adds immediately afterwards: *deliciae meae esse cum filiis hominum*[18] ("my delight is to be with the children of men"). Our Lord is playing with us! So when we feel that we are just play acting, because we feel cold and uninspired; when we find it difficult to fulfill our duties and attain the spiritual objectives we had set ourselves, then the time has come for us to realize that God is playing with us, and that he wishes us to act out our *play* with style.

I don't mind telling you that the Lord has, on occasion, given me many graces. But as a rule I have to go against the grain. I follow my plan, not because I like it, but because I've a duty to do so, for Love. "But, Father," you ask me, "can one put on an act for God? Wouldn't that be hypocritical?" Don't worry: for you the moment has arrived to play out a human comedy before a divine spectator. Persevere, for the Father, the Son, and the Holy Spirit are contemplating your act; do it all for love of God, to please him, although you find it hard.

How beautiful it is to be God's jester! How beautiful to act out such a role for Love, with

[18] *Ibid.*

a spirit of sacrifice, not seeking any personal satisfaction, but just to please our Father God who is playing with us! Turn to our Lord with confidence and say to him: "I don't feel like doing this at all, but I will offer it up for you." And then put your heart into the job you are doing, even though you think you are just play acting. Blessed play acting! I assure you it isn't hypocrisy, because hypocrites need a public for their pantomimes, whereas the spectators of our play, let me repeat, are the Father, the Son, and the Holy Spirit; the Most Holy Virgin and St Joseph and all the angels and saints in Heaven. Our interior life involves no more show than this, it is Christ who is passing by *quasi in occulto*[19] ("as if he would keep himself hidden").

Iubilate Deo. Exsultate Deo adiutori nostro.[20] **153**
("Praise God. Leap for joy in the Lord, our one and only help"). Jesus my Lord, whoever doesn't understand this, knows nothing about love, or sin, or wretchedness. Do you know what it is to be lifted up to the heart of God? Do you realize that a soul can face his Lord,

[19] Cf. Jn 7:10.
[20] Ps 80:2 (Introit of the Mass).

open his heart to him, and tell him his woes? I do it, for example, when God takes to himself people who are still young, who could still serve him and love him for many years here on earth; because I just don't understand. But my lament is one of trust, because I know that if I were ever to slip out of God's arms, I would stumble immediately. So, right away, calmly, as I accept the designs of Heaven, I add: "May the most just and most lovable Will of God be done, be fulfilled, be praised and eternally exalted above all things. Amen. Amen."

This is the way of doing things the Gospel teaches us; it is a clever move and a very holy one, the source of the effectiveness of our apostolic work. This is the fountainhead; from it our love and our peace as children of God flow and it is the way by which we can transmit affection and serenity to mankind. If only we do this, we will end our days in Love, having sanctified our work and found in it the hidden happiness of the things of God. We will go about life with the holy shamelessness of children and reject the shame, the hypocrisy, of grown-ups, who are afraid to return to their Father after experiencing the failure of a fall.

I end with our Lord's words of greeting, as found in today's Gospel: *pax vobis* ("Peace be with you")! "And the disciples rejoiced at the sight of the Lord,"[21] of this Lord who accompanies us to the Father.

[21] Jn 20:19-20.

OPEN TO GOD AND MEN*

We are here, *consummati in unum!*[1] ("perfectly made one"), united in prayer and intention, and ready to begin this period of conversation with our Lord, having renewed our desires to be effective instruments in his hands. Before Jesus in the Blessed Sacrament—how I love to make an act of explicit faith in the real presence of our Lord in the Eucharist!—use your prayer to stir up in your hearts the eagerness to spread the fervor of their resolute beating to every part of the earth, to the utmost corner of the planet where even one man may be found generously spending his life in the service of God and souls. Thanks to the inef- 154

* A homily given on November 3, 1963, 22nd Sunday after Pentecost.

[1] Jn 17:23.

fable reality of the Communion of Saints, we are indeed all joined together—"fellow workers," St John says[2]—in the task of spreading the truth and the peace of the Lord.

It is right that we should think about how we are imitating the Master. We should pause and reflect so that we can learn directly from our Lord's life some of the virtues which ought to shine out in our lives, if we are really anxious to spread the Kingdom of Christ.

Prudence, a necessary virtue

155 In the passage from St Matthew's Gospel which we read in today's Mass, it says: *tunc abeuntes pharisaei, consilium inierunt ut caperent eum in sermone*[3] ("the Pharisees went and took council that they might trap him in his talk"). Don't forget that this hypocritical approach is a common tactic even in our own times. I suspect that the tares of the Pharisees will never be wiped out in this world; they have always managed to grow at such an amazing

[2] 3 Jn 1:8.
[3] Mt 22:15.

rate. Perhaps our Lord tolerates this growth to make us, his sons, more prudent, for the virtue of prudence is essential for anyone whose job it is to judge, to strengthen, to correct, to fire with enthusiasm, or to encourage. And that is exactly what a Christian has to do, by taking advantage, as an apostle, of the situation of his ordinary work to help the people around him.

At this point, I raise my heart to God, and I ask him through the intercession of the Blessed Virgin—who is in the Church and yet above the Church, who is between Christ and the Church, protecting us and reigning over us, the Mother of all mankind, as she is of our Lord—through her, I beg that he may grant the gift of prudence to everyone of us, and especially to those who, immersed in the bloodstream of society, wish to work for God; because it will stand us in very good stead to learn to be prudent.

The scene from the Gospel continues to **156**
unfold: the Pharisees "sent their disciples with some of those who were of Herod's party, and said: Master..."[4] Note how craftily they call him

[4] *Ibid* 22:16.

"Master." They pretend to be his admirers and friends, treating him as they would a person from whom they expect to receive instruction. *Magister, scimus quia verax es*[5] ("we know that you are truthful")...What infamous guile! Have you ever come across such double-dealing! Take care then how you pass through this world. Don't be over-cautious or distrustful. But you should feel on your shoulders—remembering the image of the Good Shepherd depicted in the catacombs—the weight of the lost sheep, which represents not just a single soul, but the entire Church, the whole of humanity.

If you accept this responsibility with good grace and zest, you will become both daring and prudent in defending and proclaiming God's rights. And then, because of the integrity of your life-style, many people will come to regard you as teachers and call you so, even though you have no such ambition, for we have no interest in earthly glory. But, at the same time, don't be surprised if, among the many who approach you, there are some who sidle up to you with no other purposes than to

[5] *Ibid.*

flatter you. I would like you to register deep in your souls those words that you have so often heard from me: we must never let anything, neither slander, nor backbiting, neither human respect, nor the fear of what others may say, and much less the praise of the hypocrites, stand in the way of the fulfillment of our duty.

You remember the parable of the Good 157
Samaritan? A poor man lies by the roadside, covered with the injuries he has received from thieves who have robbed him of his last penny. A priest of the Old Law passes by, and a little later a Levite. They both continue on their way without bothering to help. "But a certain Samaritan as he journeyed came upon him, and seeing him, was moved with compassion. And he went up to him and bound up his wounds, pouring on oil and wine. And setting him on his own beast, he brought him to an inn and took care of him."[6] Note that this is not an example provided by our Lord for the benefit of just a few select people, since he immediately adds in answer to his questioner, that is

[6] Lk 10:33-34.

to each one of us: "Go and do the same yourself."[7]

Therefore, when in our own life or in that of others we notice something that isn't going well, something that requires the spiritual and human help which, as children of God, we can and ought to provide, then a clear sign of prudence is to apply the appropriate remedy by going to the root of the trouble, resolutely, lovingly, and sincerely. There is no room here for inhibitions, for it is a great mistake to think that problems can be solved by omissions or procrastination.

Prudence demands that the right medicine be used whenever the situation calls for it. Once the wound has been laid bare, the cure should be applied in full and without palliatives. When you see the slightest symptom that something is wrong, be straightforward and truthful about it, irrespective of whether it involves helping someone else or whether it is your own problem. When such help is needed, we must allow the person who, in the name of God, has the qualifications to carry out the cure, to press in on the infected wound, first from a distance,

[7] *Ibid* 10:37.

and then closer and closer until all the pus is squeezed out and the infection eradicated at its source. We must apply these procedures first to ourselves, and then to those whom, for reasons of justice or charity, we are obliged to help: I pray specially that parents, and everyone whose job it is to train and educate, may do this well.

Human respect

Don't let any hypocritical excuse hold you 158
back: apply the dose in full. But go about it with a motherly hand, with the almost infinite tenderness shown by our own mothers, when they were treating the hurts and injuries, big or little, resulting from our childhood games and falls. When it is better to wait a few hours, by all means do so. But never wait longer than is strictly necessary. Any other approach would imply cowardice or a desire not to inconvenience ourselves, which is very different from prudence. Everyone, especially those of you who have the job of training others, must put aside the fear of getting at the wound to disinfect it.

It could happen that someone might whisper cunningly in the ears of those who have to heal, but are hesitant or unwilling to face up to their obligations: "Master, we know that thou art truthful..."[8] Don't tolerate such ironical praise. Those who don't make the effort to carry out their task diligently are not masters, because they don't teach the true way. Nor are they truthful, since their false prudence leads them to despise or regard as exaggerated the clear guidelines which have been tested a thousand times over by upright conduct, by age, by the science of government, by the knowledge of human weakness, and by the love for each and every sheep of the flock. They are guidelines which impel one to speak up, to intervene, to show concern.

False teachers are afraid of getting to the bottom of things. They get uneasy at the very idea, never mind the obligation, of having to use a painful antidote when circumstances require it. You can be quite sure that in such an attitude there is no prudence: and no piety or good sense either. It reflects instead a timid disposition, a lack of responsibility, foolishness,

[8] Mt 22:16.

and stupidity. These are the people who will afterwards panic, at the sight of disaster, and try to stop the evil when it is already too late. They forget that the virtue of prudence demands that we find out and pass on *in good time* the calm advice that comes from maturity, long experience, unhindered vision, and unhampered speech.

Let us continue with the same passage **159**
from St Matthew: "we know that you are truthful, and that you teach the way of God in truth."[9] Such cynicism never ceases to surprise me. These people are motivated only by the intention of twisting our Lord's words. They want to catch him out in some slip of the tongue and, instead of explaining in simple terms what they consider to be an insoluble problem, they try to confuse the Master with compliments that should only come from friendly lips and honest hearts. I have purposely paused to consider the methods of the Pharisees, not so that we will become suspicious, but so that we learn to be prudent; so that we aren't taken in by deceit even though it comes decked out in phrases or expressions

[9] *Ibid.*

which in themselves are true, as in the Gospel passage we have been just considering. *You* don't make distinctions, they say; *you* have come for all men; nothing stops *you* from proclaiming the truth and teaching goodness.[10]

I will say it again: we have to be prudent, yes; but not suspicious. Give everyone the utmost credit for what he says. Be very noble. As far as I am concerned, the word of a Christian, of a loyal man—I trust everyone of you entirely—is worth more than the official signatures of a hundred notaries who are in unanimous agreement, even though on some occasions I may have been deceived by following this rule. But I prefer to leave myself open to the unscrupulous abuse of this confidence, rather than deprive anyone of the credit he deserves as a person and as a son of God. I can assure you that I have never been disappointed by the consequences of this way of acting.

[10] Cf. *Ibid* 22:16.

Be right-minded

If the Gospel isn't helping us constantly to draw conclusions applicable to our everyday life, the reason is that we aren't meditating on it enough. Many of you are young; some of you have already reached maturity. You all want, all of us want—otherwise we wouldn't be here—to yield good fruit in our lives. We are trying to bring a spirit of sacrifice into our actions and to turn the talent that our Lord has entrusted to us to good account, for we feel a divine zeal for souls. But, in spite of all these good intentions, it wouldn't be the first time that someone has fallen into the trap set by this alliance—*ex pharisaeis et herodianis*[11]—made up perhaps of those who ought in some way or other to be defending God's rights because they are Christians, but who, having instead become allied to and mixed in with the interests of evil forces, are treacherously laying snares to catch their brothers in the faith, who are servants with them of the same Redeemer. **160**

Be prudent and always act with simplicity, which is a very appropriate virtue for a son of

[11] Mk 12:13.

God. Behave naturally in the way you speak and in what you do. Get to the root of problems; don't stay on the surface. Remember that, if we really want to fulfill our obligations as Christians in a holy and manly way, we must anticipate unpleasant moments for others and for ourselves too.

161 I won't hide from you the fact that, when I have to correct someone or take a decision that will cause pain, I suffer before, during, and after it; and I am not a sentimental person. It consoles me to think that it is only animals that don't cry. We men, children of God, do cry. As I see it, there will be times when you too will have to suffer if you are really serious about doing your duty faithfully. Don't forget that it is more comfortable (though it is a mistake) to avoid suffering at any cost, with the excuse of not wanting to hurt others. This inhibition often hides a shameful escape on our part from suffering, since it isn't usually pleasant to correct someone in serious matter. My children, remember that hell is full of closed mouths.

A number of you here are doctors. Forgive my presumption in taking another example from medicine. What I say may not be very scientific, but the ascetical comparison will still be valid. To heal a wound, the first thing to do is to clean it well, including a wide area around it. The surgeon knows that the cleaning hurts, but he also knows that there will be worse pain later if it is not done. A disinfectant is also applied immediately. Naturally it stings (or, as they say where I come from, it *prickles*) and hurts the patient. But it's the only way if the wound is not to become infected.

If it is obvious that such measures must be taken to protect bodily health, although it may only be a relatively minor wound, then when the health of the soul is at stake—the very nerve center of a man's life—how much more necessary it is to wash, to cut away, to scrape, to disinfect, to suffer! Prudence demands that we intervene in this way and that we don't flee from duty, because to sidestep our obligations here would indicate a great lack of concern for and even a grave offense against the virtue of justice and fortitude.

You can be sure that a Christian who really wants to do everything honestly in the eyes of God and of his neighbor needs to possess all the virtues, at least potentially. But Father, you will ask me, what about my weaknesses?

And I will answer: can't a doctor who is sick cure others, even if his illness is chronic? Will his illness prevent him from prescribing proper treatment for other patients? Obviously not. In order to cure others, all he needs is to have the necessary knowledge and to apply it with the same concern as he would in his own case.

Turning our weakness to good account

162 Each day, you will find, as I do, if you examine yourselves courageously in the presence of God, that you have many defects. If we struggle, with God's help, to get rid of them we needn't give them too much importance, and we will overcome them even though it may seem that we never manage to uproot them entirely. Furthermore, over and above those weaknesses, if you are really determined to correspond to God's grace, you will be helping to cure the big shortcomings of others. When you realize you are as weak as they are and capable of any sin, no matter how horrible, you will be more understanding and gentle with others, and at the same time more demanding,

because you will want all men to make up their minds to love God with all their hearts.

We Christians, children of God, must help others by honestly putting into practice what those hypocrites perversely muttered to the Master: "You make no distinction between man and man."[12] That is to say, we must completely reject any kind of partiality (we are interested in the souls of all men!) although it is only natural that we turn first to the people whom for whatever reasons (even though at times they may appear to be only human reasons) God has placed at our side.

Et viam Dei in veritate doces[13] ("And you teach **163**
the way of God truthfully"). Teach others. Never stop teaching: that means showing the ways of God with utter truthfulness. You needn't worry about your defects being seen, yours and mine. I like making mine public, and telling of my personal struggle and my desire to correct this failing or that in my battle to be loyal to our Lord. Our efforts to banish and overcome our defects will in themselves be a way of teaching God's ways: first, and in spite

[12] Mt 22:16.
[13] *Ibid.*

of our visible errors, he wants us to strive to give witness with our lives; then, with our teaching, just like our Lord did when he *coepit facere et docere*[14] ("began with works, then afterwards he devoted himself to preaching").

Having reminded you that this priest loves you very much and that your Father in Heaven loves you more because he is infinitely good, infinitely a Father; and having shown you that there is nothing I can reproach you with, I feel all the same that I must help you to love Jesus Christ and the Church, his flock, because in this I think you are not ahead of me; you emulate me, but you are not ahead of me. When, through my preaching or in my personal conversations with each one of you, I draw attention to some defect, it is not in order to make you suffer. My only motive is to help us love our Lord more deeply. And when I impress upon you the need to practise the virtues, I never forget that I am under the same obligation myself.

164 I once heard someone say very rashly that the experience of one's lapses serves to make one fall a further hundred times into the same

[14] Acts 1:1.

error. I tell you, instead, that a prudent person makes use of these setbacks to be more careful in the future, to learn to do good, and to renew his decision to seek greater holiness. From your failures and successes in God's service, seek always to draw, together with an increase in love, a stronger determination to carry on fulfilling your rights and duties as Christian citizens, no matter what the cost. And do this manfully, without fleeing from honors or responsibilities, without being afraid of the reactions we produce in those around us, perhaps originating from false brethren, when we nobly and loyally try to seek God's glory and the good of our neighbor.

So, then, we have to be prudent. Why is this? In order to be just, in order to live charity, and to give good service to God and to all our fellowmen. Not without good reason has prudence been called *genitrix virtutum*[15] ("the mother of virtues"), and also *auriga virtutum*[16] ("the guide of every good habit").

[15] St Thomas Aquinas, *In III Sententiarum*, dist. 33, q.2, a.5.
[16] St Bernard, *Sermones in Cantica Canticorum*, 49, 5 (PL 183, 1018).

To each his due

165 Read the Gospel scene attentively, in order to take advantage of these wonderful lessons in the virtues which should throw light on the way we act. When they had finished their hypocritical and fawning preamble, the Pharisees and Herodians came to the point, " 'Tell us therefore what you think: is it lawful to give tribute to Caesar or not?' "[17] And St John Chrysostom writes: "Take note of their astuteness, for they don't say, 'Tell us what is right or suitable or permissible, but tell us what you think.' They were obsessed with the idea of betraying him and of making him hateful to the authorities."[18] "But Jesus, knowing their wickedness, said, 'Why do you test me, you hypocrites? Show me the coin of the tribute.' So they offered him a denarius. Then Jesus said to them, 'Whose are this image and this inscription?' They said to him, 'Caesar's.' Then he said to them, 'Render, therefore, to Caesar the things that are Caesar's, and to God the things that are God's.' "[19]

[17] Mt 22:17.
[18] St John Chrysostom, *In Matthaeum homiliae*, 70, 1 (PG 58, 656).
[19] Mt 22:18-21.

As you can see, the dilemma is as old as our Lord's answer is unequivocal and clear. There is no clash, no opposition, between serving God and serving men; between the exercise of our civic rights and duties and our religious ones; between the commitment to build up and improve the earthly city, and the conviction that we are passing through this world on our way to our heavenly homeland.

Here too, as I never tire of repeating, we can see that unity of life which is an essential condition for those who are trying to sanctify themselves in the midst of the ordinary situations of their work and of their family and social relationships. Jesus does not allow any division here: "No one can serve two masters, for he will either hate the one and love the other, or if he subjects himself to the first, he will despise the other."[20] The exclusive choice of God that a Christian makes when he responds fully to his call, impels him to refer everything to our Lord and, at the same time, to give his neighbor everything that justice requires.

[20] *Ibid* 6:24.

166 There is no excuse for protecting oneself with apparently pious reasons, in order to deprive others of their due. "If anyone says, 'Yes, I love God,' while at the same time he hates his brother, he is a liar."[21] But they also lie who deny our Lord the love and reverence—the adoration—due to him as our Creator and Father; or who refuse to obey his commandments with the false excuse that such obedience is incompatible with serving men, since St John clearly states that "in this we know that we love the sons of God, if we love God and keep his commandments. For loving God means keeping his commandments; and his commandments are not a burden to us."[22]

You may hear many people who, in the name of efficiency, and even of charity, make speeches and invent theories with the aim of curtailing the outward signs of respect and homage towards God. They seem to regard everything done to honor God as excessive. Take no notice of them. Keep on your way. Such speculations only lead to controversies that at best get nowhere, and quite often cause

[21] 1 Jn 4:20.
[22] *Ibid* 5:2-3.

scandal among Christians and end up hindering the fulfillment of our Lord's precept that we give everyone his due and practise the holy virtue of justice with gentle perfection.

Duties of justice towards God and men

First of all, we must be just towards God. **167**
Let this fact be firmly impressed in our hearts, so that it shows in our behavior, for it is the touchstone of the true "hunger and thirst for justice,"[23] which distinguishes this virtue from the shouting of the envious and resentful and from the outcries of the selfish and greedy...For the worst and most ungrateful injustice is to deny our Creator and Redeemer the recognition of the abundant and wonderful gifts he has given us. If you are really striving to be just, you will often reflect on your utter dependence upon God, and be filled with gratitude and the desire to repay the favors of a Father who loves us to the point of madness: "For what have you got that you have not received?"[24]

[23] Mt 5:6.
[24] 1 Cor 4:7.

This way the good spirit of filial piety will come alive in our hearts and it will bring you to address God with a tender heart. Don't be taken in by the hypocrites around you when they sow doubts as to whether our Lord has a right to ask so much of you. Instead, put yourselves obediently and unconditionally in the presence of God, like "clay in the potter's hands,"[25] and humbly confess to him: *Deus meus et omnia* ("You are my God and my all")! And if you ever have to bear unexpected blows, or undeserved tribulations at the hands of your fellowmen, you will know how to sing with a new joy: "May the most just and most lovable will of God be done, be fulfilled, be praised and eternally exalted above all things. Amen. Amen."

168 The circumstances of the servant in the parable who owed ten thousand talents,[26] are a good summary of our situation before God. We too are unable to find the wherewithal to pay the enormous debt we have contracted for so much divine goodness, which we have increased through our personal sins. Even though we fight resolutely, we can never

[25] Jer 18:6.
[26] Cf. Mt 18:24.

properly repay the great debt that God has forgiven us. However, divine mercy fully makes up for the impotence of human justice. God can say he is satisfied and remit our debt, simply "because he is good and his mercy infinite."[27]

The parable, as you will remember, ends with a second scene which is the counterpoint of the first. The servant, whose huge debt has just been cancelled, took no pity on a fellow servant who owed him only a hundred pence. And it is here that the meanness of his heart comes to light. Strictly speaking, no one will deny him the right to demand what is his. Nevertheless, there is something inside us that rebels and tells us that his intolerant attitude is very far from real justice. It is not right that a person who, only a moment previously has been treated with mercy and understanding, should not then react with at least a little patience towards his own debtor. Remember that justice does not consist exclusively in an exact respect for rights and duties, as in the case of arithmetical problems that are solved simply by addition and subtraction.

[27] Ps 105:1.

169 The Christian virtue of justice is more ambitious. It enjoins us to prove ourselves thankful, friendly, and generous. It encourages us to act as loyal and honorable friends, in hard times as well as in good ones; to obey the law and to respect legitimately authority; to amend gladly when we realize we have erred in tackling a problem. Above all, if we are just, we will fulfill our professional, family, and social commitments without fuss or display, working hard and exercising our rights, which are also duties.

I don't believe in the justice of idle people because, with their *dolce far niente* ("sweetly doing nothing"), as they say in my beloved Italy, they fail, sometimes seriously, in that most fundamental principle of equity, which is work. We must not forget that God created man *ut operatur*[28] ("that he might work"), and others (our family and our country, the whole human race) also depend on the effectiveness of our work. My children, what a poor idea of justice those people have who would reduce it to the mere redistribution of material goods!

[28] Gen 2:15.

Justice and love of freedom and truth

From early childhood (or, as Scripture says,[29] 170
as soon as I had ears to hear) I already began to hear people clamoring about the *social question*. There is nothing special about this, because it is such an old topic; it has always been around. It arose, most likely, when men first became organized in some way and began to perceive differences of age, intelligence, capacity for work, interests, and personality.

I don't know whether or not we can avoid having social classes. In any case it is not my job to speak of such matters, much less here, in this oratory, where we have come together to talk about God (I would never want to talk about anything else) and to talk *to* God.

You may think what you will about anything that Providence has left to the free and legitimate discussion of men. But in my case, my being a priest of Christ tells me I must work at a higher level and remind you that, whatever the situation, we are never exempt from practising justice, heroically if necessary.

[29] Cf. Mt 11:15.

171 We have a duty to defend the personal freedom of everyone, in the knowledge that "Jesus Christ is the one who obtained that freedom for us."[30] If we do not so behave, what right have we to claim our own freedom? We must also spread the truth, because *veritas liberabit vos*[31] ("the truth will set you free"). The truth makes us free, while ignorance enslaves. We have to uphold the right of all men to live, to own what is necessary to lead a dignified existence, to work and to rest, to choose a particular state in life, to form a home, to bring children into the world within marriage and to be allowed to educate them, to pass peacefully through times of sickness and old age, to have access to culture, to join with other citizens to achieve legitimate ends, and, above all, the right to know and love God in perfect liberty, for conscience, true conscience, will discover the imprint of the Creator in all things.

For this reason, it is urgent to repeat (and here I am not speaking politics, I am simply pointing out the Church's teaching) that Marx-

[30] Gal 4:31.
[31] Jn 8:32.

ism is incompatible with the Christian faith. Can there be anything more opposed to the faith than a system which is based on eliminating the loving presence of God from the soul? Shout it aloud, so that your voice is clearly heard, that in order to practise justice we have no need whatsoever of Marxism. On the contrary, because of its exclusively materialistic solutions, which know nothing of the God of peace, this most serious error raises all kinds of barriers to the achievement of happiness and understanding among men. It is within Christianity that we find the good light that will enable us to answer all problems: all you have to do is to strive sincerely to be Catholics, *non verbo neque lingua, sed opere et veritate*[32] ("not with words or with the tongue, but with the works and in truth"). Speak up fearlessly, whenever the occasion arises (and, if necessary, look for such opportunities), without being in any way shy.

[32] 1 Jn 3:18.

Justice and charity

172 Read Holy Scripture. Meditate one by one on the scenes depicting our Lord's life and teachings. Consider especially the counsels and warnings with which he prepared the handful of men who were to become his Apostles, his messengers from one end of the earth to the other. What is the key to his teaching? Is it not the new commandment of charity? It was Love that enabled them to make their way through that corrupt pagan world.

Be convinced that justice alone is never enough to solve the great problems of mankind. When justice alone is done, don't be surprised if people are hurt. The dignity of man, who is a son of God, requires much more. Charity must penetrate and accompany justice because it sweetens and deifies everything: "God is love."[33] Our motive in everything we do should be the Love of God, which makes it easier for us to love our neighbor and which purifies and raises all earthly loves on to a higher level.

There is a long road to travel from the demands of strict justice to the abundance of

[33] *Ibid* 4:16.

charity. And there are not many who persevere to the end. Some are content to go as far as the threshold: they leave aside justice and limit their actions to a bit of welfare work, which they define as charitable, without realizing that they are doing only a small part of what in fact they have a strict duty to do. And they are as satisfied with themselves as the Pharisee who thought he had fulfilled the law perfectly because he fasted twice a week and gave tithes of all he possessed.[34]

Charity, which is like a generous overflowing of justice, demands first of all the fulfillment of one's duty. The way to start is to be just; the next step is to do what is most equitable...; but in order to love, great refinement is required, and much thoughtfulness, and respect, and kindliness in rich measure. In other words, it involves following the Apostle's advice: "carry one another's burdens, and thus you will fulfill the law of Christ."[35] Then, indeed we shall be living charity fully and carrying out the commandment of Jesus. **173**

For me there is no clearer example of this practical union of justice and charity than the

[34] Cf. Lk 18:12.
[35] Gal 6:2.

behavior of mothers. They love all their children with the same degree of affection, and it is precisely this same love that impels them to treat each one differently, with an *unequal justice,* since each child is different from the others. So, in the case of our fellowmen, charity perfects and completes justice. It moves us to respond differently to different people, adapting ourselves to their specific circumstances so as to give joy to those who are sad, knowledge to those who lack it, affection to the lonely ...Justice says that each person should receive his due, which does not mean giving the same to everyone. Utopian egalitarianism can give rise to the greatest injustice.

In order to act in this way always, the way good mothers do, we need to forget about ourselves and aspire to no other honor than that of serving others, in the same way as Jesus Christ, who preached that "the Son of man has not come to be served but to serve."[36] This requires the integrity of being able to submit our own wills to that of our divine model, working for all men, and fighting for their eternal happiness and well-being. I know of no

[36] Mt 20:28.

better way to be just than that of a life of self-surrender and service.

Perhaps someone will think I am naive. It 174
doesn't worry me. Although I may be labelled as such, because I still believe in charity, I assure you I will believe in it, always! And, while God gives me life, I shall continue, as a priest of Jesus Christ, to work for unity and peace among those who are brothers by the very fact that they are children of the same Father, God. I shall continue to work with the aim of getting men to understand each other, and to share the same ideal, the ideal of the Faith!

Let us turn to our Lady, the prudent and faithful virgin, and to St Joseph, her husband, the perfect model of the just man.[37] They, who lived the virtues we have just contemplated in the presence of Jesus, the Son of God, will obtain for us the grace we need to have the same virtues rooted in our souls, so that we may resolve always to behave as good disciples of the Master: prudent, just and full of charity.

[37] Cf. *Ibid* 1:19.

FOR THEY SHALL SEE GOD*

Jesus Christ is our model, the model for every Christian. You are well aware of this because you have heard it and reflected on it so often. You have also taught this to many people in the course of your apostolate of friendship (true friendship, with a divine meaning) which by now has become a part of you. And you have recalled this fact, when necessary, when using the wonderful means of fraternal correction, so that the person who was listening to you might compare his behavior with that of our first-born Brother, the Son of Mary, Mother of God and our Mother also. **175**

* A homily given on March 12, 1954.

Jesus is the model for us. He himself has told us so: *discite a me*[1] ("learn from me"). Today I want to talk to you about a virtue which, while it is neither the only virtue, nor the most important one, nevertheless operates in a Christian's life like salt, preserving it from corruption; it is also the touchstone of the apostolic soul. The virtue is holy purity.

We know full well that theological charity is the highest virtue. But chastity is a means *sine qua non* ("an indispensable condition"), if we are to establish an intimate dialogue with God. When people do not keep to it, when they give up the fight, they end up becoming blind. They can no longer see anything, because "the animal man cannot perceive the things that are of the Spirit of God."[2]

We, however, wish to look through unclouded eyes, encouraged as we are by our Lord's teaching: "Blessed are the pure of heart, for they shall see God."[3] The Church has always understood these words as an invitation to chastity. As St John Chrysostom writes, "Those

[1] Mt 11:29.
[2] 1 Cor 2:14.
[3] Mt 5:8.

who love chastity, whose consciences are completely clear, keep their hearts pure. No other virtue is so necessary in order to see God."[4]

The example of Christ

During the course of his life on earth, Jesus our Lord had all manner of insults heaped upon him and was mistreated in every way possible. Remember the way it was rumored that he was a troublemaker and how he was said to be possessed?[5] At other times, demonstrations of his infinite Love were deliberately misinterpreted, and he was accused of being a friend of sinners.[6] 176

Later on he, who personified penance and moderation, was accused of haunting the tables of the rich.[7] He was also contemptuously referred to as *fabri filius*,[8] ("the carpenter's son"), the worker's son, as if this were an insult. He

[4] St John Chrysostom, *In Matthaeum homiliae*, 15, 4 (PG 57, 227).

[5] Cf. Mt 11:18.

[6] Cf. *Ibid* 9:11.

[7] Cf. Lk 19:7.

[8] Mt 13:55.

allowed himself to be denounced as a glutton and a drunkard...He let his enemies accuse him of everything, except that he was not chaste. On this point he sealed their lips, because he wanted us to keep a vivid memory of his immaculate example: a wonderful example of purity, of cleanness, of light, of a love that can set the whole world on fire in order to purify it.

For myself, I always like to consider holy purity in the light of our Lord's own behavior. In practicing this virtue, what refinement he showed! See what St John says about Jesus when *fatigatus ex itinere, sedebat sic supra fontem*[9] ("wearied as he was from the journey, he was sitting by the well").

Recollect yourselves and go over the scene again slowly in your minds. Jesus Christ, *perfectus Deus, perfectus homo*[10] is tired out from his travels and his apostolic work. Perhaps there have been times when the same thing has happened to you and you have ended up worn out, because you have reached the limit of your resources. It is a touching sight to see our

[9] Jn 4:6.
[10] Symbol *Quicumque.*

Master so exhausted. He is hungry too—his disciples have gone to a neighboring village to look for food. And he is thirsty.

But tired though his body is, his thirst for souls is even greater. So, when the Samaritan woman, the sinner, arrives, Christ with his priestly heart, turns eagerly to save the lost sheep, and he forgets his tiredness, his hunger, and his thirst.

Our Lord was busy with this great work of charity when the apostles came back from the village, and they *mirabantur quia cum muliere loquebatur*[11] ("they were astonished to find him talking to a woman alone"). How careful he was! What love he had for the beautiful virtue of holy purity, that virtue which helps us to be stronger, manlier, more fruitful, better able to work for God, and more capable of undertaking great things!

"For this is the will of God, your **177**
sanctification...Let every one of you learn how to make use of his body in holiness and honor, not yielding to the promptings of passion, as the heathen do, who do not know God."[12] We

[11] Jn 4:27.
[12] 1 Thess 4:3-5.

belong to God completely, soul and body, flesh and bones, all our senses and faculties. Ask him, confidently: Jesus, guard our hearts! Make them big and strong and tender, hearts that are affectionate and refined, overflowing with love for you and ready to serve all mankind.

Our bodies are holy. They are *temples of God*, says St Paul. This cry of the apostle brings to mind the universal call to holiness which our Lord addresses to all men: *estote vos perfecti sicut et Pater vester caelestis perfectus est*[13] ("you are to be perfect, as your heavenly Father is perfect"). Our Lord asks everyone, without distinction of any kind, to cooperate with his grace. He demands that each of us, in accordance with his particular state in life, should put into practice the virtues proper to the children of God.

Thus, when I remind you now that Christians must keep perfect chastity, I am referring to everyone: to the unmarried, who must practise complete continence; and to those who are married, who practise chastity by fulfilling the duties of their state in life.

[13] Mt 5:48.

If one has the spirit of God, chastity is not a troublesome and humiliating burden, but a joyful affirmation. Will power, dominion, self-mastery do not come from the flesh or from instinct. They come from the will, especially if it is united to the Will of God. In order to be chaste (and not merely continent or decent) we must subject our passions to reason, but for a noble motive, namely, the promptings of Love.

I think of this virtue as the wings which enable us to carry God's teaching, his commandments, to every environment on this earth, without fear of getting contaminated in the process. Wings, even in the case of those majestic birds which soar higher than the clouds, are a burden and a heavy one. But without wings, there is no way of flying. I want you to grasp this idea clearly, and to decide not to give in when you feel the sting of temptation, with its suggestion that purity is an unbearable burden. Take heart! Fly upwards, up to the sun, in pursuit of Love!

Bearing God in our bodies

178 It has always made me very sorry to hear some teachers (so many alas!) going on and on about the dangers of impurity. The result, as I have been able to verify in quite a few souls, is the opposite of what was intended, for it's a sticky subject, stickier than tar, and it deforms people's consciences with all kinds of fears and complexes, so that they come to imagine that the obstacles in the way of attaining purity of soul are almost insurmountable. This is not our way. Our approach to holy purity must be healthy and positive, and expressed in modest and clear language.

To discuss purity is really to talk about Love. I have just pointed out to you that I find it helpful in this regard to have recourse to the most holy Humanity of our Lord, that indescribable marvel where God humbles himself to the point of becoming man, and in doing so does not feel degraded for having taken on flesh like ours, with all its limitations and weaknesses, sin alone excepted. He does all this because he loves us to distraction! He does not in fact lower himself when he empties himself. On the contrary, he raises up and deifies us in body and soul. The virtue of chastity is simply to say "Yes" to his Love, with an affection that is clear, ardent, and properly ordered.

We must proclaim this loud and clear to the whole world, by our words and by the witness of our lives: "Let us not poison our hearts as if we were miserable beasts governed by our lower instincts!" A Christian writer once expressed it thus: "Consider that man's heart is no small thing, for it can embrace so much. Do not measure its greatness by its physical dimensions, but by the power of its thought, whereby it is able to attain the knowledge of so many truths. In the heart it is possible to prepare the way of the Lord, to lay out a straight path where the Word and the Wisdom of God may pass. With your honorable conduct and your irreproachable deeds, prepare the Lord's way, smooth out his path so that the Word of god may act in you without hindrance and give you the knowledge of his mysteries and of his coming."[14]

Holy Scripture reveals to us that the great work of our sanctification, which is accomplished in a marvellous hidden manner by the

[14] Origen, *In Lucam homiliae*, 21 (PG 13, 1856).

Paraclete, takes place in both the soul and the body. "Do you not know that your bodies are members of Christ?" cries the Apostle, "Shall I then take the members of Christ and make them members of a harlot? (...) Or do you not know that your bodies are temples of the Holy Spirit, who dwells in you, whom you have received from God, and that you are no longer your own? For you have been bought at a great price. Glorify God and bear him in your bodies."[15]

179 There are people who smile when they hear chastity mentioned. Theirs is a joyless and dead smile, the product of a sick mind. And they tell you: "Hardly anyone believes in *that* anymore!" One of the things I used to say to the young men who accompanied me when I used to go, so very many years ago, to the slums and hospitals on the outskirts of Madrid was: "As you know, there is a mineral kingdom; then, on a higher plane, a vegetable kingdom, where we find life as well as existence. Higher still there is the animal kingdom, comprised of beings endowed, for the most part, with sensitivity and movement."

[15] 1 Cor 6:15, 19-20.

Then I would explain to them, in a manner that may not have been very scientific, although it made the point, that we ought to establish another kingdom, the *hominal* kingdom, made up of human beings. This is because rational creatures possess a wonderful intelligence, a spark of the Divine Wisdom which enables them to reason on their own. And they also have the marvellous gift of freedom whereby they can accept or reject one thing or another, as they see fit.

Now in this kingdom of human beings (I would tell them, drawing on the experience gained from all my priestly work) for normal people, sex comes in fourth or fifth place. First come spiritual ideals, with each person choosing his own. Next, a whole series of matters that concern ordinary men and women: their father and mother, home, children, and so on. After that, one's job or profession. Only then, in fourth or fifth place, does the sexual impulse come in.

For this reason, whenever I have met people who make sex the central topic of their conversation and interests, I have felt they were abnormal, wretched people, even sick perhaps. And I would add (and the young people to whom I was speaking would burst out laughing at this point) that these poor things made me feel as much pity as would the sight of a deformed child with a big, enormous head, one yard round. They are unhappy individuals. For our part, besides praying for them, we should feel a brotherly compassion for them because we want them to be cured of their pitiful illness. But what is quite clear is that they are in no way more manly or womanly than people who don't go around obsessed with sex.

Chastity is possible

180 We are, all of us, subject to passions, and we all come up against the same sort of difficulties, no matter how old we are. That is why we have to fight. Remember what St Paul wrote: *datus est mihi stimulus carnis meae, angelus Satanae, qui me colaphizet*[16] ("he was given a sting for his flesh, which was like an angel of Satan, to buffet him, otherwise he would have become proud").

[16] 2 Cor 12:7.

It is not possible to lead a clean life without God's assistance. He wants us to be humble and to ask for his aid. At this very moment, you should trustingly beg our Lady, as you accompany her in the solitude of your hearts, without saying anything out loud: "Mother, this poor heart of mine rebels so foolishly...If you don't protect me..." And she will help you to keep it pure and to follow the way to which God has called you.

Be humble, very humble, my children. Let us learn to be humble. We need prudence to protect our Love. We must keep a careful watch and not be overcome by fear. Many of the classical spiritual authors compare the devil to a mad dog tied down by a chain. If we don't go near him, he cannot bite us, no matter how much he barks. If you foster humility in your souls, you will certainly avoid the occasions of sin, and you will react by having the courage to run away from them. You will have daily recourse to the help that comes from Heaven, and will make lively progress along this path of true love.

Don't forget that when someone is cor- **181**
rupted by the concupiscence of the flesh, he cannot make any spiritual progress. He cannot

do good works. He is a cripple, cast aside like an old rag. Have you ever seen patients suffering from progressive paralysis and unable to help themselves or get up? Sometimes they cannot even move their heads. Well, in the supernatural order, the same thing happens to people who are not humble and have made a cowardly surrender to lust. They don't see, or hear, or understand anything. They are paralyzed. They are like men gone mad. Each of us here ought to invoke our Lord, and his Blessed Mother, and pray that he will grant us humility and a determination to avail ourselves devoutly of the divine remedy of confession. Do not let even the smallest focal point of corruption take root in your souls, no matter how tiny it may be. Speak out. When water flows, it stays clean; blocked up, it becomes a stagnant pool full of repugnant filth. What was once drinking water becomes a breeding ground for insects.

You know as well as I do that chastity is possible and that it is a great source of joy. You also realize that now and then it requires a little bit of struggle. Let us listen again to St Paul: "For I am delighted with the law of God according to the inner man, but I see another law in my members, warring against the law of my mind and making me prisoner to the law of sin that is in my members. Unhappy man that I am! Who will deliver me from this body of death?"[17] Cry out yourself more than he, if you have to, although without exaggerating. *Sufficit tibi gratia mea*[18] ("my grace is sufficient for you"), is our Lord's answer.

I have noticed at times how an athlete's eyes **182**
light up at the sight of the obstacles he has to overcome. What a victory there is in store! See how he conquers the difficulties! God our Lord looks at us that way. He loves our struggle: we will win through always, because he will never deny us his all-powerful grace. Thus, it doesn't matter if we have to fight, because he does not abandon us.

It is a battle, but not a renunciation. We respond with a joyful affirmation, and give ourselves to him freely and cheerfully. Your conduct should not be limited to simply evading falls and occasions of sin. In no way should you let it come down to a cold and calculating negation. Are you really convinced that chastity is a virtue and that, as such, it ought to grow

[17] Rom 7:22-24.
[18] 2 Cor 12:9.

and become perfect? Then I insist once again, that it is not enough merely to be continent according to one's state in life. We must practice, we must live chastity, even to a heroic degree. This attitude involves a positive act whereby we gladly accept God's summons when he says: *Praebe, fili mi, cor tuum mihi et oculi tui vias meas custodiant*[19] ("Son, give me your heart, and turn your gaze upon my ways of peace").

And now I ask you, how are you facing up to this battle? You know very well that a fight which is kept up from the beginning is a fight already won. Get away from danger as soon as you are aware of the first sparks of passion, and even before. Also, speak about it at once to the person who directs your soul. Better if you talk about it beforehand, if possible, because, if you open you heart wide, you will not be defeated. One such act after another leads to the forming of a habit, and inclination, and ends up making things easy. That is why we have to struggle to make this virtue a habit, making mortification a habit so that we do not reject the Love of Loves.

[19] Prov 23:26.

Reflect on this advice of St Paul to Timothy: *te ipsum castum custodi*[20] ("keep yourself chaste"), so that we too may be ever vigilant, determined to guard this treasure that God has entrusted to us. During the course of my life, how often have I heard people exclaim: "Oh, if only I had broken it off at the start!" They said it full of sorrow and shame.

Giving one's whole heart

I must remind you that you will not find happiness if you don't fulfill your Christian duties. If you were to leave them aside, you would feel terrible remorse and would be thoroughly miserable. Even the most ordinary things, which are licit and which bring a bit of happiness, would then become as bitter as gall, as sour as vinegar, and as repugnant as arum. **183**

Let each of us, myself included, put our trust in Jesus, saying to him: "Lord, I am ready to struggle and I know that you do not lose battles. I realize too that if at times I lose, it

[20] 1 Tim 5:22.

is because I have gone away from you. Take me by the hand. Don't trust me. Don't let go of me."

You may be thinking: "But, Father, I am so happy! I love Jesus! Even though I am made of clay, I do want to become a saint with the help of God and his Blessed Mother!" I don't doubt you. I am only forewarning you with these words of advice just in case, just supposing a difficulty were to arise.

At the same time, I would remind you that for Christians (for you and me) our life is a life of Love. This heart of ours was born to love. But when it is not given something pure, clean, and noble to love, it takes revenge and fills itself with squalor. True love of God, and consequently purity of life, is as far removed from sensuality as it is from insensitivity, and as far from sentimentality as it is from heartlessness or hardheartedness.

It is such a pity not to have a heart. How unfortunate are those people who have never learned to love with tenderness! We Christians are in love with Love: our Lord does not want us to be dry and rigid, like inert matter. He wants us to be saturated with his love! People who, for the sake of God, say "No" to a human love are not bachelors or spinsters, like those sad, unhappy, crestfallen men and women who have despised the chance of a pure and generous love.

Chastity and human love

As I have often told you, and I don't care who knows it, I have also used the words of popular songs, that almost always treat of love, to keep up my conversation with our Lord. I like them, I really do. Our Lord has chosen me and some of you as well to belong totally to himself; so we translate the noble love expressed in human love songs into something that is divine. The Holy Spirit does this in the Song of Songs; and the great mystics of all ages have done the same. **184**

Look at these verses of St Teresa of Avila:

"If you would have me idling
For love of you I will be idle;
But if you bid me work, my
Sole desire is to die working.
Tell me the when, the how,
  the where;

O sweetest love I beg of you
To say what you would have
me do."[21]

Or that song of St John of the Cross, which begins so charmingly:

"A little shepherd boy
Is all alone and far from joy
Full of sorrow and distress
From thinking of his shepherdess
Love unrequited in his breast."[22]

Human love, when it is pure, fills me with immense respect and inexpressible veneration.

[21] *"Si queréis que este holgando,*
Quiero por amor holgar;
si me mandais trabajar,
morir quiero trabajando.
Decid ¿ donde, como y cuándo?
Decid, dulce Amor, decid:
¿ Que mandáis hacer de mi?"
(St Teresa of Avila, *Vuestra soy, para Vos naci, in Poems,* 5, 9.)

[22] *"Un pastorcico solo está penado,*
ajeno de placer y de contento,
y en su pastora puesto el pensamiento
y el pecho del amor muy lastimado."
(St John of the Cross, *Otras canciones a lo divino de Cristo y el alma, in Poems,* 10.)

How could we fail to appreciate the holy and noble love shared by our parents, to whom we owe a great part of our friendship with God? I bless such love with my two hands, and if anyone asks me why I say *with my two hands,* I reply at once: "Because I don't have four."

Blessed be human love! But our Lord has asked something more of me. And, as Catholic theology clearly states, to give oneself out of love for the Kingdom of Heaven to Jesus alone and, through Jesus, to all men, is a love more sublime than married love, even though marriage is a sacrament and indeed *sacramentum magnum*[23] ("a great sacrament").

But, whatever the calling, the fact is that each person, in his own place, according to the vocation which God has inspired in his soul (be he single, married, widowed, or priest) must strive to live chastity with great refinement, because it is a virtue for everyone. It calls on everyone to struggle, to be delicate, sensitive, and strong. It calls for a degree of refinement which can only be fully appreciated when we come close to the loving Heart of Christ on the

[23] Eph 5:32.

Cross. Don't worry if at times you feel threatened by temptation. One thing is to feel temptation, quite another to consent. Temptation can be rejected easily with God's help. What we must never do is to dialogue with temptation.

The means to conquer

185 Let us now take a look at the resources we Christians can count on at all times to conquer in the struggle to guard our chastity; a struggle we must undertake not as angels but as women and men who are strong and healthy and *normal!* I have a great devotion for the angels, and I venerate this army of God with all my heart. But I do not like comparing ourselves to them, for angels have a different nature from ours and any comparison would only confuse the issue.

Many places are affected by a general climate of sensuality which, taken together with confused ideas about doctrine, leads many people to justify all types of aberrations, or at least to show a very careless tolerance towards all kinds of depraved customs.

We must be as clean and pure as we can as far as the body is concerned and without being afraid, because sex is something noble and holy—a participation in God's creative power—which was made for marriage. And thus, pure and fearless, you will give testimony by your behavior that it is possible and beautiful to live holy purity.

First, we will strive to refine our conscience. We must go sufficiently deep, until we can be sure our conscience is well formed and we can distinguish between a delicate conscience, which is a true grace from God, and a scrupulous conscience, which is not the same.

Take very special care of chastity and also of the other virtues which accompany it: modesty and refinement.* They are as it were the safeguard of chastity. Don't take lightly those norms of conduct which help so much to keep us worthy in the sight of God: keeping a watchful guard over our senses and our heart; the courage—the courage to be a *coward*—to flee from the occasions of sin; going to the sacra-

* *Pudor*, in the original, a word used here not so much in its sense of shyness, as in that of creating a protective atmosphere for holy purity (Translator's note).

ments frequently, particularly to the sacrament of Confession; complete sincerity in our own spiritual direction; sorrow, contrition, and reparation after one's falls. And all this imbued with a tender devotion to our Lady so that she may obtain for us from God the gift of a clean and holy life.

186 If, alas, one falls, one must get up at once. With God's help, which will never be lacking if the proper means are used, one must seek to arrive at repentance as quickly as possible, to be humbly sincere and to make amends so that the momentary failure is transformed into a great victory for Jesus Christ.

You should also get into the habit of taking the battle to areas that are far removed from the main walls of the fortress. We cannot go about doing balancing acts on the very frontiers of evil. We have to be firm in avoiding the indirect voluntary. We must reject even the tiniest failure to love God, and we must strive to develop a regular and fruitful Christian apostolate, which will have holy purity both as a necessary foundation and also as one of its most characteristic fruits. We ought as well to fill all our time with intense and responsible work, in which we seek God's presence, because we must never forget that we have been bought at a great price and that we are temples of the Holy Spirit.

What other advice do I have for you? Well, simply to do what the Christians who have really tried to follow Christ have always done, and to use the same means employed by the first men who felt prompted to follow Jesus: developing a close relationship with our Lord in the Eucharist, a childlike recourse to the Blessed Virgin, humility, temperance, mortification of the senses ("it is not good to look at what it is not licit to desire,"[24] was St Gregory the Great's warning) and penance.

You might well tell me that all this is nothing but a summary of the whole Christian life. The fact is that purity, which is love, cannot be separated from the essence of our faith, which is charity, a constant falling in love with God, who created and redeemed us, and who is constantly taking us by the hand, even though time and again we may not even notice it. He cannot abandon us. "Sion said: 'The Lord has forsaken me, my Lord has forgotten me.' Can a mother forget her infant, be without tender-

[24] St Gregory the Great, *Moralia*, 21, 2, 4, (PL 76, 190).

ness to the child of her womb? Even should she forget, I will never forget you."[25] Don't these words fill you with immense joy?

187 I like to say that there are three things that fill us with gladness in this life and which will bring us the eternal happiness of Heaven: a firm, refined, joyful, and unquestioning fidelity to the faith, to the vocation that each of us has received, and to purity. The person who gets entangled in the brambles along the way (sensuality, pride, etc.) does so because he wants to and, if he doesn't change, he will be miserable all his life because he will have turned his back on Christ's Love.

As I have already said, we all have our defects. But our defects should never be a reason for us to turn away from God's Love. Rather should they lead us to cling to that Love, sheltering within his divine goodness, as the warriors of old did by climbing into their suits of armor. Our defense is the cry, *ecce ego, quia vocasti me*[26] ("here I am, because you have called me"). Just because we discover how fragile we are is no reason to run away

[25] Is 49:14-15.
[26] 1 Kings 3:6, 8.

from God. What we must do is to attack our defects, precisely because we know that God trusts us.

How shall we be able to overcome our meanness? Let me make the point again because it is so important: by being humble and by being sincere in spiritual direction and in the Sacrament of Penance. Go to those who direct your souls with your hearts open wide. Do not close your hearts, for if the dumb devil gets in, it is very difficult to get rid of him. 188

Forgive me for insisting on these points, but I believe it is absolutely necessary for you to have deeply impressed on your minds the fact that humility, together with its immediate consequence, sincerity, are the thread which links the other means together. These two virtues act as a foundation on which a solid victory can be built. If the dumb devil gets inside a soul, he ruins everything. On the other hand, if he is cast out immediately, everything turns out well; we are happy and life goes forward properly. Let us always be *brutally sincere,* but in a good-mannered way.

I want one thing to be clear: I am not as worried about the heart or the flesh as I am about pride. Be humble. If ever you think you are completely and utterly right, you are not right at all. Go to spiritual direction with your soul wide open. Don't close it because, I repeat, the dumb devil will get in, and it is difficult to get him out again.

Remember the poor boy who was possessed by a devil, and the disciples were unable to set him free. Only our Lord could free him, by prayer and fasting. On that occasion the Master worked three miracles. The first enabled the boy to hear because, when the dumb devil gets control, the soul refuses to listen. The second made him speak, and the third expelled the devil.

189 Tell first what you would not like to be known. Down with the dumb devil! By turning some small matter over and over in your mind, you will make it snowball into something big, with you trapped inside. What's the point of doing that? Open up your soul! I promise that you will be happy, that is faithful to your Christian way, if you are sincere. Clarity and simplicity: they are absolutely necessary dispositions. We have to open up our souls completely, so that the sun of God and the charity of Love can enter in.

It is not necessarily bad will that prevents people from being utterly sincere. Sometimes they may simply have an erroneous conscience. Some people have so formed, or rather deformed their consciences that they think their dumbness, their lack of simplicity, is something good. They think it is good to say nothing. This can even happen to people who have received an excellent training and know the things of God. This may indeed be what is convincing them that they should not speak out. But they are wrong. Sincerity is a must, always. There are no valid excuses, no matter how good they seem.

Let us end this period of conversation in which you and I have been praying to our Father, asking him to grant us the grace to live the Christian virtue of chastity as a joyful affirmation.

We ask this of him through the intercession of our Lady, she who is immaculate purity. Let us turn to her, *tota pulchra* ("all beautiful"), taking to heart the advice I gave many years ago to those who felt uneasy in their daily struggle to be humble, pure, sincere, cheerful, and generous. "All the sins of your life seem to be rising up against you. Don't give up hope!

On the contrary, call your holy Mother Mary, with the faith and abandonment of a child. She will bring peace to your soul."[27]

[27] *The Way*, no. 498.

LIVING BY FAITH*

You hear people saying sometimes that there 190
are fewer miracles nowadays. Might it not rather be that there are fewer people living a life of faith? God cannot go back on his promise, "Ask of me, and I will give you the nations for your inheritance, and the ends of the earth for your possession."[1] Our God is Truth itself, the very foundation of all that exists: nothing takes place independently of his almighty will.

"As it was in the beginning, is now, and ever shall be, world without end."[2] The Lord does not change. He does not need to go after things he might not have, for he is all motion, all beauty, all greatness. Today as always. "The

* A homily given on October 12, 1947.

[1] Ps 2:8.

[2] Doxology, *Gloria Patri...*

heavens will vanish like smoke, and the earth will wear out like a garment...but my salvation will last forever and my justice will have no end."[3]

In Jesus Christ God has established a new and everlasting covenant with mankind. He has placed his almighty power at the service of our salvation. When his creatures lose confidence and are afraid through lack of faith, we hear once again the voice of Isaias who speaks out in the name of the Lord: "Is my hand too short to redeem? Have I not strength to save? With one threat I can dry the sea and turn rivers to desert; so that their fish shrivel up for want of water and die of thirst. I clothe the heavens with darkness, and make sackcloth their covering."[4]

191 Faith is a supernatural virtue which disposes our intelligence to give assent to the truths of revelation, to say "Yes" to Christ, who has brought us full knowledge of the Blessed Trinity's plan for our salvation. "In old days, God spoke to our fathers in many ways and by many means, through the prophets; now at

[3] Is 51:6.
[4] Is 50:2-3.

last in these times, he has spoken to us through his Son, whom he has appointed heir of all things, through whom also he created this world of time; a Son who is the splendor of his glory and the figure of his substance; all things depend, for their support, on his word of power. Now, making atonement for our sins, he has taken his place on high, at the right hand of God's majesty."[5]

By the pool of Siloe

I would like Jesus himself to talk to us about **192**
faith, to give us lessons in faith. So let us open the New Testament and relive with him some of the events of his life. For he did not disdain to teach his disciples, showing them, little by little, how to give themselves wholeheartedly to carrying out the Will of his Father. He taught them both by words and by deeds.

Consider chapter nine of St John. "And Jesus saw, as he passed on his way, a man who had been blind from birth. Whereupon his disciples asked him, 'Master, was this man guilty of sin,

[5] Heb 1:1-3.

or was it his parents, that he should have been born blind?' "[6] These men, even though they were so close to Christ, could still think badly about that poor blind man. So do not be surprised if, as you go through life seeking to serve the Church, you also come across disciples of our Lord behaving in a similar manner towards you or towards others. Don't let it worry you and, like the blind man, take no notice; just place yourselves wholeheartedly in Christ's hands. He does not accuse, he pardons. He does not condemn, he forgives. He is not cold and indifferent towards illness, but instead cures it with divine diligence.

Our Lord "spat on the ground, and made clay with the spittle. Then he spread the clay on the man's eyes, and said to him, 'Go and wash in the pool of Siloe (a name that means *Sent*).' So he went and washed there, and came back with his sight restored."[7]

193 What an example of firm faith the blind man gives us! A living, operative faith. Do you behave like this when God commands, when so often you can't see, when your soul is

[6] Jn 9:1-2.
[7] *Ibid* 9:6-7.

worried and the light is gone? What power could the water possibly contain that when the blind man's eyes were moistened with it they were cured? Surely some mysterious eye salve, or a precious medicine made up in the laboratory of some wise alchemist, would have done better? But the man believed; he acted upon the command of God, and he returned with eyes full of light.

St Augustine, commenting on this passage, wrote: "It seems appropriate that the Evangelist should have explained the meaning of the name of the pool saying that it meant *Sent*. Now you know who has been sent. If our Lord had not been sent to us, none of us would have been freed from sin."[8] We must have complete faith in the one who saves us, in this divine Doctor who was sent with the express purpose of curing us; and the more serious or hopeless our illness is, the stronger our faith has to be.

We must learn to acquire the divine measure **194**
of things, never losing our supernatural outlook, and realizing that Jesus makes use also of our weaknesses to reveal his glory. So,

[8] St Augustine, *In Ioannis Evangelium tractatus*, 44, 2 (PL 35, 1714).

whenever your conscience feels the stirrings of self-love, of weariness, of discouragement, or the weight of your passions, you must react immediately and listen to the Master, without letting the sad truth about our lives frighten us, because as long as we live our personal failings will always be with us.

This is the way we Christians must travel. We have to cry out ceaselessly with a strong and humble faith, "Lord, put not your trust in me. But I, I put my trust in you." Then, as we sense in our hearts the love, the compassion, the tenderness of Christ's gaze upon us, for he never abandons us, we shall come to understand the full meaning of those words of St Paul, *virtus in infirmitate perficitur*[9] ("power is made perfect in weakness"). If we have faith in our Lord, in spite of our failings—or, rather, with our failings—we shall be faithful to our Father, God; his divine power will shine forth in us, sustaining us in our weakness.

[9] 2 Cor 12:9.

The faith of Bartimaeus

If we turn now to St Mark we will find he tells us about another blind man being cured. As Jesus "was leaving Jericho, with his disciples and a great multitude, Bartimaeus, the blind man, Timaeus' son, was sitting there by the wayside, begging."[10] Hearing the commotion the crowd was making, the blind man asked, "What is happening?" They told him, "It is Jesus of Nazareth." At this his soul was so fired with faith in Christ that he cried out, "Jesus, Son of David, have pity on me."[11] 195

Don't you too feel the same urge to cry out? You who also are waiting at the side of the way, of this highway of life that is so very short? You who need more light, you who need more grace to make up your mind to seek holiness? Don't you feel an urgent need to cry out, "Jesus, Son of David, have pity on me?" What a beautiful aspiration for you to repeat again and again!

I recommend you to meditate slowly on the events preceding the miracle, to help you keep this fundamental idea clearly engraved upon

[10] Mk 10:46.
[11] *Ibid* 10:47.

your minds: what a world of difference there is between the merciful Heart of Jesus and our own poor hearts! This thought will help you at all times, and especially in the hour of trial and temptation, and also when the time comes to be generous in the little duties you have, or in moments when heroism is called for.

"Many of them rebuked him, telling him to be silent."[12] As people have done to you, when you sensed that Jesus was passing your way. Your heart beat faster and you too began to cry out, prompted by an intimate longing. Then your friends, the need to do the done thing, the easy life, your surroundings, all conspired to tell you: "Keep quiet, don't cry out. Who are you to be calling Jesus? Don't bother him."

But poor Bartimaeus would not listen to them. He cried out all the more: "Son of David, have pity on me." Our Lord, who had heard him right from the beginning, let him persevere in his prayer. He does the same with you. Jesus hears our cries from the very first, but he waits. He wants us to be convinced that we need him. He wants us to beseech him, to persist, like the blind man waiting by the road from Jericho.

[12] *Ibid* 10:48.

"Let us imitate him. Even if God does not immediately give us what we ask, even if many people try to put us off our prayers, let us still go on praying."[13]

"And Jesus stopped, and told them to call him." Some of the better people in the crowd turned to the blind man and said, "Take heart. Rise up, he is calling you."[14] Here you have the Christian vocation! But God does not call only once. Bear in mind that our Lord is seeking us at every moment: Get up, he tells us, put aside your indolence, your easy life, your petty selfishness, your silly little problems. Get up from the ground, where you are lying prostrate and shapeless. Acquire height, weight and volume, and a supernatural outlook. **196**

"Whereupon the man threw away his cloak and leapt to his feet, and so came to him."[15] He threw aside his cloak! I don't know if you have ever lived through a war, but many years ago I had occasion to visit a battlefield shortly after an engagement. There, strewn all over the ground, were greatcoats, water bottles, haver-

[13] St John Chrysostom, *In Matthaeum homiliae*, 66, 1 (PG 58, 626).
[14] Mk 10:49.
[15] *Ibid* 10:50.

sacks stuffed with family souvenirs, letters, photographs of loved ones...which belonged, moreover, not to the vanquished, but to the victors! All these items had become superfluous in the bid to race forward and leap over the enemy defenses. Just as happened to Bartimaeus, as he raced towards Christ.

Never forget that Christ cannot be reached without sacrifice. We have to get rid of everything that gets in the way: greatcoat, haversack, water bottle. You have to do the same in this battle for the glory of God, in this struggle of love and peace by which we are trying to spread Christ's kingdom. In order to serve the Church, the Pope, and all souls, you must be ready to give up everything superfluous, to be left without a cloak to shelter you from the bitter cold of night, without your much-loved family souvenirs, without water to refresh you. This is the lesson taught us by faith and love. This is the way that we must love Christ.

Faith and deeds

197 And now begins a dialogue with God, a marvellous dialogue that moves us and sets our

hearts on fire, for you and I are now Bartimaeus. Christ, who is God, begins to speak and asks, *Quid tibi vis faciam* ("What do you want me to do for you")? The blind man answers, "Lord, that I may see."[16] How utterly logical! How about yourself, can you really see? Haven't you too experienced at times what happened to the blind man of Jericho? I can never forget how, when meditating on this passage many years back, and realizing that Jesus was expecting something of me, though I myself did not know what it was, I made up my own aspirations: "Lord, what is it you want? What are you asking of me?" I had a feeling that he wanted me to take on something new and the cry *Rabboni, ut videam* ("Master, that I may see"), moved me to beseech Christ again and again, "Lord, whatever it is that you wish, let it be done."

Pray with me now to our Lord: *doce me facere* **198**
voluntatem tuam, quia Deus meus es tu[17] ("teach me to do your will, for you are my God"). In short, our lips should express a true desire on our part to correspond effectively to our

[16] *Ibid* 10:51.
[17] Ps 142:10.

Creator's promptings, striving to follow out his plans with unshakable faith, being fully convinced that he cannot fail us.

If we love God's Will in this way, we shall come to understand that the value of our faith lies not only in how clearly we can express it, but also in our determination to defend it by our deeds, and we shall act accordingly.

But let us go back to the scene outside Jericho. It is now to you that Christ is speaking. He asks you, "What is it you want of me?" "That I may see, Lord, that I may see." Then Jesus answers, "Away home with you. Your faith has brought you recovery. And all at once he recovered his sight and followed Jesus on his way."[18] Following Jesus on his way. You have understood what our Lord was asking from you and you have decided to accompany him on his way. You are trying to walk in his footsteps, to clothe yourself in Christ's clothing, to be Christ himself: well, your faith, your faith in the light our Lord is giving you, must be both operative and full of sacrifice. Don't fool yourself. Don't think you are going to find new ways. The faith he demands of us is as

[18] Mk 10:52.

I have said. We must keep in step with him, working generously and at the same time uprooting and getting rid of everything that gets in the way.

Faith and humility

Now it is St Matthew who tells us about a most touching episode. "And behold a woman, who for twelve years had been troubled with an issue of blood, came up behind him and touched the hem of his cloak."[19] What great humility she shows! "She said to herself, 'If only I can touch the hem of his garment, I shall be healed.' "[20] There are always sick people who, like Bartimaeus, pray with great faith and have no qualms about confessing their faith at the top of their voices. But notice how, among those whom Christ encounters, no two souls are alike. This woman, too, has great faith, but she does not cry aloud; she draws near to Jesus without anyone even noticing. For her it is enough just to touch his garment, because she is quite **199**

[19] *Ibid* 9:20.
[20] Mt 9:21.

certain she will be cured. No sooner has she done so than our Lord turns round and looks at her. He already knows what is going on in the depths of her heart and has seen how sure she is: "Have no fear, my daughter, your faith has saved you."[21]

"She delicately touched the hem of his garment. She came forward with faith. She believed, and she knew she had been cured...We too, if we want to be saved, should touch Christ's garment with faith."[22] Do you see now how our faith must be? It must be humble. Who are you, and who am I, to deserve to be called in this way by Christ? Who are we, to be so close to him? As with that poor woman in the crowd, he has given us an opportunity. And not just to touch his garment a little, to feel for a moment the fringe, the hem of his cloak. We actually have Christ himself. He gives himself to us totally, with his Body, his Blood, his Soul, and his Divinity. We eat him each day. We speak to him intimately as one does to a father, as one

[21] *Ibid* 9:22.

[22] St Ambrose, *Expositio Evangelii secundum Lucam*, 6, 56, 58 (PL 15, 1682-1683).

speaks to Love itself. And all this is true. It is no fantasy.

Let us try to become more humble. For only 200
a truly humble faith will allow us to see things from a supernatural point of view. We have no other alternative. There are only two possible ways of living on this earth: either we live a supernatural life, or else an animal life. And you and I can only live the life of God, a supernatural life. "For what does it profit a man, if he gains the whole world and suffers the loss of his own soul?"[23] What use to man are all the things of the earth, all that our intelligence and will can aspire to? What is the point of all that, if it is all to come to an end and sink out of sight; if all the riches of this world are mere theater props and scenery, and if after all this there is eternity forever, and ever, and ever?

The phrase "forever" made St Teresa of Avila great. One day, as a child, she set out from Avila with her brother Rodrigo through the Adaja gate. As they left behind the city walls, intending to reach the land of the Moors where they could be beheaded for love of

[23] Mt 16:26.

Christ, she kept whispering to her brother, who was beginning to get tired, "forever, forever, forever."[24]

Men lie when they say "forever" about things on earth. The only true, totally true, "forever" is that which we say with reference to God. This is how you ought to live your life, with a faith that will help you to taste the honey, the sweetness of Heaven whenever you think about eternal life which is indeed "forever."

Contemplation in our everyday life

201 Let us go back to the Gospels and take a look at what St Matthew tells us in chapter twenty-one. He described how Jesus, "returning to the city, was hungry. And seeing a fig tree by the wayside he went up to it."[25] How wonderful, Lord, to see you hungry! To see you thirsty, too, by the well of Sichar![26] I contemplate you who are *perfectus Deus, perfectus homo*[27] truly God, yet

[24] Cf. St Teresa, *Life*, 1,6.
[25] Mt 21:18-19.
[26] Cf. Jn 4:7.
[27] Symbol *Quicumque*.

truly man, with flesh like my flesh. "He emptied himself, taking the form of a slave,"[28] so that I should never have the slightest doubt that he understands me and loves me.

"He was hungry." Whenever we get tired—in our work, in our studies, in our apostolic endeavors—when our horizon is darkened by lowering clouds, then let us turn our eyes to Jesus, to Jesus who is so good, and who also gets tired; to Jesus who is hungry and suffers thirst. Lord, how well you make yourself understood! How lovable you are! You show us that you are just like us, in everything but sin, so that we can feel utterly sure that, together with you, we can conquer all our evil inclinations, all our faults. For neither weariness nor hunger matters, nor thirst, nor tears...since Christ also grew weary, knew hunger, was thirsty, and wept. What is important is that we struggle to fulfill the will of our heavenly Father,[29] battling away good heartedly, for our Lord is always at our side.

Jesus approaches the fig tree: he approaches 202
you, he approaches me. Jesus hungers, he

[28] Phil 2:7.
[29] Cf. Jn 4:34.

thirsts for souls. On the Cross he cried out *Sitio*[30] ("I thirst")! He thirsts for us, for our love, for our souls and for all the souls we ought to be bringing to him, along the way of the Cross which is the way to immortality and heavenly glory.

He reached the fig tree "and found nothing but leaves on it."[31] How deplorable. Does the same thing happen to us? Is it a sad fact that we are lacking in faith, in dynamism in our humility? Have we no sacrifices, no good works to show? Is our Christianity just a facade, with nothing real behind it? This would be terrible, because Jesus goes on to command, " 'Let no fruit ever grow on you hereafter.' Whereupon the fig tree withered away."[32] This Gospel passage makes us feel sorry, yet at the same time encourages us to strengthen our faith, to live by faith, so that we may always be ready to yield fruit to our Lord.

Let us not deceive ourselves: our Lord does not depend in any way on the human results of our efforts. Our most ambitious projects are,

[30] Jn 19:28.
[31] Mt 21:19.
[32] *Ibid.*

for him, but child's play. What he wants are souls, he wants love. He wants all men to come to him, to enjoy his Kingdom forever. We have to work a lot on this earth and we must do our work well, since it is our daily tasks that we have to sanctify. But let us never forget to do everything for his sake. If we were to do it for ourselves, out of pride, we would produce nothing but leaves, and no matter how luxuriant they were, neither God nor our fellowmen would find any good in them.

When they saw the tree had withered "his **203**
disciples were amazed, saying 'How did it wither so suddenly?' "[33] The first twelve, who had seen Christ work so many miracles, were completely astonished once again. Their faith was not yet a burning faith, so our Lord went on to assure them, "I promise you, if you have faith, and do not hesitate, you will be able to do more than I have done over the fig tree. If you say to this mountain, 'Remove and be cast into the sea,' it will come about."[34] Christ lays down one condition: we must live by faith; then we will be able to move mountains. And so

[33] *Ibid* 21:20.
[34] *Ibid* 21:21.

many things need moving...in the world, but, first of all, in our own hearts. So many obstacles placed in the way of grace! We have to have faith, therefore: faith and works, faith and sacrifice, faith and humility. For faith makes us all powerful: "If you will only believe, every gift you ask for in your prayer will be granted."[35]

The man of faith sees the things of this life in their proper perspective. He knows that our stay on earth is, to use a phrase of St Teresa, "a bad night in a bad inn."[36] He becomes convinced once again that our time on earth is a time to work and to struggle, a time to purify ourselves in order to wipe out the debt we owe to God's justice for our sins. He knows too that worldly possessions are but a means, and he uses them generously, heroically.

204 Faith is not only a virtue to be preached. Above all it is to be practised. Often, perhaps, we just don't have the strength. If this happens (once more we go to the Gospels) let us do as the father of the lunatic boy did. He very much wanted his son to be saved; he hoped Christ would cure him, but he could not bring himself

[35] *Ibid* 21:22.
[36] Cf. St Teresa, *Way of Perfection*, 40,9 (70,4).

to believe that such happiness was possible. Jesus, who always asks us to have faith and who knows at the same time what is troubling the man's soul, helps him saying: "If you can believe, all things are possible to him who believes."[37] Everything is possible, we are all powerful! But only if we have faith. The man feels his faith wavering and he is afraid that his lack of trust will prevent his son from being cured. He weeps. Don't be ashamed of tears like these, for they are the fruit of our love of God, of contrite prayer, of true humility. "Whereupon the father of the boy cried aloud with tears, Lord, I do believe. Help my unbelief."[38]

We too now, after this time of meditation, can speak the same words to him: "Lord, I do believe! I have been brought up to believe in you. I have decided to follow you closely. Repeatedly during my life I have implored your mercy. And repeatedly too I have thought it impossible that you could perform such marvels in the hearts of your children. Lord, I do believe, but help me to believe more and better!"

[37] Mk 9:23.
[38] *Ibid* 9:24.

Let us address this same plea to our Lady, Mother of God and our Mother, and Teacher of faith: "Blessed art thou for thy believing; the message that was brought to thee from the Lord shall have fulfillment."[39]

[39] Lk 1:45.

THE CHRISTIAN'S HOPE*

A good number of years ago, with a sense of conviction that was growing stronger in me each day, I wrote: "Put all your hope in Jesus. You yourself have nothing, are worth nothing, can do nothing. He will act, if only you abandon yourself in him."[1] Time has gone by, and that conviction of mine has grown even stronger and deeper. I have seen many souls with such hope in God that it has set them marvellously ablaze with love, with a fire that makes the heart beat strong and keeps it safe from discouragement and dejection, even though along the way they may suffer and at times suffer greatly. 205

* A homily given on June 8, 1968, Ember Saturday after Pentecost.

[1] *The Way*, no. 731.

I was deeply moved by the Epistle in today's Mass, and I imagine the same will have happened to you. I realized that God was helping us, through the words of the Apostle, to contemplate the divine interlacing of the three theological virtues which form the backing upon which the true life of every Christian man or woman has to be woven.

Let us listen once again to the words of St Paul: "Since we are justified by faith, let us enjoy peace with God through our Lord Jesus Christ. Through him we have obtained access, by faith, to that grace in which we stand and we rejoice in the hope of attaining glory as the sons of God. More than that, we rejoice even in our afflictions, knowing well that affliction gives rise to patience, and patience brings perseverance, and perseverance brings hope, and this hope does not disappoint us: for the love of God has been poured into our hearts by the Holy Spirit."[2]

206 Here in the presence of God who is presiding over us right now from the tabernacle (how reassuring it is to have Jesus so very close to us!) we are going to meditate today on the

[2] Rom 5:1-5.

virtue of hope, that gentle gift from God which makes our hearts overflow with gladness, *spe gaudentes*[3] ("rejoicing in hope"), joyful, for if we are faithful an everlasting Love awaits us.

Let us never forget that for all men, and, therefore, for each and every one of us, there are only two ways of living on this earth: either we lead a divine life, striving to please God; or we set him aside and live an animal-like existence, guided to a greater or lesser degree by human enlightenment. I have never given too much credit to the "do-gooders" who pride themselves on their unbelief. I love them truly, as I do all mankind who are my brothers. I admire their goodwill which in certain aspects may even be heroic. But I also feel sorry for them because they have the immense misfortune of lacking the light and the warmth of God, and the indescribable joy which comes from the theological virtue of hope.

The true Christian, who acts according to his faith, always has his sights set on God. His outlook is supernatural. He works in this world of ours, which he loves passionately; he is

[3] *Ibid* 12:12.

involved in all its challenges, but all the while his eyes are fixed on Heaven. St Paul brings this out very clearly: *quae sursum sunt quaerite* "('seek the things that are above'), where Christ is sitting at the right hand of God. Savor the things of Heaven, not the things that are upon the earth. For you are dead," to worldliness, through Baptism, "and your life is hidden with Christ in God."[4]

Earthly expectations and Christian hope

207 There are many who repeat that hackneyed expression "while there's life there's hope," as if hope were an excuse for ambling along through life without too many complications or worries on one's conscience. Or as if it were a pretext for postponing indefinitely the decision to mend one's ways and the struggle to attain worthwhile goals, particularly the highest goal of all which is to be united with God.

If we follow this view, we will end up confusing hope with comfort. Fundamentally, what is wrong with it is that there is no real

[4] Col 3:1-3.

desire to achieve anything worthwhile, either spiritual or material. Thus, some people's greatest ambition boils down to avoiding whatever might upset the apparent calm of their mediocre existence. These timid, inhibited, lazy souls, full of subtle forms of selfishness, are content to let the days, the years, go by *sine spe nec metu* ("neither hoping nor fearing"), without setting themselves demanding targets, nor experiencing the hopes and fears of battle: the important thing for them is to avoid the risk of disappointment and tears. How far one is from obtaining something, if the very wish to possess it has been lost through fear of the demands involved in achieving it!

Then there is the superficial attitude of those for whom hope is a sort of idyllic fantasy, often presented under the guise of culture and learning. As they are incapable of facing up to themselves squarely and of choosing to do good, they say that hope is merely an illusion, a utopian dream, a bit of relief from the anxieties of a hard life. For these people hope has become frivolous wishful thinking, leading nowhere. What a false idea of hope!

But along with these timid and frivolous **208**
types, we also find here on earth many upright

individuals pursuing noble ideals, even though their motives are often not supernatural, but merely philanthropic. These people face up to all kinds of hardship. They generously spend themselves serving others, helping them overcome suffering and difficulties. I am always moved to respect and even to admiration by the tenacity of those who work wholeheartedly for noble ideals. Nevertheless, I consider I have a duty to remind you that everything we undertake in this life, if we see it exclusively as our own work, bears from the outset the stamp of perishability. Remember the words of Scripture: "I considered all that my hands had done and the effort I had spent doing it, and I saw that all was vanity and a striving after wind, with nothing gained under the sun."[5]

This precariousness does not stifle hope. On the contrary, once we recognize the insignificant and contingent nature of our earthly endeavors, the way is then open for true hope, a hope which upgrades all human work and turns it into a meeting point with God. An inexhaustible light then bathes everything we do and chases away the dark shadows of

[5] Eccles 2:11.

disappointment. But if we transform our temporal projects into ends in themselves and blot out from our horizon our eternal dwelling place and the end for which we have been created, which is to love and praise the Lord and then to possess him forever in Heaven, then our most brilliant endeavors turn traitor, and can even become a means of degrading our fellow creatures. Remember that sincere and well-known exclamation of St Augustine, who had such bitter experience when God was unknown to him and he was seeking happiness outside God: "You have made us for yourself, O Lord, and our hearts are restless till they rest in you!"[6] Perhaps there is no greater tragedy for man than the sense of disillusionment he suffers when he has corrupted or falsified his hope, by placing it in something other than the one Love which satisfies without ever satiating.

In my case, and I wish the same to happen to you, the certainty I derive from feeling—from knowing—that I am a son of God fills me with real hope which, being a supernatural virtue, adapts to our nature when it is infused in us, and so is also a very human virtue. I am

[6] St Augustine, *Confessiones*, 1, 1, 1 (PL 32, 661).

happy because I am certain we will attain Heaven if we remain faithful to the end; I rejoice in the thought of the bliss that will be ours, *quoniam bonus*[7] ("because my God is good and his mercy infinite"). This conviction spurs me on to grasp that only those things that bear the imprint of God can display the indelible sign of eternity and have lasting value. Therefore, far from separating me from the things of this earth, hope draws me closer to these realities in a new way, a Christian way, which seeks to discover in everything the relation between our fallen nature and God, our Creator and Redeemer.

What to hope for

209 Perhaps some of you are wondering, "What should a Christian hope for?" After all, the world has many good things to offer that attract our hearts, which crave happiness and anxiously run in search of love. Besides, we want to sow peace and joy at every turn. We are not content to achieve prosperity just for ourselves.

[7] Ps 105:1.

We want to make everyone around us happy as well.

Some people, alas, whose aims are worthy but limited and their ideals only perishable and fleeting, forget that Christians have to aspire to the highest peaks of all, to the infinite. Our aim is the very Love of God, to enjoy that Love fully, with a joy that never ends. We have seen in so many ways that things here below have to come to an end for all of us, when this world ends; and even sooner, for each individual, when he dies, for we cannot take wealth and prestige with us to the grave. That is why, buoyed up by hope, we raise our hearts to God himself and have learned to pray, *in te Domine speravi, non confundar in aeternum*[8] ("I have placed my hope in you, O Lord: may your hand guide me now and at every moment, forever and ever").

God did not create us to build a lasting city 210
here on earth,[9] because "this world is the way to that other, a dwelling place free from care."[10] Nevertheless, we children of God ought not to

[8] *Ibid* 30:2.
[9] Cf. Heb 13:14.
[10] Jorge Manrique, *Coplas*, 5.

remain aloof from earthly endeavors, for God has placed us here to sanctify them and make them fruitful with our blessed faith, which alone is capable of bringing true peace and joy to all men wherever they may be. Since 1928 I have constantly preached that we urgently need to Christianize society. We must imbue all levels of mankind with a supernatural outlook, and each of us must strive to raise his daily duties, his job or profession, to the order of supernatural grace. In this way all human occupations will be lit up by a new hope that transcends time and the inherent transience of earthly realities.

Through Baptism we are made bearers of the word of Christ, a word which soothes, enkindles, and reassures the wounded conscience. For our Lord to act in us and for us, we must tell him that we are ready to struggle each day, even though we realize we are feeble and useless, and the heavy burden of our personal shortcomings and weakness weighs down upon us. We must tell him again and again that we trust in him and in his help: if necessary, like Abraham, hoping "against all hope".[11] Thus, we

[11] Rom 4:18.

will go about our work with renewed vigor, and we will teach others how to live free from worry, hate, suspicion, ignorance, misunderstandings, and pessimism because God can do everything.

Wherever we may be, our Lord urges us to 211
be vigilant. His plea should lead us to hope more strongly in our desires for holiness and to translate them into deeds. "Give me your heart, my son,"[12] he seems to whisper in our ears. Stop building castles in the air. Make up your mind to open your soul to God, for only in our Lord will you find a real basis for your hope and for doing good to others. If we don't fight against ourselves; if we don't rebuff once and for all the enemies lodged within our interior fortress—pride, envy, the concupiscence of the flesh and of the eyes, self-sufficiency, and the wild craving for licentiousness; if we abandon this inner struggle, our noblest ideals will wither "like the bloom on the grass; and when the scorching sun comes up the grass withers, and the bloom falls, and all its fair show dies away."[13] Then, all you need is

[12] Prov 23:26.
[13] Jm 1:10-11

a tiny crevice and discouragement and gloom will creep in, like encroaching poisonous weeds.

Jesus is not satisfied with a wavering assent. He expects, and has a right to expect, that we advance resolutely, unyielding in the face of difficulties. He demands that we take firm, specific steps; because, as a rule, general resolutions are just fallacious illusions, created to silence the divine call which sounds within our hearts. They produce a futile flame that neither burns nor gives warmth, but dies out as suddenly as it began.

You will convince me that you sincerely want to achieve your goals when I see you go forward unwaveringly. Do good and keep reviewing your basic attitudes to the jobs that occupy you each moment. Practise the virtue of justice, right where you are, in your normal surroundings, even though you may end up exhausted. Foster happiness among those around you by cheerfully serving the people you work with and by striving to carry out your job as perfectly as you can, showing understanding, smiling, having a Christian approach to life. And do everything for God, thinking of his glory, with your sights set high and longing for the definitive homeland, because there is no other goal worthwhile.

I can do all things

If you're not struggling, it's no use telling 212
me that you are really trying to become more closely identified with Christ, to know him and love him. When we set out seriously along the *royal highway*, that of following Christ and behaving as children of God, we soon realize what awaits us: the Holy Cross. We must see it as the central point upon which to rest our hope of being united with our Lord.

Let me warn you that the program ahead is not an easy one. It takes an effort to lead the kind of life our Lord wants. Listen to the account St Paul gives of the incidents and sufferings he encountered in carrying out the will of Jesus: "Five times the Jews scourged me, and spared me but one lash in forty; three times I was beaten with rods, once I was stoned; I have been shipwrecked three times, I have spent a night and a day as a castaway at sea. What journeys I have undertaken, in danger from rivers, in danger from robbers, in danger from my own people, in danger from the Gentiles; danger in cities, danger in the wilderness, danger in the sea, danger among false brethren! I have met with toil and weariness, so often been sleepless, hungry, and thirsty; so often denied myself food, gone cold and naked. And all this, over and above something else which I do not count; I mean the burden I carry every day, my anxious care for all the churches."[14]

In these conversations we have with our Lord, I like to keep very close to everyday reality and avoid dreaming up theories or imagining great hardships and heroic exploits, which seldom happen. What is important is to make good use of time, that time which is always slipping from our grasp and which to a Christian is more precious than *gold*, because it represents a foretaste of the glory that will be granted us hereafter.

Naturally, the difficulties we meet in our daily lives will not be as great or as numerous as St Paul encountered. We will, however, discover our own meanness and selfishness, the sting of sensuality, the useless, ridiculous smack of pride, and many other failings be-

[14] 2 Cor 11:24-28.

sides: so very many weaknesses. But are we to give in to discouragement? Not at all. Together with St Paul, let us tell our Lord, "I am well content with these humiliations of mine, with the insults, the hardships, the persecutions, the times of difficulty I undergo for Christ; for when I am weakest, then I am strongest of all."[15]

Sometimes, when things turn out the very opposite of what we intended, we cry out spontaneously: "Lord, it's all going wrong, every single thing I'm doing!" The time has come for us to rectify our approach and say: "With you, Lord, I will make steady headway, because *quia tu es Deus fortitudo mea*[16] (for you, O Lord, are my strength)". 213

I have asked you to keep on lifting your eyes up to Heaven as you go about your work, because hope encourages us to grasp hold of the strong hand which God never ceases to reach out to us, to keep us from losing our supernatural point of view. Let us persevere even when our passions rear up and attack us, attempting to imprison us within the narrow confines of our selfishness; or when puerile

[15] *Ibid* 12:10.
[16] Ps 42:2.

vanity makes us think we are the center of the universe. I am convinced that unless I look upward, unless I have Jesus, I will never accomplish anything. And I know that the strength to conquer myself and to win comes from repeating that cry, "I can do all things in him who strengthens me,"[17] words which reflect God's firm promise not to abandon his children if they do not abandon him.

Our wretchedness and God's forgiveness

214 Our Lord has come so close to his creatures that we all hunger in our hearts for higher things, to be uplifted, to do good. If I am now prompting similar aspirations in you, it is because I want you to be convinced of the confidence he has placed in your soul. If you let him work in you, you will become, right where you are, a useful instrument, more useful than you could ever have imagined. But to make sure that cowardice does not make you betray the confidence God has placed in you, you must avoid the presumption of naively

[17] Phil 4:13.

underestimating the difficulties that you will meet in your Christian life.

These difficulties shouldn't surprise us. As a consequence of our fallen nature, we carry within us a principle of opposition, of resistance to grace. It comes from the wounds inflicted by original sin, and is aggravated by our own personal sins. Therefore, we have to strive ever upwards, by means of our everyday tasks, which are both divine and human and always lead to the love of God. In this we must be humble and contrite of heart and we must trust in God's help, while at the same time devoting our best efforts to those tasks as if everything depended on us.

As we fight this battle, which will last until the day we die, we cannot exclude the possibility that enemies both within and without may attack with violent force. And, as if this burden were not enough, you may at times be assailed by the memory of your own past errors, which may have been very many. I tell you now, in God's name: don't despair. Should this happen (it need not happen; nor will it usually happen), then turn it into another motive for uniting yourself more closely to our Lord, for he has chosen you as his child and he will not abandon you. He has allowed that trial to befall you so that you may love him the more and may discover even more clearly his constant protection and Love.

Take heart, I insist, because Christ, who pardoned us on the Cross, is still offering us his pardon through the Sacrament of Penance. We always "have an advocate to plead our cause before the Father: the Just One, Jesus Christ. He, in his own person, is the atonement made for our sins, and not only for ours, but for the sins of the whole world,"[18] so that we may win the Victory.

Forward, no matter what happens! Cling tightly to our Lord's hand and remember that God does not lose battles. If you should stray from him for any reason, react with the humility that will lead you to begin again and again; to play the role of the prodigal son every day, and even repeatedly during the twenty-four hours of the same day; to correct your contrite heart in Confession, which is a real miracle of God's Love. In this wonderful Sacrament our Lord cleanses your soul and fills you with joy and strength to prevent you from

[18] 1 Jn 2:1-2.

giving up the fight, and to help you keep returning to God unwearied, when everything seems black. In addition, the Mother of God, who is also our Mother, watches over you with motherly care, guiding your every step.

God never tires of forgiving

Holy Scripture points out that even "the just man falls seven times."[19] Whenever I read this phrase my soul trembles with love and sorrow. This divine indication shows us our Lord once again setting out to meet us and speak to us about his mercy, his tenderness and clemency that know no limits. Be sure of this: God does not want our wretchedness, but he is aware of it, and indeed he makes use of our weakness to make saints of us. 215

As I was saying, I tremble out of love. Looking at my life, I see quite honestly that I myself am nothing, am worth nothing and have nothing, that I can do nothing and, even more, that I am nothingness itself! But he is everything and, at the same time, he belongs to me

[19] Prov 24:16.

and I to him because he does not reject me and has given himself up for me. Have you ever seen a greater love than this?

I tremble also out of sorrow, because when I look back at what I have done, I am amazed at the extent of my failings. All I have to do is to examine my behavior in the few hours since I woke up this morning to discover so much lack of love, so little faithful correspondence. This truly saddens me, but it does not take away my peace of mind. I prostrate myself before God and I state my situation clearly. Immediately he helps me, he reassures me, and I hear him repeat slowly in the depths of my heart, *meus es tu*[20] ("you are mine"). I know the way you are, as I have always known it. Forward!

It cannot be otherwise. If we strive continually to place ourselves in our Lord's presence, our confidence will increase when we realize that his Love and his call are always present. God never tires of loving us. Hope shows us that without him we cannot carry out even the most insignificant duty. But with God, with his grace, our wounds will quickly heal; clothed

[20] Is 43:1.

with his strength we shall be able to ward off the attacks of the enemy, and we shall improve. To sum up, the realization that we are made of clay, and cheap clay at that, has to lead us, above all, to strengthen our hope in Christ Jesus.

Make it a habit to mingle with the characters **216**
who appear in the New Testament. Capture the flavor of those moving scenes where the Master performs works that are both divine and human, tells us, with human and divine touches, the wonderful story of his pardon for us and his enduring Love for his children. Those foretastes of Heaven are renewed today, for the Gospel is always true: we can feel, we can sense, we can even say we touch God's protection with our own hands; a protection that grows stronger as long as we keep advancing despite our stumbles, as long as we begin again and again, for this is what interior life is about, living with our hope placed in God.

Unless we aspire to overcome the obstacles both within and without, we will not obtain the reward. "No athlete wins a crown, if he has not fought in earnest;"[21] "and the fight would not

[21] 2 Tim 2:5.

be genuine if there were no opponent to fight with. Therefore, if there is no opponent, there will be no crown; for there can be no victor without someone vanquished."[22]

Far from discouraging us, the difficulties we meet have to spur us on to mature as Christians. This fight sanctifies us and gives effectiveness to our apostolic endeavors. As we contemplate those moments when Jesus, in the Garden of Olives and later mocked and abandoned on the Cross, accepts and loves the Will of his Father, all the while feeling the enormous weight of the Passion, we must be convinced that in order to imitate Christ, and be good disciples of his, we must take his advice to heart, "If any man has a mind to come my way, let him renounce self, and take up his cross, and follow me."[23] That is why I like to ask Jesus, for myself, "Lord, no day without a cross!" Then, through God's grace, our characters will grow strong and we will become a point of support for our God, over and above our own wretchedness.

[22] St Gregory of Nyssa, *De perfecta christiani forma* (PG 46, 286).

[23] Mt 16:24.

Take a nail, for instance. If you meet no resistance when you hammer it into a wall, what can you expect to hang on it? Likewise, if we do not let God toughen us through sacrifice, we will never become our Lord's instruments. On the other hand, if we decide to accept difficulties gladly and make use of them for the love of God, then in the face of what is difficult and unpleasant, when things are hard and uncomfortable, we will be able to exclaim with the apostles James and John, "Yes, we can!"[24]

It is important to struggle

I ought to put you on your guard against a trick that Satan does not hesitate to use in order to rob us of our peace. He never takes a holiday! A time may come when he sows doubts in our minds, tempting us to think that we are slipping sadly backwards and are making scarcely any progress. The conviction may grow upon us that, in spite of all our efforts to improve, we are getting worse. I can assure you that normally this pessimistic judg- 217

[24] Mk 10:39.

ment is mere fantasy, a deception that needs to be rejected. What has happened, as a rule, is that our souls have become more attentive, our consciences more sensitive, and our love more demanding. It can also be that the light of grace is shining more intensely and exposing to our view many details that would otherwise remain unnoticed in the shadows. In any case, we have to examine our uneasiness carefully, because through these insights our Lord is asking us to be more humble or more generous. It is good to remember that God in his providence is continuously leading us forward and he spares no effort, whether in the form of portentous signs or of tiny miracles, to make his children progress.

Militia est vita hominis super terram, et sicut dies mercenarii, dies eius[25] ("Man's life on earth is warfare, and his days are spent under the burden of work"). No one escapes this law, not even the easygoing who try to turn a deaf ear to it. They desert the ranks of Christ, and then take up other battles to satisfy their laziness, their vanity, or their petty ambitions. They become enslaved to their every whim.

[25] Job 7:1.

Since to be in a state of struggle is part and parcel of the human condition, let us try to fulfill our obligations with determination. Let us pray and work with good will, with upright motives, and with our sights set on what God wants. This way our longing for Love will be satisfied and we shall progress along the path to sanctity, even if we find at the end of the day that we still have a long way to go.

Renew your decision each morning, with a very determined *Serviam* ("I will serve you, Lord")! Renew your resolution not to give in, not to give way to laziness or idleness; to face up to your duties with greater hope and more optimism, convinced that if we are defeated in some small skirmish we can overcome this setback by making a sincere act of love.

The virtue of hope assures us that God **218**
governs us with his all-powerful providence and that he gives us all the means we need. Hope makes us aware of our Lord's constant goodwill towards mankind, towards you and me. He is always ready to hear us, because he never tires of listening. He is interested in your joys, your successes, your love, and also in your worries, your suffering, and your failures. So do not hope in him only when you realize you

are weak. Call upon your heavenly Father in good times and in bad, taking refuge in his merciful protection. And our conviction that we are nothing (it doesn't take a high degree of humility to recognize the truth that we are nothing but a row of zeros) will turn into irresistible strength, because Christ will be the one to the left of these zeros, converting them into an immeasurable figure! "The Lord is my strength and my refuge; whom shall I fear?"[26]

Get used to seeing God behind everything, realizing that he is always waiting for us, that he is contemplating us and quite rightly demands that we follow him faithfully without abandoning the place assigned to us in the world. In order not to lose his divine company, we must walk with loving vigilance and with a sincere determination to struggle.

219 The struggle of a child of God cannot go hand in hand with a spirit of sad-faced renunciation, somber resignation or a lack of joy. It is, on the contrary, the struggle of the man in love who, whether working or resting, rejoicing or suffering, is always thinking of the one he

[26] Ps 26:1.

loves, for whose sake he is happy to tackle any problems that may arise. Besides, in our case, being united with God, we can call ourselves victors because, I insist, he does not lose battles. My own experience is that when I strive faithfully to meet his demands, "he gives me a resting place where there is green pasture, leads me out to the cool water's brink, refreshed and content. As in honor pledged, by sure paths he leads me; dark be the valley about my path, hurt I fear none while he is with me; thy rod, thy crook are my comfort."[27]

To win the battles of the soul, the best strategy often is to bide one's time and apply the suitable remedy with patience and perseverance. Make more acts of hope. Let me remind you that in your interior life you will suffer defeats and you will have ups and downs —may God make them imperceptible—because no one is free of these misfortunes. But our all-powerful and merciful Lord has granted us the precise means with which to conquer. As I have already mentioned, all we have to do is to use them, resolving to begin again and again at every moment, should it prove necessary.

[27] *Ibid* 22:2-4.

I would like to see you going to the holy Sacrament of Penance, the sacrament of divine forgiveness, every week, and indeed whenever you need it, without giving in to scruples. Clothed in grace, we can cross mountains,[28] and climb the hill of our Christian duty, without halting on the way. If we use these resources with a firm purpose and beg our Lord to grant us an ever-increasing hope, we will possess the infectious joy of those who know they are children of God: "If God is with us, who can be against us?"[29] Let us be optimists. Moved by the power of hope, we will fight to wipe away the trail of filth and slime left by the sowers of hatred. We will find a new joyful perspective to the world, seeing that it has sprung forth beautiful and fair from the hands of God. We will give it back to him with that same beauty, if we learn how to repent.

With our eyes on Heaven

220 Let us grow in hope, thereby strengthening our faith which is truly "that which gives

[28] Cf. *Ibid* 103:10.
[29] Rom 8:31.

substance to our hopes, which convinces us of things we cannot see."[30] Let us grow in this virtue, let us beg our Lord to increase his charity in us; after all, one can only really trust that which one loves with all one's might. And it is certainly worthwhile to love our Lord. You and I know from experience that people in love surrender themselves unhesitatingly. Their hearts beat in a wonderful unison, with a single love. What then will the Love of God be like? Do you not realize that Christ has died for each and every one of us? Yes, for this poor little heart of ours, Jesus consummated his redeeming sacrifice.

Our Lord speaks frequently to us of the reward which he won for us by his Death and Resurrection. "I am going away to prepare a home for you. And though I do go away, to prepare you a home, I am coming back; and then I will take you to myself, so that you too may be where I am."[31] Heaven is the final destination of our path on earth. Jesus has gone ahead of us and awaits us there, in the company of our Lady and of St Joseph, whom I so much revere, and of all the angels and saints.

[30] Heb 11:1.
[31] Jn 14:2-3.

Even in the times of the Apostles there were heretics who tried to tear hope away from Christians. "If what we preach about Christ, then, is that he rose from the dead, how is it that some of you say the dead do not rise again? If the dead do not rise, then Christ has not risen either; and if Christ has not risen, then our preaching is groundless, and your faith too is groundless..."[32] Our way is divine, Jesus himself being the way, the truth, and the life,[33] and, thus, we have a sure token that it ends in eternal happiness, provided we do not separate ourselves from him.

221 How marvellous it will be when we hear our Father tell us, "Well done, my good and faithful servant, because you have been faithful over a few things, I will set you over many; enter into the joy of your Lord!"[34] Let us be full of hope! This is the great thing about being a contemplative soul. We live by Faith, Hope, and Love; and Hope makes us powerful. Do you remember what St John says? "I am writing to you, young men, because you are strong and the

[32] 1 Cor 15:12-14.
[33] Cf. Jn 14:6.
[34] Mt 25:21.

word of God abides in you, and you have conquered the evil one."[35] God is urging us on, for the sake of the eternal youthfulness of the Church and of all mankind. You have the power to transform everything human into something divine, just as King Midas turned everything he touched into gold!

Do not ever forget that after death you will be welcomed by Love itself. And in the love of God you will find as well all the noble loves which you had on earth. Our Lord has arranged for us to spend this brief day of our earthly existence working and, like his only-begotten Son, "doing good."[36] Meanwhile, we have to be on our guard, alert to the call St Ignatius of Antioch felt within his soul as the hour of his martyrdom approached. "Come to the Father,"[37] come to your Father, who anxiously awaits you.

Let us ask Holy Mary, *Spes Nostra* ("our hope"), to kindle in us a holy desire that we may all come together to dwell in the house of the Father. Nothing need to disturb us if we

[35] 1 Jn 2:14.
[36] Acts 10:38.
[37] St Ignatius of Antioch, *Epistola ad Romanos*, 7 (PG 5, 694).

make up our minds to anchor our hearts in a real longing for our true fatherland. Our Lord will lead us there with his grace, and he will send a good wind to carry our ship to the bright shores of our destination.

THE STRENGTH OF LOVE*

From his position in the multitude a man asks our Lord a question. He was one of those learned men who were no longer able to understand the teaching that had been revealed to Moses, so entangled had it become because of their own sterile casuistry. Jesus opens his divine lips to reply to this doctor of the law and answers him slowly, with the calm assurance of one who knows what he is talking about: " 'You shall love the Lord your God with your whole heart, and your whole soul, and your whole mind. This is the greatest of the commandments and the first. And the second, its like, is this, You shall love your neighbor as yourself. On these two commandments all the law and the prophets depend.' "[1] 222

* A homily given on April 6, 1967.

[1] Mt 22:37-40.

Let us now consider the Master and his disciples gathered together in the intimacy of the Upper Room. The time of his Passion is drawing close and he is surrounded by those he loves. The fire in the Heart of Christ bursts into flame in a way no words can express and he confides in them, "I give you a new commandment: that you love one another, just as I have loved you, you also must love one another. By this shall all men know that you are my disciples, if you have love for one another."[2]

If you wish to get close to our Lord through the pages of the Gospels, I always recommend that you try to enter in on the scene taking part as just one more person there. In this way (and I know many perfectly ordinary people who live this way) you will be captivated like Mary was, who hung on every word that Jesus uttered or, like Martha, you will boldly make your worries known to him, opening your heart sincerely about them all no matter how little they may be.[3]

[2] Jn 13:34-35.
[3] Cf. Lk 10:39-40.

Lord, why do you call it a *new* commandment? As we have just heard, it was already laid down in the Old Testament that we should love our neighbor. You will remember also that, when Jesus had scarcely begun his public life, he broadened the scope of this law with divine generosity: "You have heard that it was said, 'you shall love your neighbor and hate your enemy.' But I tell you, Love your enemies, do good to those who hate you, pray for those who persecute and slander you."[4] **223**

But, Lord, please allow us to insist. Why do you still call this precept new? That night, just a few hours before offering yourself in sacrifice on the Cross, during your intimate conversation with the men who—in spite of being weak and wretched, like ourselves—accompanied you to Jerusalem, you revealed to us the standard for our charity, one we could never have suspected: "as I have loved you." How well the apostles must have understood you, having witnessed for themselves your unbounded love.

The Master's message and example are clear and precise. He confirmed his teaching with deeds. Yet I have often thought that, after

[4] Mt 5:43-44.

twenty centuries, it is indeed still a *new* commandment because very few people have taken the trouble to practise it. The others, the majority of men, both in the past and still today, have chosen to ignore it. Their selfishness has led them to the conclusion: "Why should I complicate my life? I have more than enough to do just looking after myself."

Such an attitude is not good enough for us Christians. If we profess the same faith and are really eager to follow in the clear footprints left by Christ when he walked on this earth, we cannot be content merely with avoiding doing unto others the evil that we would not have them do unto us. That is a lot, but it is still very little when we consider that our love is to be measured in terms of Jesus' own conduct. Besides, he does not give us this standard as a distant target, as a crowning point of a whole lifetime of struggle. It is—it ought to be, I repeat so that you may turn it into specific resolutions—the starting point, for our Lord presents it as a sign of Christianity: "By this shall all men know that you are my disciples."

224 Our Lord Jesus Christ became incarnate and took on our nature to reveal himself to mankind as the model of all virtues, "Learn from me," he says to us, "for I am meek and humble of heart."[5]

Later, when he explains to the apostles the mark by which they will be known as Christians, he does not say, "Because you are humble." He is purity most sublime, the immaculate Lamb. Nothing could stain his perfect, unspotted holiness.[6] Yet he does not say, "You will be known as my disciples because you are chaste and pure."

He passed through this world completely detached from earthly goods. Though he is the Creator and Lord of the whole universe, he did not even have a place to lay his head.[7] Nevertheless, he does not say, "They will know that you are mine because you are not attached to wealth." Before setting out to preach the Gospel he spent forty days and forty nights in the desert keeping a strict fast.[8] But, once again, he does not tell his disciples, "Men will recognize you as God's servants because you are not gluttons or drunkards."

[5] *Ibid* 11:29.
[6] Cf. Jn 8:46.
[7] Cf. Mt 8:20.
[8] Cf. *Ibid* 4:2.

No, the distinguishing mark of the Apostles and of true Christians in every age is, as we have heard: "By this," precisely by this, "shall all men know that you are my disciples, if you have love for one another."[9]

I think it is perfectly understandable that God's children have always been deeply moved, as you and I are now, by our Master's insistence on this point. "The Lord does not say that the proof of his disciples' faithfulness will be the working of wondrous miracles and prodigies, although he gave them the power to perform them, in the Holy Spirit. What does he tell them? 'You shall be known as my disciples if you love one another.' "[10]

God's way of teaching

225 Not to hate one's enemies, not to return evil for evil, to refrain from vengeance, and to forgive ungrudgingly were all considered at that time unusual behavior, too heroic for normal men. The same thing, let's be honest about it, is true today. Such is the small-

[9] Jn 13:35.
[10] St Basil, *Regulae fusius tractatae*, 3, 1 (PG 31, 918).

mindedness of men. But Christ, who came to save all mankind and who wishes Christians to be associated with him in the work of redemption, wanted to teach his disciples—you and me—to have a great and sincere charity, one which is more noble and more precious: that of loving one another in the same way as Christ loves each one of us. Only then, by imitating the divine pattern he has left us, and notwithstanding our own rough ways, will we be able to open our hearts to all men and love in a higher and totally new way.

How well the early Christians practised this ardent charity which went far beyond the limits of mere human solidarity or natural kindness. They loved one another, through the heart of Christ, with a love both tender and strong. Tertullian, writing in the second century tells us how impressed the pagans were by the behavior of the faithful at that time. So attractive was it both supernaturally and humanly that they often remarked: "See how they love one another."[11]

If you think, looking at yourself now or in so many things you do each day, that you do

[11] Tertullian, *Apologeticus*, 39, 7 (PL 1, 471).

not deserve such praise; that your heart does not respond as it should to the promptings of God, then consider that the time has come for you to put things right. Listen to St Paul's invitation, "Let us do good to all men, and especially to those who are of one family with us in the faith,"[12] who make up the Mystical Body of Christ.

226 The principal apostolate we Christians must carry out in the world, and the best witness we can give of our faith, is to help bring about a climate of genuine charity within the Church. For who indeed could feel attracted to the Gospel if those who say they preach the Good News do not really love one another, but spend their time attacking one another, spreading slander, and quarrelling?

It is all too easy, and very fashionable, to say that you love everyone, Christians and non-Christians alike. But if those who maintain this ill-treat their brothers in the faith, I don't see how their behavior can be anything but "pious hypocrisy." By contrast, when in the Heart of Christ we love those "who are children of the same Father, and with us share the same faith

[12] Gal 6:10.

and are heirs to the same hope"[13] then our hearts expand and become fired with a longing to bring everyone closer to our Lord.

I am reminding you here of the demands of charity, and perhaps someone might object that it is precisely the virtue of charity which is lacking in what I have just said. Nothing could be further from the truth. I can assure you with a holy pride and without any false ecumenism that I was overjoyed when in the recent Second Vatican Council the Church expressed with renewed intensity its concern to bring the Truth to those who walk outside the one Way, that of Jesus; because I am consumed by a hunger that all may be saved.

Yes, I was very glad; glad too because it 227
confirmed anew a favorite apostolate of Opus Dei, the apostolate *ad fidem*, which rejects no one and admits non-Christians, atheists, and pagans, allowing them to share as far as they are able in the spiritual benefits of our Association.[14] As I have mentioned on other occa-

[13] Minucius Felix, *Octavius*, 31 (PL 3, 338).

[14] Msgr. Escrivá calls Opus Dei an Association because it was not erected as a Personal Prelature until 1982.

Nevertheless, it is but a matter of justice to point out that as early as the 1930's, Msgr. Escrivá had already foreseen that the

sions, this apostolate has a long history, involving both suffering and loyalty. So I am not afraid to repeat that I think it is a false and hypocritical zeal that leads some to be friendly towards those who are far away from us, while they trample on or despise those who share our same faith. In the same way, I don't believe that you are genuinely concerned about the poorest of the poor, if you persist in mortifying the people you live with; if you are indifferent to their joys, sorrows, or grief; if you are not trying to understand or overlook their defects, provided they do not offend God.

228 Doesn't it move you to find the Apostle John in his old age devoting the best part of one of his epistles to exhorting us to follow this divine teaching? The love that ought to exist amongst us Christians is born of God who is Love. "Beloved, let us love one another; for charity comes from God, and he who loves is born of God and knows God. He who has no love does not know God, for God is Love."[15] He focuses

juridical configuration of Opus Dei would have to be found among the institutions of personal and secural jurisdiction. Thus he guided Opus Dei towards this juridical solution and, before his death in 1975, had prepared everything.

[15] 1 Jn 4:7-8.

on fraternal charity because through Christ we have become children of God: "See what love the Father has shown towards us, that we should be called children of God, and should be such."[16]

At the same time as he raps sharply on our consciences to make them sensitive to God's grace, he also insists that we have received a marvellous proof of the Father's love for men, "By this was made manifest the charity of God for us, that God sent his only begotten Son into the world, so that we might live through him."[17] It was the Lord who took the initiative by coming out to meet us. He gave us this example so that we might join him in serving others, generously placing our hearts on the ground, as I am fond of saying, so that others may tread softly and find their struggle more pleasant. This is how we should behave because we have been made children of the same Father, that Father who did not hesitate to give us his dearly beloved Son.

Charity is not something we ourselves build **229**
up. It invades us along with God's grace,

[16] *Ibid* 3:1.
[17] *Ibid* 4:9.

"because he has loved us first."[18] We would do well to fill, to saturate ourselves with this most beautiful truth: "If we are able to love God, it is because we have been loved by God."[19] You and I are able to lavish affection upon those around us, because we have been born to the Faith, through the Father's love for us. Ask God boldly for this treasure, for the supernatural virtue of charity, so that you may practise it even in the smallest details.

Too often we Christians have not known how to correspond to this gift. At times we have debased it, as if it could be confined to a soulless and cold almsgiving; or we have reduced it to more or less stereotyped good works. This distortion of charity was well expressed once by a sick woman when she commented with sad resignation, "Yes, they treat me with 'charity' here, but my mother used to look after me with affection." A love that springs from the Heart of Christ could never countenance such distinctions.

In order that you might grasp this truth very clearly, I have preached on countless occasions

[18] *Ibid* 4:10.
[19] Origen, *Commentarii in Epistolam ad Romanos*, 4, 9 (PG 14, 977).

that we do not have one heart to love God with and another with which to love men. This poor heart of ours, made of flesh, loves with an affection which is human and which, if it is united to Christ's love, is also supernatural. This, and no other, is the charity we have to cultivate in our souls, a charity which will lead us to discover in others the image of our Lord.

Charity with everyone

St Leo the Great says that "the term 'neighbor' includes not only those with whom we have ties of friendship or family, but all our fellowmen with whom we share a common nature...A single Creator has made us and given us our souls. We all live under the same sky and breathe the same air, and we live through the same days and nights. Although some people are good and others bad, some just and others unjust, God nevertheless is generous and kind towards all."[20] **230**

We grow up as children of God by practising the new commandment. In the Church we learn

[20] St Leo the Great, *Sermo XII*, 2 (PL 54, 170).

to serve and not to be served,[21] and we find we have the strength to love all mankind in a new way, which all will recognize as stemming from the grace of Christ. Our love is not to be confused with sentimentality or mere good fellowship, nor with that somewhat questionable zeal to help others in order to convince ourselves of our superiority. Rather, it means living in peace with our neighbor, venerating the image of God that is found in each and every man and doing all we can to get them in their turn to contemplate that image, so that they may learn how to turn to Christ.

Charity with everyone means, therefore, apostolate with everyone. It means we, on our part, must translate into deeds and truth the great desire of God "who wishes all men to be saved and to come to the knowledge of truth."[22]

If we must also love our enemies (here I mean those who regard us as such, for I do not consider myself an enemy of anyone or of anything) we have all the more reason for loving those who are simply distant from us,

[21] Cf. Mt 20:28.
[22] 1 Tim 2:4.

those whom we find less attractive, those who seem the opposite of you or me on account of their language, culture, or upbringing.

What kind of love are we talking about? **231**
Sacred Scripture uses the Latin word *dilectio*, to make us understand clearly that it does not simply mean the feeling of affection. It signifies, rather, a firm determination on the part of the will. *Dilectio* comes from *electio*, choice. I would add that, for Christians, loving means "wanting to love,"* making up one's mind in Christ to work for the good of souls, without discrimination of any kind; trying to obtain for them, before any other good, the greatest good of all, that of knowing Christ and falling in love with him.

Our Lord spurs us on: "Do good to those who hate you, pray for those who persecute and insult you."[23] We might not feel humanly attracted to those who would reject us were we to approach them. But Jesus insists: we must not return evil for evil; we must not waste any

* In the original *querer*, playing on the two meanings ("to want" and "to love") of the Spanish verb. (Translator's note)

[23] Mt 5:44.

opportunities we have of serving them wholeheartedly, even if we find it difficult to do so; we must never cease keeping them in mind in our prayers.

This *dilectio*, this charity, becomes even more affectionate when its object is our brothers in the faith and particularly those who, by God's will, work close beside us: our parents, husbands or wives, children, brothers and sisters, friends and colleagues, neighbors. Without this affection, which is a noble and pure human love directed towards God and based on him, there would be no charity.

Expressing our love

232 I like to repeat what the Holy Spirit tells us through the prophet Isaias, *discite benefacere*[24] ("learn how to do good"). I like to apply this advice to all the different aspects of our interior struggle, because we can never consider our lives as Christians as something finished and complete. The Christian virtues develop as a consequence of real effort, each day.

[24] Is 1:17.

Take any job in life; how do we set about learning it? First, we find out what we want to achieve and what means we have to obtain it. Then we use those means, perseveringly, over and over again, until we have formed a well-rooted habit. As soon as we learn one thing, we discover other things hitherto unknown to us and they in turn stimulate us to continue working without ever giving up.

Charity towards our neighbor is an expression of our love of God. Accordingly, when we strive to grow in this virtue, we cannot fix any limits to our growth. The only possible measure for the love of God is to love without measure; on the one hand, because we will never be able to thank him enough for what he has done for us; and on the other, because this is exactly what God's own love for us, his creatures, is like: it overflows without calculation or limit.

In his Sermon on the Mount, Jesus teaches his divine command of charity to all who are ready to listen with an open mind. At the end, by way of summary, he says, "Love your enemies, and do good to them, and lend to them, without any hope of return; then your reward will be a rich one, and you will be children of the most High, generous like him towards the thankless and unjust. Be merciful, then, as your Father is merciful."[25]

Mercy is more than simply being compassionate. Mercy is the overflow of charity, which brings with it also an overflow of justice. Mercy means keeping one's heart totally alive, throbbing in a way that is both human and divine, with a love that is strong, self-sacrificing, and generous. Here is what St Paul has to say about charity in his hymn to this virtue, "Charity is patient, is kind; charity feels no envy; charity is never perverse or proud, never insolent; does not claim its rights, cannot be provoked, does not brood over an injury; takes no pleasure in wrong-doing, but rejoices at the victory of truth; sustains, believes, hopes, endures, to the last."[26]

233 One of its first expressions is to initiate the soul into the ways of humility. When we sincerely see ourselves as nothing; when we understand that, without God's help, the weakest and most puny of creatures would be better than we are; when we see we are capable of every kind of error and every kind of abomi-

[25] Lk 6:35-36.
[26] 1 Cor 13:4-7.

nation; when we realize we are sinners, even though we are earnestly struggling to turn our back on our many infidelities, how could we possibly think badly of others? Or how could we harbor fanaticism, intolerance, or haughtiness in our hearts?

Humility leads us as it were by the hand to treat our neighbor in the best way possible, that is, being understanding towards everyone, living at peace with everyone, forgiving everyone; never creating divisions or barriers; and behaving—always!—as instruments that foster unity. Not in vain is there in the depths of man's being a strong longing for peace, for union with his fellowman, for a mutual respect for personal rights, so strong that it seeks to transform human relations into fraternity. This longing reflects something which is most deeply imprinted upon our human condition: since we are all children of God, our fraternity is not a cliché or an empty dream; it beckons as a goal which, though difficult, is really ours to achieve.

As Christians we must show that affection of this kind is in fact possible whatever the cynics or sceptics, those disappointed in love or those with a cowardly outlook on life might say. It may be quite difficult to be truly affectionate, for man was created free and he can rebel against God in a useless and bitter way. But it is possible and people can attain it, because it flows as a necessary consequence of God's love for us and our love for God. If you and I want it, Jesus also wants it. Then we will obtain a full and fruitful understanding of the meaning of suffering, sacrifice, and unselfish dedication in ordinary life.

Practising charity

234 It would be naive to think that the demands of Christian charity are easy to fulfill. Our day-to-day experience of the affairs of men, even unfortunately within the Church itself, tells us a very different story. If love did not bid us keep silence, each could tell a lengthy tale of disunity, personal attacks, injustice, slander, and intrigue. Let us admit it openly, and try for our part to apply the right solution to the problem, which should consist in our personal efforts not to wound or ill-treat anyone, and not to humiliate others when we have to correct them.

The problem, of course, is not new. Only a few years after Christ's Ascension into Heaven, when most of the Apostles were still alive and active and there was a wonderful atmosphere of faith and hope, there were already quite a number who had begun to lose their way, failing to follow the charity of their Master.

To the Corinthians St Paul writes, "Do not these rivalries, these dissensions among you show that nature is still alive, that you are guided by human standards? When one of you says, 'I am for Paul,' and another, 'I am for Apollo,' are not these human thoughts,"[27] of men who do not understand that Christ came to do away with all these divisions? "Why, what is Apollo, what is Paul? Only the ministers of the God in whom your faith rests, who have brought that faith to each of you in the measure God granted."[28]

The apostle is not condemning diversity. Each person has his own gift from God, some in one thing, some in another.[29] These differences, however, must serve the good of the

[27] *Ibid* 3:3-4.
[28] *Ibid* 3:4-5.
[29] Cf. *Ibid* 7:7.

Church. I feel moved right now to ask our Lord (and if you wish you can join in my prayer) not to permit uncharitableness to sow its cockle in the Church. Charity is the salt of the Christian apostolate. If it should lose its taste, how can we come to the world and proclaim: "Here is Christ?"

235 Therefore, I repeat to you with St Paul, "I may speak with every tongue that men and angels use; yet, if I lack charity, I am no better than echoing bronze, or the clash of cymbals. I may have powers of prophecy, no secret hidden from me, no knowledge too deep for me; I may have utter faith, so that I can move mountains; yet if I lack charity, I count for nothing. I may give away all that I have to feed the poor; I may give myself up to be burnt at the stake; if I lack charity, it goes for nothing."[30]

Some people have reacted to these words of the Apostle to the Gentiles like those disciples who, on hearing our Lord promise the Sacrament of his Body and Blood, commented: "This is a hard saying. Who can listen to it?"[31] It is indeed hard, because the charity described by

[30] *Ibid* 13:1-3.
[31] Jn 6:61.

St Paul is not just philanthropy, humanitarianism, or an understandable sympathy for the sufferings of others. Rather it requires the practice of the theological virtue of loving God and of loving others for the sake of God. This is why "charity never fails, whereas prophecies will disappear, and tongues will cease, and knowledge will be destroyed...So there abide faith, hope, and charity, these three; but the greatest of these is charity."[32]

The only way

We are now convinced that charity has nothing whatever in common with the caricature that sometimes has been made of this central virtue of the Christian life. Why, then is it necessary to preach about it so constantly? Is it just a topic that has to be preached about, but has little chance of being put into practice in everyday life? 236

If we look about us we could find reasons for believing that charity is a phantom virtue. But if we then consider things from a super-

32 1 Cor 13:8, 13.

natural point of view, we can also see what is the root cause of this sterility: the absence of a continuous and intense, person-to-person relationship with our Lord Jesus Christ, and an ignorance of the work of the Holy Spirit in the soul, whose very first fruit is precisely charity.

In commenting on St Paul's advice, "bear one another's burdens and so you will fulfill the law of Christ,"[33] one of the Fathers of the Church says, "By loving Christ we can easily bear the weaknesses of others, including those people whom we do not love as yet because they are lacking in good works."[34]

This is the direction taken by the path that makes us grow in charity. We would be mistaken were we to believe that we must first engage in humanitarian activities and social works, leaving the love for God to one side. "Let us not neglect Christ out of concern for our neighbor's illness, for we ought to love the sick for the sake of Christ."[35]

Turn your gaze constantly to Jesus who, without ceasing to be God, humbled himself

[33] Gal 6:2.

[34] St Augustine, *De diversis quaestionibus LXXXIII*, 71, 7 (PL 40, 83).

[35] St Augustine, *ibid.*

and took the nature of a slave,[36] in order to serve us. Only by following in his direction will we find ideals that are worthwhile. Love seeks union, identification with the beloved. United to Christ, we will be drawn to imitate his life of dedication, his unlimited love, and his sacrifice unto death. Christ brings us face to face with the ultimate choice: either we spend our life in selfish isolation, or we devote ourselves and all our energies to the service of others.

Let us now ask our Lord, as we finish these **237**
moments of conversation with him, to enable us to say with St Paul, "in all this we are conquerors, through him who has granted us his love. Of this I am fully persuaded: neither death nor life, nor angels or principalities or powers, neither what is present nor what is to come, no force whatever, neither the height above us nor the depth beneath us, nor any other created thing, will be able to separate us from the love of God, which comes to us in Christ Jesus our Lord."[37]

Scripture sings the praises of this love with burning words: "Many waters cannot quench

[36] Cf. Phil 2:6-7.
[37] Rom 8:37-39.

charity, neither can the floods drown it."[38] So thoroughly did this love fill Mary's Heart that it enriched her to the point of making her a Mother for all mankind. In the Virgin Mary, her love of God is one with her concern for all her children. Her most sweet Heart, which was sensitive to the smallest details—"they have no wine"[39]—must have suffered immensely on seeing the collective cruelty and the ferocity of the executioners that led to the Passion and Death of Jesus. Mary, however, does not speak. Like her Son, she loves, keeps silent, and forgives. Here we see the strength of love!

[38] Cant 8:7.
[39] Jn 2:3.

A LIFE OF PRAYER*

Whenever we feel in our hearts a desire to improve, a desire to respond more generously to our Lord, and we look for something to guide us, a north star to guide our lives as Christians, the Holy Spirit will remind us of the words of the Gospel that we "ought to pray continually and never be discouraged."[1] Prayer is the foundation of any supernatural endeavor. With prayer we are all powerful; without it, if we were to neglect it, we would accomplish nothing. 238

I would like us, in our meditation today, to make up our minds once and for all that we need to aspire to become contemplative souls, in the street, in the midst of our work, by

* A homily given on April 4, 1955.
[1] Lk 18:1.

maintaining a constant conversation with our God and not breaking it off at any time of the day. If we really want to be loyal followers of our Master, this is the only way.

239 Let us turn our gaze to Jesus Christ, who is our model, the mirror in which we should see ourselves. How does he act, even in his outward behavior, in the great moments of his life? What does the holy Gospel tell us about him? I am moved by our Lord's habitual attitude of prayer, the way he turns to the Father before beginning his public life, retiring to the desert for forty days and forty nights, to pray.[2]

Forgive me if I insist, but it is very important to note carefully what the Messiah did, because he came to show us the path that leads to the Father. With our Lord we will discover how to give a supernatural dimension to all our actions, even those that seem least important. We will learn to live every moment of our lives with a lively awareness of eternity, and we will understand more deeply man's need for periods of intimate conversation with his God, so as to get to know him, to invoke him, to praise him, to break out into acts of

[2] Cf. Mt 4:2.

thanksgiving, to listen to him or, quite simply, to be with him.

Many years ago, as I reflected upon our Lord's way of doing things, I came to the conclusion that the apostolate, of whatever kind it be, must be an overflow of the interior life. This is why the passage which relates how Christ decided to choose the first twelve seems to me to be so natural and at the same time so supernatural. St Luke tells us that before choosing them "he spent the whole night in prayer."[3] Think also of the events at Bethany. Before he raises Lazarus from the dead, after having wept over his friend, he lifts his eyes to Heaven and says, "Father, I thank you for hearing my prayer."[4] This is his message for us: if we wish to help others, if we really wish to encourage them to discover the true meaning of their life on earth, we must base everything on prayer.

There are so many Gospel scenes where 240
Jesus talks to his Father that we cannot stop to consider them all. But I do feel we must pause to consider the intense hours preceding his

[3] Lk 6:12.
[4] Jn 11:41.

Passion and Death, when Christ prepares himself to carry out the Sacrifice that will bring us back once more to God's Love. In the intimacy of the Upper Room, the Heart of Jesus overflows with love; he turns to the Father in prayer, announces the coming of the Holy Spirit, and encourages his disciples to maintain the fervor of their charity and their faith.

Our Redeemer's mood of fervent recollection continues in the Garden of Gethsemani, as he perceives that his Passion is about to begin, with all its humiliation and suffering close at hand, the harsh Cross on which criminals are hanged and which he has longed for so ardently. "Father, if it pleases thee, take away this chalice from before me."[5] And immediately he adds, "Yet not my will but thine be done."[6] Later, nailed to the Cross, alone, with his arms opened wide in a gesture of an eternal priest, he continues his dialogue with his Father, "Into thy hands I commend my spirit."[7]

241 Let us also contemplate his blessed Mother, who is our Mother too. We find her on Calvary,

[5] Lk 22:42.
[6] *Ibid.*
[7] *Ibid* 23:46.

at the foot of the Cross, praying. This is nothing new for Mary. She has always acted like this, as she fulfilled her duties and looked after her home. As she went about the things of this earth she kept her attention on God. Christ, who is *perfectus Deus, perfectus homo,*[8] wanted us also to have the example of his Mother, the most perfect of creatures, she who is full of grace, to strengthen our desire to lift our eyes up to the love of God at every moment. Remember the scene at the Annunciation? The Archangel comes down bearing a divine message—the announcement that Mary is to be the Mother of God—and he finds her withdrawn in prayer. When Gabriel greets her, she is totally absorbed in God. "Hail, full of grace, the Lord is with thee."[9] A few days later she breaks out into the joy of the *Magnificat,* a Marian hymn which the Holy Spirit has transmitted to us through the loving faithfulness of St Luke. It reveals Mary's constant and intimate conversation with God.

Our Mother had meditated deep and long on the words of the holy men and women of

[8] Symbol, *Quicumque.*
[9] Lk 1:28.

the Old Testament who awaited the Savior, and on the events that they had taken part in. She must have marvelled at all the great things that God, in his boundless mercy, had done for his people, who were so often ungrateful. As she considers the tenderness shown time after time by God towards his people, Mary's immaculate Heart breaks out in loving words, "My soul magnifies the Lord, and my spirit has rejoiced in God my Savior, for he has looked graciously upon the lowliness of his handmaid."[10] The early Christians, children of this good Mother, learned from her; we can, and we ought to do likewise.

242 The Acts of the Apostles describe a scene I love to contemplate because it gives us a clear, abiding example of prayer: "They persevered, all of them, in the apostles' teaching, in their fellowship in the breaking of bread, and in prayer."[11] We are told this time and again in the passage narrating the lives of the first followers of Christ. "All these, with one mind, gave themselves up to prayer."[12] Again when

[10] *Ibid* 1:46-48.
[11] Acts 2:42.
[12] *Ibid* 1:14.

Peter was imprisoned because he had boldly preached the truth, they decided to pray. "There was a continual stream of prayer going up to God from the Church on his behalf."[13]

Prayer was then, as it is today, the only weapon, the most powerful means, for winning the battles of our interior struggle. "Is one of you sad?" asks St James. "Let him pray."[14] St Paul sums it up by saying, "Pray without ceasing."[15] Never get tired of praying.

How to pray

How should we pray? I would go as far as **243**
to say, without fear of being mistaken, that there are many, countless ways of praying. But I would like all of us to pray genuinely, as God's children, not gabbling away like hypocrites who will hear from Jesus' lips "Not everyone who says to me, 'Lord, Lord!' shall enter into the Kingdom of Heaven."[16] People who live by hypocrisy can perhaps achieve "the

[13] *Ibid* 12:5.
[14] Jm 5:13.
[15] 1 Thess 5:17.
[16] Mt 7:21.

sound of prayer," says St Augustine, "but they cannot possess its voice, because there is no life in them."[17] They lack the desire to fulfill the Father's Will. When we cry "Lord!" we must do so with an effective desire to put into practice the inspirations the holy Spirit awakens in our soul.

We must strive to eliminate any shadow of deceit on our part. If we are to banish this evil, which is condemned so severely by our Lord, we must first try to ensure that our dispositions, both habitual and actual, are those of a clear aversion to sin. Sincerely, in a manly way, we must develop, both in our hearts and in our minds, a sense of horror for mortal sin. We must also cultivate a deep-seated hatred of deliberate venial sin, those negligences which, while they don't deprive us of God's grace, do serve to obstruct the channels through which grace comes to us.

244 I have never gotten tired of talking about prayer and with God's grace I never will. I remember back in the thirties, as a young priest, people of all kinds used to come to me looking for ways of getting closer to our Lord. To all

[17] St Augustine, *Enarrationes in Psalmos*, 139, 10 (PL 37, 1809).

of them, university students and workers, healthy and sick, rich and poor, priests and laymen, I gave the same advice: "Pray." If anyone replied, "I don't even know how to begin," I would advise him to put himself in God's presence and tell him of his desires and anxiety, with that very same complaint: "Lord, I don't know how to pray!" Often, humble admissions like that were the beginning of an intimate relationship with Christ, a lasting friendship with him.

Many years have gone by, and I still don't know of a better recipe. If you think you're not quite ready to pray, go to Jesus as his disciples did and say to him, "Lord, teach us how to pray."[18] You will discover how the Holy Spirit "comes to the aid of our weakness; when we do not know what prayer to offer, to pray as we ought, the Spirit himself intercedes for us, with groans beyond all utterance,"[19] which are impossible to describe, for no words are adequate to express their depth.

What a great source of confidence the Word of God should be for us! When, throughout my

[18] Lk 11:1.
[19] Rom 8:26.

priestly ministry, I have time and again counselled people to pray, I have not been inventing anything. It's all there in Holy Scripture. That is where I learned to say, "Lord, I don't know how to talk to you! Lord, teach us how to pray!" When we pray, thus, we receive all the loving assistance of the Holy Spirit—that light, fire, and driving wind which sets the flame alight and makes it capable of enkindling a great fire of love.

Prayer is dialogue

245 We have already entered upon the ways of prayer. But how do we go forward? You must have noticed how many people, both men and women, appear to be talking just to themselves, listening complacently to their own voices. It is an almost continuous chatter of words, a monologue that goes on and on about the problems that worry them, while they do nothing to solve them. It would seem as if all they really wanted was the morbid satisfaction of getting others to feel sorry for them, or admire them. That's all they seem to be aiming for.

If we truly want to unburden our hearts, and are honest and sincere about it, we seek the advice of those who love and understand us: our father or mother, wife or husband, our brother or friend. Even though often what we want isn't so much to listen as to express our feelings and say what has happened to us, a dialogue has already begun. Let us begin to do the same with God; we can be quite sure he listens to us and answers us. Let us pay attention to him and open up our soul in humble conversation, telling him in confidence everything that is on our minds and in our hearts: our joys, sorrows, hopes, annoyances, successes, failures, even the most trivial happenings in our day. We will discover that our Heavenly Father is interested in everything about us.

Overcome any sluggishness you may feel, 246
and the false excuse that prayer can wait for later. Let us never put off this vital source of grace until tomorrow. Now is the right time. God, who is a loving spectator of everything we do, watches over our most intimate needs. You and I, I tell you once again, we need to confide in him as we might confide in a brother, a friend, a father. Tell him, as I am telling him now, that he is all greatness, all goodness, all

mercy. Tell him also, "This is why I want to fall in love with you, despite my rough manners and poor hands, soiled and ill-treated by the dust and grime of this earth."

In this way, almost without realizing it, we will go forward at God's pace, taking strong and vigorous strides. We will come to sense deep in our hearts that when we are close to our Lord we are able to find joy in suffering, self-denial, and sorrow. What a great source of strength it is for a son of God to know that he is so close to his Father! This is why, my Lord and Father, no matter what happens, I stand firm and secure with you, because you are my rock and my strength.[20]

247 For some of you, all this may sound quite familiar; for others, it may be something new; for everybody, it is demanding. As for me, as long as I have strength to breathe, I will continue to preach that it is vitally necessary that we be souls of prayer *at all times*, at every opportunity, and in the most varied of circumstances, because God never abandons us. It is not a proper Christian attitude to look upon friendship with God only as a last resort. Do

[20] Cf. 2 Kings 22:2.

we think it normal to ignore or neglect the people we love? Obviously not! Those we love figure constantly in our conversations, desires, and thoughts. We hold them ever present. So it should be with God.

When we seek our Lord in this way, our whole day becomes one intimate and trusting conversation with him. I have said and written this so many times, but I don't mind saying it again, because our Lord has shown us by his example that this is exactly what we have to do: we have to pray at all times, from morning to night and from night to morning. When everything goes well: "Thank you, my God!" If we are having a hard time, "Lord, do not abandon me!" Then this God of ours, who is "meek and humble of heart"[21] will not ignore our petitions or remain indifferent. For he himself has told us, "Ask, and it shall be given to you; seek, and you shall find; knock, and it shall be opened for you."[22]

Let us try, therefore, never to lose our supernatural outlook. Let us see the hand of God in everything that happens to us: both in

[21] Mt 11:29.
[22] Lk 11:9.

pleasant and unpleasant things, in times of consolation and in times of sorrow, as in the death of someone we love. Your first instinct always should be to talk to your Father God, whom we should seek in the depths of our souls. And we cannot consider this a trivial or unimportant matter. On the contrary, it is a clear sign of a deep interior life, of a true dialogue of love. Far from being psychologically deforming, constant prayer should be for a Christian as natural as the beating of his heart.

Vocal prayers and mental prayer

248 Upon this living fabric of our Christian faith are woven in the vocal prayers, like jewels. Some are of divine composition: "Our Father...," "Hail Mary...," "Glory be to the Father, and to the Son, and to the Holy Spirit." There is as well that crown of praise to God and to our Mother, the Holy Rosary, and then so many other acclamations, full of devotion, that fellow Christians, our brothers in the faith, have recited from the very earliest times.

St Augustine, quoting a verse from Psalm 85, "Take pity on me, Lord, I have cried to you all day long," comments: "Not 'one day': understand 'all day' to mean all the time, without ceasing...A single man reaches out to the end of the world; for it is the members of the one Christ who call out to God, some of them already resting in him, others invoking him now, and others who will come and implore him when we will have died, and still others who will follow them in prayer."[23] Are you not moved when you consider that you can share in this never-ending homage to the Creator? How great is man when he acknowledges that he is a privileged creature of God and has recourse to him *tota die*, at every moment of his journey on earth!

Each day without fail we should devote **249**
some time especially to God, raising our minds to him, without any need for the words to come to our lips, for they are being sung in our heart. Let us give enough time to this devout practice; at a fixed hour, if possible. Before the tabernacle, close to him who has remained there out of Love. If this is not possible, we can pray anywhere because our God is ineffably present in the heart of every soul in grace. Still I would

[23] St Augustine, *Enarrationes in Psalmos*, 85, 5 (PL 37, 1085).

advise you to go to the oratory whenever you can. I make a point of calling it an oratory and not a chapel, to emphasize that it is not a place where you adopt a formal, ceremonial manner, but rather one where you can raise up your mind in an intimate and recollected way, to Heaven, and you can be sure that Jesus sees us and hears us, that he is waiting for us and presides over us from the tabernacle where he is truly present, hidden under the sacramental species.

Each one of you, if he wants, can find his own way to converse with God. I do not like to talk about methods or formulas, because I have never wished to straitjacket anyone. What I have always tried to do is to encourage everyone to come closer to our Lord, respecting each soul as it is, each with its own characteristics. Ask him to introduce his ideas and plans into our lives: not only into our heads, but also into the depths of our hearts and into all our outward actions. I assure you that you will, thus, be spared many of the disappointments and sorrows of selfishness, and you will find you have the strength to do good to all around you. How many obstacles vanish when in our hearts we place ourselves next to this God of ours, who never abandons us! Jesus' love for his own, for the sick, and for the lame, is renewed, expressed in different ways, "What is the matter?" he asks, and we reply, "It's my..." At once there is light, or at least the acceptance of his will, and inner peace.

When I encourage you to open your heart in confidence to the Master, I am referring especially to your own difficulties, because most of the obstacles to our happiness come from our pride, which may be hidden to a greater or less degree. We had thought we were worth a great deal and had a lot of exceptional qualities; then, when others didn't agree, we felt humiliated. This is a good time to pray and to correct our mistaken attitude. We can be sure it is never too late to change our course. But it's wise to start changing it as soon as possible.

In prayer, with God's grace, pride can be transformed into humility. Then, true joy wells up in our hearts, even though we feel that the wings of our souls are still clogged with the mud, the clay of our wretchedness which is now beginning to dry out. If we practise mortification the mud will fall off, allowing us to soar very high, because the wind of God's mercy will be blowing in our favor.

250 Look: our Lord is anxious to guide us at a marvellous pace, both human and divine, and which leads to joyful abandonment, happiness in suffering and self-forgetfulness. "If any man has a mind to come my way, let him renounce self."[24] This is a counsel we have all heard. Now we have to make a firm decision to put it into practice. May our Lord be able to use us so that, placed as we are at all the crossroads of the world—and at the same time placed in God—we become salt, leaven, and light. Yes, you are to be in God, to enlighten, to give flavor, to produce growth and new life.

But don't forget that we are not the source of this light: we only reflect it. It is not we who save souls and move them to do good. We are quite simply instruments, some more, some less worthy, for fulfilling God's plans for salvation. If at any time we were to think that we ourselves are the authors of the good we do, then our pride would return, more twisted than ever. The salt would lose its flavor, the leaven would rot, and the light would turn to darkness.

[24] Mt 16:24.

Among the followers of our Lord

During my thirty years as a priest I have constantly insisted that we need to pray, and that it is possible to convert our whole life into an unceasing clamor of prayer. Naturally, some people have asked me if this can really be done, all the time. It can. Union with our Lord does not cut us off from the world we live in. It does not make us strange beings, out of touch with what is going on around us. 251

If it is true that God has created us, that he has redeemed us, that he loves us so much that he has given up his only-begotten Son for us,[25] that he waits for us—everyday—as eagerly as the father of the prodigal son did,[26] how can we doubt that he wants us to respond to him with all our love? The strange thing would be not to talk to God, to draw away and forget him, and busy ourselves in activities which are closed to the constant promptings of his grace.

Besides, let me remind you that nobody 252
escapes the tendency to imitate others. Even unconsciously we tend to imitate one another.

[25] Cf. Jn 3:16.
[26] Cf. Lk 15:11-32.

Are we then going to refuse the invitation to imitate Jesus? Everyone strives to identify himself little by little with what he admires, with the model he has chosen for himself. Our way of acting is geared to the ideal we have set for ourselves. Our teacher is Christ, the Son of God and the Second Person of the Blessed Trinity. If we imitate Christ, we will attain the marvellous possibility of sharing in that current of love, which is the mystery of God, One in Three.

If at times you don't feel strong enough to follow in the footsteps of Jesus Christ, say a few loving words to those who knew him well during his life on earth. To Mary, first of all, for she it was who brought him to us. Then to the Apostles. "And there were certain Gentiles who approached Philip, the man from Bethsaida in Galilee, and made a request of him: Sir, they said, we desire to see Jesus. Philip came and told Andrew, and together, Andrew and Philip, went and told Jesus."[27] Don't you find this scene encouraging? Those foreigners didn't dare to approach the Master directly, so they looked for a good intercessor.

[27] Jn 12:20-22.

Are you worried that your sins are so many that our Lord will not listen to you? It is not so, because Jesus is full of mercy. But if despite this marvellous truth you still feel how wretched you are, go to him like the publican did,[28] and say, "Lord, here I am. It's up to you!" See, too, what St Matthew tells us when Jesus had a paralyzed man brought before him. The sick man doesn't say a word. He is simply there, in the presence of God. And Christ, moved by the man's contrition, by the sorrow of one who knows he deserves nothing, responds immediately, as merciful as ever, "Take courage, your sins are forgiven."[29] 253

My advice is that, in your prayer, you actually take part in the different scenes of the Gospel, as one more among the people present. First of all, imagine the scene or mystery you have chosen to help you recollect your thoughts and meditate. Next, apply your mind, concentrating on the particular aspect of the Master's life you are considering—his merciful Heart, his humility, his purity, the way he fulfills his Father's Will. Then tell him what happens to

[28] Cf. Lk 18:13.
[29] Mt 9:2.

you in these matters, how things are with you, what is going on in your soul. Be attentive, because he may want to point something out to you, and you will experience suggestions deep in your soul, realizing certain things and feeling his gentle reprimands.

254 As a way of giving outlet to my prayer—this may be helpful for some of you as well—I often materialize even the most spiritual of things. It is a method that our Lord used. He liked to teach through parables, using images from life around him: a shepherd and his flock, the vine and its branches, boats and nets, seed scattered by the sower...

The seed of God's Word has been sown in our heart. What kind of ground have we prepared for him? Are there many stones? Is it full of thorns? Are we letting petty and exclusively human cares trample all over it? Lord, make my plot of ground be good, fertile, and generously exposed to sun and rain. Let your seed take root in it and produce a fine crop of good wheat.

"I am the vine, you are the branches."[30] September comes and the vines are rich with

[30] Jn 15:5.

long, lissom branches, flexibly intertwining and bending under the weight of the grapes now ready for the harvest. You see, the branches are full of fruit, because they share in the sap that comes from the stem. Otherwise, from the tiny buds we knew just a few months back, they could not have produced the sweet ripe fruit that gladdens the eye and makes the heart rejoice.[31] Here and there on the ground we may find some dry twigs, lying half-buried in the soil. Once they too were branches of the vine; now they lie there withered and dead, a perfect image of barrenness: "separated from me, you can do nothing."[32]

Then there is the treasure. You can imagine the immense joy of the lucky man who finds it. The hard times, the sufferings are over. He sells everything he has and buys the field. His whole heart is there, where his treasure lies hidden.[33] Our treasure is Christ. We shouldn't mind having to throw overboard everything that impedes our following him. Our boat, once freed of its useless cargo, will sail directly to the safe harbor of God's Love.

[31] Cf. Ps 103:15.
[32] Jn 15:5.
[33] Cf. Mt 6:21.

255 There are countless ways of praying, as I have already told you. We children of God don't need a method, an artificial system, to talk with our Father. Love is inventive, full of initiative. If we truly love, we will discover our own intimate paths to lead us to a continuous conversation with our Lord.

May God grant that what we have contemplated today will not pass over our souls like a summer downpour—a few drops of rain, then once again the baking sun and the fields are as dry as before. The water of God's grace needs to settle, to seep through to the roots and bear fruit in virtues. If we let it do this, our years on earth—made up of days of work and prayer—will be spent in the presence of our Father. If we falter, let us turn to Holy Mary who loves us and teaches us how to pray; and to St Joseph, our father and lord, whom we venerate so much. In this world he was the one who was closest to the Mother of God and, after Mary, to her Divine Son. Together they will bring our weakness to Jesus, so that he may turn it into strength.

THAT ALL MAY BE SAVED[*]

Our Christian vocation, this calling which our Lord makes to each of us personally, leads us to become identified with him. But we should not forget that he came on earth to redeem everyone, because "he wishes all men to be saved."[1] There is not a single soul in whom Christ is not interested. Each soul has cost him the price of his Blood.[2] 256

As I think about these truths, there comes to mind a conversation which took place between the apostles and the Master shortly before the miracle of the feeding of the five thousand. A great multitude had followed Jesus. Our Lord looked up and said to Philip,

[*] A homily given on April 16, 1954.

[1] 1 Tim 2:4.

[2] Cf. 1 Pt 1:18-19.

" 'Where shall we buy bread for these to eat?' "[3] Philip made a rapid calculation and answered: " 'Two hundred silver pieces would not buy enough bread for them, even to give each a little.' "[4] They didn't have that kind of money; what they could find was paltry in comparison. "One of his disciples, Andrew, the brother of Simon Peter, said to him: 'There is a boy here who has five barley loaves and two fishes; but what is that among so many?' "[5]

Leavening the dough

257 We want to follow our Lord. We are anxious to spread his Word. From a human point of view, it's only natural that we should ask ourselves: who are we, for so many people? Compared with the total population of the world, even though there are millions of us, we are few in number. We must, therefore, see ourselves as a tiny measure of yeast, prepared and ready to do good to the whole of mankind, remembering the words of the Apostle: "a little

[3] Jn 6:5.
[4] *Ibid* 6:7.
[5] *Ibid* 6:8-9.

leaven is enough to leaven all the dough,"[6] transforming it completely. We have to learn to become that yeast, that leaven, and so modify and transform the multitude.

Is yeast, by its nature, better than dough? No. But it is what makes the dough rise and become good and nourishing food.

Reflect a moment, even if only in general terms, on the way yeast works in the making of bread—that simple, staple food which is available to everyone. In many places (you yourselves may have seen it done) the baking process is like a real ceremonial, ending up with a splendid product that you can almost taste with your eyes.

They start with good flour, of top quality if possible. Then the dough is worked in the kneading trough and the yeast is mixed in. It is a long and patient job. The dough must now be left to rest; this is essential for the leaven to do its work and make the dough rise.

Meanwhile the oven is made ready, its temperature rising as the logs of wood burn bright. The risen dough is placed in the glowing oven and turns into high-quality bread, wonderfully

[6] 1 Cor 5:6.

light and fresh. This result would never have been possible had it not been for the small amount of leaven, which dissolved and disappeared among the other ingredients, working effectively and passing unnoticed.

258 If we pray and meditate on these words of St Paul, we will realize that we have no alternative but to work, in the service of all souls. Anything else would be selfishness. If we look at ourselves humbly, we will see clearly that, in addition to his gift of faith, our Lord has also granted us a number of talents and qualities. None of us has been mass-produced. Our Father has created us one by one and shared out different goods among his children. It is up to us to use these talents, these qualities, in the service of all men. We are called to use the gifts God has given us as instruments to help others discover Christ.

Please don't think that the desire to help others is in the nature of an extra, a lace trimming for our ordinary lives as Christians. If leaven is not used for fermenting, it rots. There are two ways leaven can disappear, either by giving life to dough, or by being wasted, a perfect tribute to selfishness and barrenness. We are not doing Jesus a favor when we make him known to others: "When I preach the Gospel, I take no credit for that; I act under constraint," obliged by Jesus' command; "it would go hard with me indeed if I did not preach the Gospel."[7]

Going fishing

" 'Behold, I will send many fishermen,' says 259
the Lord, 'and I will catch those fishes.' "[8] That is his way of explaining the great task we have before us: we must become fishermen. The world is often compared, in conversation or in books, with the sea. It is a good comparison, for in our lives, just as in the sea, there are quiet times and stormy seasons, periods of calm and gusts of strong wind. One often finds souls swimming in difficult waters, in the midst of heavy waves. They travel through stormy weather, their journey one sad rush, despite their apparently cheerful expressions and their boisterousness. Their bursts of laughter are a cover for their discouragement and ill-temper.

[7] *Ibid* 9:16.
[8] Jer 16:16.

Their lives are bereft of charity and understanding. Men, like fish, devour each other.

Our task as children of God is to get all men to enter, freely, into the divine net; to get them to love each other. If we are Christians, we must seek to become fishermen like those described by the prophet Jeremiah with a metaphor which Jesus also often used: "Follow me and I will make you fishers of men,"[9] he says to Peter and Andrew.

260 Let us accompany our Lord as he goes about his divine task of fishing. We find Jesus by the Lake of Genesareth, with the crowds pressing upon him, eager "to hear the word of God."[10] Just as they do today! Can't you see? they want to hear God's message, even though outwardly they may not show it. Some perhaps have forgotten Christ's teachings. Others, through no fault of their own, have never known them and they think that religion is something odd. But of this we can be sure, that in every man's life there comes a time sooner or later when his soul draws the line. He has had enough of the usual explanations. The lies of the false prophets no

[9] Mt 4:19.
[10] Lk 5:1.

longer satisfy. Even though they may not admit it at the time, such people are longing to quench their thirst with the teachings of our Lord.

Let us follow St Luke's description. "At this he saw two boats moored by the lake, whose fishermen had gone ashore, and were washing their nets. And he went on board one of the boats, which belonged to Simon, and asked him to stand off a little from the land; and so, sitting down, he began to teach the multitudes from the boat."[11] When he had finished his catechizing, he told Simon: " 'Put out into the deep, and lower your nets for a catch.' "[12] Christ is the master of this boat. He it is that prepares the fishing. It is for this that he has come into the world, to do all he can so that his brothers may find the way to glory and to the love of the Father. It is not we who have invented the Christian apostolate. If anything, we get in its way, through our clumsiness and lack of faith.

"Simon answered him, 'Master, we have **261**
toiled all the night, and caught nothing.' "[13] A reasonable enough reply. The night hours were

[11] *Ibid* 5:2-3.
[12] *Ibid* 5:4.
[13] *Ibid* 5:5.

their normal time for fishing, and this time the catch had yielded nothing. What was the point of fishing by day? But Peter has faith: " 'nevertheless, at thy word I will let down the net.' "[14] He decides to act on Christ's suggestion. He undertakes to work relying entirely on the Word of our Lord. And what happened? "When they had done this, they took a great quantity of fish, so that the net was near breaking, and they must needs beckon to their partners who were in the other boat to come and help them. When these came, they filled both boats, so that they were ready to sink."[15]

When Jesus went out to sea with his disciples he was not thinking only about the catch of fishes. And so when Peter falls down at his feet and humbly confesses: " 'Depart from me, Lord, for I am a sinful man,' " our Lord replies: " 'Do not be afraid; henceforth you shall be a fisher of men.' "[16] In this new task of fishing, all the power and effectiveness of God will also be at hand: the apostles are instruments for the working of great wonders, in spite of their personal shortcomings.

[14] *Ibid.*
[15] *Ibid* 5:6-7.
[16] *Ibid* 5:8, 10.

Miracles will multiply

The same is true of us. If we struggle daily 262
to become saints, each of us in his own situation in the world and through his own job or profession, in our ordinary lives, then I assure you that God will make us into instruments that can work miracles and, if necessary, miracles of the most extraordinary kind. We will give sight to the blind. Who could not relate thousands of cases of people, blind almost from the day they were born, recovering their sight and receiving all the splendor of Christ's light? And others who were deaf, or dumb, who could not hear or pronounce words fitting to God's children...Their senses have been purified and now they listen and speak as man, not animals. *In nomine Iesu!*[17] ("In the name of Jesus"), his Apostles enable the cripple to move and walk, when previously he had been incapable of doing anything useful; and that other lazy character, who knew his duties but didn't fulfill them...In the Lord's name, *surge et ambula*[18] ("rise up and walk").

[17] Acts 3:6.
[18] *Ibid* 3:6.

Another man was dead, rotting, smelling like a corpse: he hears God's voice, as in the miracle of the son of the widow at Naim: " 'Young man, I say to you, rise up.' "[19] We will work miracles like Christ did, like the first Apostles did. Maybe you yourself, and I, have benefited from such wonders. Perhaps we were blind, or deaf, or paralyzed; perhaps we had the stench of death, and the word of our Lord has lifted us up from our abject state. If we love Christ, if we follow him sincerely, if we stop seeking ourselves and seek him alone, then in his name we will be able to give to others, freely, what we have freely received.

263 I have constantly preached about this opportunity that is both supernatural and human and which is offered by God our Father to us his children: we can share in Christ's work of Redemption. How glad am I when I find this teaching in the writings of the Fathers of the Church. St Gregory the Great explains: "Christians free men from serpents, when they uproot evil from their hearts by exhorting them to do good...They lay their hands on the sick and cure them, when they see their neighbor flagging in

[19] Lk 7:14

his good work and they offer to help in so many ways, strengthening him with their example. These miracles are all the greater in that they are worked in spiritual things and give life not to bodies but to souls. You too, if you do not weaken, will be able to work these wonders, with the help of God."[20]

God wants all men to be saved. This is an invitation to us and also a responsibility that weighs upon each one of us. The Church is not a place of refuge for a privileged few. "Who says the great Church is only a small part of the earth? The great Church is the whole world." [21] That is how St Augustine describes it. And he adds: "Wherever you go, Christ is there. Your inheritance reaches to the ends of the earth; come take possession of it with me."[22] Remember the nets? They were full to overflowing, bursting with fish. God ardently longs to see this house full.[23] He is a Father and likes to live surrounded by all his children.

[20] St Gregory the Great, *Homiliae in Evangelia*, 29, 4 (PL 76, 1215-1216).

[21] St Augustine, *Enarrationes in Psalmos*, 21, 2, 26 (PL 36, 177).

[22] *Ibid* 211, 2, 30 (PL 36, 180).

[23] Cf. Lk 14:23.

Apostolate in our daily life

264 Let us turn now to the second catch of fish, after Jesus' Passion and Death. Peter, having denied his Master three times, later wept in humble sorrow. The cock with its crowing reminded him of our Lord's prediction and with all his heart he asked to be forgiven. While with contrite heart he waits for the promise of the Resurrection, he goes about his ordinary work: he goes fishing. "Regarding this catch of fish, we are often asked why Peter and the sons of Zebedee returned to the jobs they had before our Lord called them. They were fishermen when Jesus told them: 'Follow me, and I will make you fishers of men.' To those who are surprised by this behavior, we must answer that the Apostles were not forbidden to exercise their profession, it being a legitimate and honest thing to do."[24]

The apostolic concern which burns in the heart of ordinary Christians is not something separate from their everyday work. It is part and parcel of one's work, which becomes a source of opportunities for meeting Christ. As

[24] St Augustine, *In Ioannis Evangelium tractatus*, 122, 2 (PL 35, 1959).

we work at our job, side by side with our colleagues, friends, and relatives and sharing their interests, we can help them come closer to Christ who awaits us on the shore. Before becoming apostles, we are fishermen. After becoming Apostles, we are fishermen still. The same profession, before and after.

What has changed? There is a change inside 265
our souls, now that Christ has come aboard, as he went aboard Peter's boat. Its horizon has opened wider. It feels a greater ambition to serve and an irrepressible desire to tell all creation about the *magnalia Dei*[25] ("the marvellous doings of our Lord"), if only we let him work. Here I would like to make the point that the *professional work*, to put it that way, of priests, is a *divine and public ministry*, so demanding that it embraces everything they do, and to such an extent that it can be stated as a general rule that, if a priest has time to spare for other occupations that are not strictly priestly, he can be sure that he is not fulfilling the duties of his ministry.

"Simon Peter was there, and with him were Thomas, who is also called Didymus, and

[25] Acts 2:11.

Nathanael, from Cana of Galilee, and the sons of Zebedee, and two more of his disciples. Simon Peter told them, 'I am going out fishing;' and they said, 'We too, will go with you.' So they went out and embarked on the boat; and all that night they caught nothing. But when morning came, there was Jesus standing on the shore."[26]

He passes by, close to his Apostles, close to those souls who have given themselves to him and they don't realize he is there. How often Christ is not only near us, but in us; yet we still live in such a human way! Christ is so close to us and yet we can't spare him an affectionate glance, a loving word, a good deed done by his children.

266 "The disciples," writes St John, "did not know that it was Jesus. 'Have you caught anything, friends,' Jesus asked them, 'to season your bread with?' "[27] The close, family nature of this scene fills me with happiness and joy. That Jesus, my God, should say this! He, who already has a glorified body! " 'Cast to the right of the boat, and you will have a catch.' So they

[26] Jn 21:2-4.
[27] *Ibid* 21:4-5.

cast the net, and found before long they had no strength to haul it in, such a shoal of fish was in it."[28] Now they understand. They, the disciples, recall what they have heard so often from their Master's lips: fishers of men, Apostles. And they realize that all things are possible, because it is he who is directing their fishing.

"Whereupon the disciple whom Jesus loved said to Peter, 'It is the Lord.' "[29] Love, love is farsighted. Love is the first to appreciate kindness. The adolescent Apostle, who felt a deep and firm affection for Jesus, because he loved Christ with all the purity and tenderness of a heart that had never been corrupted, exclaimed: " 'It is the Lord!' "

"Simon Peter, hearing him say that it was the Lord, girded up the fisherman's coat, and sprang into the sea."[30] Peter personifies faith. Full of marvellous daring, he leaps into the sea. With a love like John's and a faith like Peter's, what is there that can stop us?

[28] *Ibid* 21:6.
[29] *Ibid* 21:7.
[30] *Ibid*.

Souls belong to God

267 "The other disciples followed in the boat (they were not far from land, only some hundred yards away), dragging their catch in their net behind them."[31] They bring in the catch and immediately place it at our Lord's feet, because it is his. This is a lesson for us, so that we may learn that souls belong to God; that no one on earth has that right over souls; and that the Church's apostolate, by which it announces and brings about salvation, is not based on the prestige of any human beings but on the grace of God.

Jesus questions Peter, three times, as if to give him a triple chance to atone for his triple denial. Peter has learned his lesson from the bitter experience of his wretchedness. Aware of his weakness, he is deeply convinced that rash claims are pointless. Instead he puts everything in Christ's hands. " 'Lord, you know well that I love you. Lord, you know all things; you know that I love you.' "[32] What is Christ's reply? " 'Feed my lambs, feed my sheep.' "[33] "Not

[31] *Ibid* 21:8.
[32] *Ibid* 21:15-17.
[33] *Ibid.*

yours, Peter; not yours: mine!" Because he created man; he redeemed man; he has bought each soul, one by one, at the cost, I say once again, of his Blood.

In the fifth century, when the Donatists were orchestrating their attacks against the Catholics, they claimed that Augustine, the Bishop of Hippo, couldn't possibly profess the truth because he had previously been a great sinner. St Augustine suggested to his brothers in the faith that they could reply as follows: "Augustine is a bishop in the Catholic Church. He bears his burden and he will have to give an account of it to God. I met him in the company of good men. If he is a bad man, he will know it. But even if he is good, it is not in him that I have put my trust, because the first thing I learned in the Catholic Church is not to put my hope in any man."[34]

We are not doing *our* apostolate. If we were, what could we possibly say? We are doing Christ's apostolate, because God wants it to be done and because he has commanded us to do it: "Go out all over the world, and preach the

[34] St Augustine, *Enarrationes in Psalmos*, 36, 3, 20 (PL 36, 395).

Gospel to the whole of creation."[35] The errors are ours; the fruits are his.

Daring to speak about God

268 How are we to carry out this apostolate? First of all, by our example, by living according to the Will of the Father, as Jesus, with his life and teaching, taught us to do. True faith does not permit our actions to contradict what we say. Let us examine our own behavior, to see how genuine our faith is. We are not sincere believers if we are not striving to put into practice what we preach with our lips.

269 This is a good moment to recall and reflect on an event that demonstrates the wonderful apostolic zeal of the early Christians. Scarcely a quarter of a century had passed since Jesus had gone up to Heaven and already his fame had spread to many towns and villages. In the city of Ephesus a man arrived, Apollo by name, "an eloquent man, well grounded in the Scriptures. He had had instruction in the name of the Lord; and, with a spirit full of zeal, used

[35] Mk 16:15.

to preach and teach about the life of Jesus, accurately enough, although he knew of no baptism except that of John."[36]

A glimmer of Christ's light had already filtered into the mind of this man. He had heard about our Lord and he passed the news on to others. But he still had some way to go. He needed to know more if he was to acquire the fulness of the faith and so come to love our Lord truly. A Christian couple, Aquila and Priscilla, hear him speaking; they are not inactive or indifferent. They do not think: "This man already knows enough; it's not our business to teach him." They were souls who were really eager to do apostolate and so they approach Apollo and "made friends with him, and gave him a fuller explanation of the way of the Lord."[37]

Then there is St Paul. How admirably he **270**
behaves! Imprisoned for spreading the teachings of Christ, he misses no opportunity of preaching the Gospel. Brought before Festus and Agrippa, he declares unflinchingly: "Thanks to God's help, I still stand here today,

[36] Acts 18:24-25.
[37] *Ibid* 18:26.

bearing my witness to great and small alike. Yet there is nothing in my message which goes beyond what the prophets spoke of, and Moses spoke of, as things to come; a suffering Christ, and one who should show light to his people and to the Gentiles by being the first to rise from the dead."[38]

The Apostle doesn't silence or hide his faith, or his apostolic propaganda that had brought down on him the hatred of his persecutors. He continues preaching salvation to everyone he meets. And, with marvellous daring, he boldly asks Agrippa: " 'Do you believe the prophets, King Agrippa? I know you do.' "[39] When Agrippa comments: " 'You would have me turn Christian with very little ado.' 'Why,' said Paul, 'it would be my prayer to God that, whether it were with much ado or little, both you and all those who are listening to me today should become just as I am, but for these chains.' "[40]

271 Where did St Paul get all his strength from? *Omnia possum in eo qui me confortat!*[41] I can do all things, because God alone gives me this

[38] *Ibid* 26:22-23.
[39] *Ibid* 26:27.
[40] *Ibid* 26:28-29.
[41] Phil 4:13.

faith, this hope, this charity. I find it very hard to believe in the supernatural effectiveness of an apostolate that is not based, is not solidly centered, on a life of constant conversation with our Lord. Yes, right there in our work; in our own home, or in the street, with all the small or big problems that arise daily. Right there, not taken away from those things, but with our hearts fixed on God. Then our words, our actions—our defects!—will give forth the *bonus odor Christi*[42] the sweet fragrance of Christ, which other men will inevitably notice and say: "Here is a Christian."

If you were to fall into the temptation of **272**
wondering, "who's telling me to embark on this?" We would have to reply: "Christ himself is telling you, is begging you." " 'The harvest is plentiful enough, but the laborers are few. You must ask the Lord to whom the harvest belongs to send laborers out for the harvesting.' "[43] Don't take the easy way out. Don't say, "I'm no good at this sort of thing; there are others who can do it; it isn't my line." No, for this sort of thing, there is no one else: if you

[42] 2 Cor 2:15.
[43] Mt 9:37-38.

could get away with that argument, so could everyone else. Christ's plea is addressed to each and every Christian. No one can consider himself excused, for whatever reason: age, health, or occupation. There are no excuses whatsoever. Either we carry out a fruitful apostolate, or our faith will prove barren.

273 Besides, whoever said that to speak about Christ and to spread his doctrine, you need to do anything unusual or remarkable? Just live your ordinary life; work at your job, trying to fulfill the duties of your state in life, doing your job, your professional work properly, improving, getting better each day. Be loyal; be understanding with others and demanding on yourself. Be mortified and cheerful. This will be your apostolate. Then, though you won't see why, because you're very aware of your own wretchedness, you will find that people come to you. Then you can talk to them, quite simply and naturally—on your way home from work, for instance, or in a family gathering, on a bus, walking down the street, anywhere. You will chat about the sort of longings that everyone feels deep down in his soul, even though some people may not want to pay attention to them: they will come to

understand them better, when they begin to look for God in earnest.

Ask Mary, *Regina Apostolorum* ("Queen of the Apostles"), to help you make up your mind to share the desires of *sowing and fishing* that fill the Heart of her Son. I can assure you that if you begin, you will see the boat filled, just like the fishermen from Galilee did. And you will find Christ on the shore, waiting for you. Because the catch belongs to him.

MOTHER OF GOD AND OUR MOTHER*

All the feasts of our Lady are great events, because they are opportunities that the Church gives us to show with deeds that we love Mary. But if I had to choose one among all her feasts, I would choose today's, the feast of the divine Motherhood of the Blessed Virgin. 274

Today's celebration brings us to consider some of the central mysteries of our faith. We meditate on the Incarnation of the Word, which is the work of the three Persons of the Blessed Trinity. Through the Incarnation of our Lord in her immaculate womb, Mary, the Daughter of God the Father, is also the Spouse of God the Holy Spirit and the Mother of God the Son.

*A homily given on October 11, 1964, the Feast of the Motherhood of the Blessed Virgin Mary.

When the Blessed Virgin said "Yes", freely, to the plans revealed to her by the Creator, the divine Word assumed a human nature: a rational soul and a body, which was formed in the most pure womb of Mary. The divine nature and the human were united in a single Person: Jesus Christ, true God and, thenceforth, true Man; the only-begotten and eternal Son of the Father and, from that moment on, as Man, the true son of Mary. This is why our Lady is the Mother of the Incarnate Word, the second Person of the Blessed Trinity who has united our human nature to himself forever, without any confusion of the two natures. The greatest praise we can give to the Blessed Virgin is to address her loud and clear by the name that expresses her very highest dignity: Mother of God.

The faith of the Christian people

275 This has always been the true belief of Christians. Against those who denied it, the Council of Ephesus proclaimed that "if anyone should deny that the Emmanuel is truly God, and that, therefore, the most Blessed Virgin is the Mother of God, since she gave birth according to the flesh to the Incarnate Word of God, let him be anathema."[1]

History has handed down to us eyewitness accounts of the joy felt by the Christians when they received such clear, precise definitions, which reaffirmed what everyone believed. In the words of St Cyril, "The entire community of the city of Ephesus, from the first hours of the day until nightfall, waited anxiously for the resolution...When it became known that the author of the blasphemies had been deposed, with one voice we began to glorify God and to acclaim the Synod, for the enemy of the faith had fallen. On leaving the church we went by torchlight to our houses. It was night time and the whole city was joyful and illuminated."[2] I must say that, even at a distance of sixteen centuries, their outburst of piety impresses me deeply.

God grant that this same faith may burn in our hearts, and that a hymn of thanksgiving may rise from our lips: for the Blessed Trinity, in choosing Mary as the Mother of Christ, a Man like us, has brought each one of us under

[1] Council of Ephesus, can. 1 (Denzinger-Schön. 252/113).
[2] St Cyril of Alexandria, *Epistolae*, 24 (PG 77, 138).

the shelter of her maternal cloak. She is the Mother of God and our Mother.

276 The divine Motherhood of Mary is the source of all the perfections and privileges with which she is endowed. Because of it, she was conceived immaculate and is full of grace; because of it, she is ever virgin, she was taken up body and soul to Heaven and has been crowned Queen of all creation, above the angels and saints. Greater than she, none but God. "The Blessed Virgin, from the fact that she is the Mother of God, has a certain infinite dignity which comes from the infinite good, which is God."[3] There is no danger of exaggerating. We can never hope to fathom this inexpressible mystery; nor will we ever be able to give sufficient thanks to our Mother for bringing us into such intimacy with the Blessed Trinity.

We were sinners and enemies of God. Redemption has not only freed us from sin and reconciled us with our Lord. It has also made us into children of God and has given us a Mother, the very Mother who gave birth to the Word when he took human nature. Could there

[3] St Thomas Aquinas, *Summa Theologiae,* I, q.25,a.6.

ever be a greater, more generous, outpouring of love? God longed to redeem us and, in his infinite wisdom, could have chosen many different ways of carrying out his most holy Will. He chose one which dispels all possible doubts about our salvation and glorification. "Just as the first Adam was not born of man and woman, but was formed of earth, so also the last Adam, who was to heal the wound of the first, took a body formed in the womb of the Blessed Virgin, in order to be, in his flesh, equal to the flesh of those who sinned."[4]

Mother of Fair Love

Ego quasi vitis fructificavi...:("Like the vine I **277**
sprouted beautiful branches and my blossoms gave forth savory and rich fruits").[5] We have read these words in today's Epistle. May our souls and the souls of all Christians be full of that sweet fragrance which is devotion to our Mother, and may it bring us to trust entirely in her who watches over us at all times.

[4] St Basil, *Commentarius in Isaiam*, 7, 201 (PG 30, 466).
[5] Ecclus 24:23.

"I am the Mother of fair love, and of fear, and of knowledge, and of holy hope."[6] These are the lessons which Mary reminds us of today. The lesson of fair love, of living a clean life, of having a sensitive and passionate heart, so that we may learn to be faithful in our service to the Church. This is no ordinary love. It is Love itself. There is no room here for betrayal, or calculation, or forgetfulness. It is a fair, a beautiful love, because its beginning and end is God, who is thrice Holy, who is all Beauty, all Goodness, and all Greatness.

But there is also a reference to fear. For myself, the only fear I can imagine is that of turning away from Love. God our Lord certainly does not want us to be inhibited, timid, or lukewarm about our dedication to him. He wants us to be daring, courageous, and refined. When the sacred text speaks of fear here, I am reminded of a complaint we find elsewhere in Scripture, "I searched for my heart's love, but found him not."[7]

This can happen, if one has not yet fully understood what it means to love God. Then

[6] *Ibid* 24:24.
[7] Cant 3:1.

our hearts can be swayed by things which do not lead to our Lord and so we lose sight of him. At other times it may be our Lord who hides himself. He knows the reason why. In such cases, he will be encouraging us to seek him more earnestly and, when we find him, we shall be able to cry out with joy, "I took hold of him and I will never let him go."[8]

The Gospel in today's Mass has called to our 278
minds a moving scene in Jesus' life, when he stayed behind in Jerusalem teaching in the temple. Mary and Joseph "had gone a whole day's journey before they made enquiry for him among their kinsfolk and acquaintances. When they could not find him, they made their way back to Jerusalem in search of him."[9] The Mother of God, who looked for her Son so anxiously when he was lost through no fault of her own, and experienced such great joy in finding him, will help us retrace our steps and put right whatever may be necessary when, because of our carelessness or our sins, we have been unable to recognize Christ. With her help we will know the happiness of holding him in

[8] *Ibid* 3:4.
[9] Lk 2:44-45.

our arms once more, and telling him we will never lose him again.

Mary is also the Mother of knowledge, for it is with her that we learn the most important lesson of all, that nothing is worthwhile if we are not close to our Lord. All the wonders of this earth, the fulfillment of our every ambition, all this is worthless unless the living flame of love burns within us, unless there is the light of holy hope giving us a foretaste of never-ending love in our true homeland in Heaven.

279 "In me is to be found every grace of doctrine and of truth, every hope of life and of virtue."[10] How wise the Church is to put these words on our Mother's lips so that we Christians do not forget them. She is our safety, the Love that never fails, the refuge ever open to us, the hand ever ready to caress and console.

One of the Fathers of the early Church said that we should try to keep in our minds and in our memories a clear summary of the life of the Mother of God.[11] I expect you have often looked up points in handbooks on medicine,

[10] Ecclus 24:25.

[11] Cf. St John Damascene, *Homiliae in dormitionem B.V. Mariae*, 2, 19 (PG 96, 751).

mathematics, or other subjects, where they list, for quick reference, the immediate remedies or measures to be taken so as to avoid elementary mistakes in these subjects.

We should often meditate, in the calm and 280
quiet of our prayer, on all we have heard about our Mother. The reward will be that the story of her life will become engraved on our souls; we will find ourselves going to her without hesitation, especially when we have no one else to turn to. This may sound like self-interest on our part. It is, of course; but then don't all mothers know that we children tend to be somewhat self-interested, and that we often turn to them only as a last resort? They know this very well, but it doesn't really worry them. That comes with being a mother, and their disinterested love is able to discern, through our apparent selfishness, our filial affection and our trusting confidence.

I am not suggesting, either for myself or for you, that our devotion to Mary should be limited to times of urgent need. I feel, nevertheless, that we should not feel humiliated if this happens to us from time to time. Mothers don't keep a record of their chidren's tokens of affection; nor do they weigh them up or measure them with petty calculations. A tiny sign of affection is as sweet as honey to them, and they give themselves generously in return, bestowing much more than they receive. If good earthly mothers react in this way, just imagine what we can expect from our Holy Mother Mary.

Mother of the Church

281 I like to go back in my imagination to the years Jesus spent close to his Mother, years which span almost the whole of his life on earth. I like to picture him as a little child, cared for by Mary who kisses him and plays with him. I like to see him growing up before the loving eyes of his Mother and of Joseph, his father on earth. What tenderness and care Mary and the Holy Patriarch must have shown towards Jesus, as they looked after him during his childhood, all the while, silently, learning so much from him. Their souls would become more and more like the soul of that Son, who was both man and God. This is why his Mother, and after her, St Joseph, understand better than anyone the feelings of the Heart of Christ; and

the two of them are, thus, the best way, I would say the only way, to reach the Savior.

"May the soul of Mary," writes St Ambrose, "be in each of you, so that you may praise our Lord; may the spirit of Mary be in each one of you, so that you may rejoice in God." This Father of the Church goes on to say something which at first sight seems bold, but which has a clear spiritual meaning for the life of the Christian. "According to the flesh, there is only one Mother of Christ; according to the faith, Christ is the fruit of all of us."[12]

If we become identified with Mary and imitate her virtues, we will be able to bring Christ to life, through grace, in the souls of many who will in turn become identified with him through the action of the Holy Spirit. If we imitate Mary, we will share in some way in her spiritual motherhood. And all this silently, like our Lady; without being noticed, almost without words, through the true and genuine witness of our lives as Christians, and the generosity of ceaselessly repeating her *fiat* ("be it done" cf. Lk 1:38), which we renew as an intimate link between ourselves and God.

[12] St Ambrose, *Expositio Evangelii secundum Lucam,* 2, 26 (PL 15, 1561).

282 I want to tell you something that was said to me by a good Christian, who has a great love for our Lady, though he is no expert in theology. I am going to tell it to you just as he said it, because in its simplicity it is the natural reaction of an untutored mind.

"I needed to talk about this to someone," he said. "I get terribly upset at some of the things that are going on nowadays. In the preparatory meetings for the present Council and during the Council itself proposals were made to include the 'theme of the Blessed Virgin.' Just like that, 'the theme!' Is that the proper way for children to speak of their mothers? Is that the way our fathers professed their faith? Since when has love for the Blessed Virgin become a 'theme' to be discussed as to whether or not it is appropriate?

"There is nothing more at odds with love than stinginess. I am not afraid of speaking out clearly," he continued, "in fact, if I didn't, I would feel I was insulting our Holy Mother. It has been discussed whether or not it was right to call Mary the Mother of the Church. It hurts me to have to spell this out, but surely, since she is the Mother of God and the Mother of all Christians, she must be the Mother of the

Church, which gathers together all those who have been baptized and reborn in Christ, the Son of Mary.

"I can't understand," he went on, "where the pettiness comes from which hesitates at giving that title of praise to our Lady. How different the faith of the Church is! The 'theme' of the Blessed Virgin! Do children discuss the 'theme' of love for their mother? They love her, and that's all there is to it. If they are good children, they will love her a lot. Only strangers approaching the matter with clinical coldness, as if it were a case to be studied, could speak about 'themes' or 'drafts.' " That was how that simple and devout soul put it. A well-intentioned and pious outpouring, although not altogether fair.

Let us now return to our consideration of 283
this mystery of the divine Motherhood of Mary, praying quietly and affirming from the bottom of our hearts, "Virgin Mother of God, he whom the whole world cannot contain, enclosed himself in your womb to take the flesh of man."[13]

See what the liturgy proposes for our prayer today: "Blessed be the womb of the Virgin

[13] Alleluia of the Mass of the divine Motherhood of Mary.

Mary, which bore the Son of the eternal Father."[14] An exclamation both old and new, human and divine. We are telling our Lord, as they do in some places when they want to praise someone, "Blessed be the mother who brought you into the world!"

Teacher of faith, hope, and charity

284 "The charity of Mary brought about the birth of the faithful into the Church, who are members of that head of which she is effectively the mother according to the flesh."[15] Mary teaches us as a mother does, and, being a mother, she does so quietly. We need to have a sensitivity of soul, a touch of refinement, in order to understand what she is showing us, by what she does more than by what she promises.

She teaches us to have faith. " 'Blessed art thou for thy believing,' "[16] were the words of greeting uttered by her cousin Elizabeth when

[14] Communion antiphon of the Common Mass of the Blessed Virgin Mary.

[15] St Augustine, *De Sancta Virginitate*, 6 (PL 40, 399).

[16] Lk 1:45.

our Lady went up into the hill country to visit her. Mary's act of faith had been a wonderful one, " 'Behold the handmaid of the Lord, be it done unto me according to thy word.' "[17] When her Son was born she contemplated the greatness of God on earth: a choir of angels was present, and not only the shepherds, but also important men of this world came to adore the Child. Afterwards, however, the Holy Family had to flee to Egypt, to escape Herod's murderous intent. Then, silence; thirty long years of simple, ordinary life, just like that of any other home in a small village in Galilee.

In a few brief words, the Holy Gospel points **285**
the way for us to understand our Mother's example: "Mary treasured up all these sayings, and reflected on them in her heart."[18] Let us try to imitate her, talking to our Lord, conversing like two people in love about everything that happens to us, even the most insignificant incidents. Nor should we forget that we have to weigh them, consider their value, and see them with the eyes of faith, in order to discover the Will of God.

[17] *Ibid* 1:38.
[18] *Ibid* 2:19.

If our faith is weak, we should turn to Mary. St John tells us that it was because of the miracle at the marriage feast at Cana, which Christ performed at his Mother's request, that "his disciples learned to believe in him."[19] Our Mother is always interceding with her Son so that he may attend to our needs and show himself to us in such a way that we can cry out, "You are the Son of God."

286 Mary teaches us to hope. She proclaimed: "all generations will call me blessed."[20] Humanly speaking, how could she hope for such a thing? Who was she, in the eyes of the men and women of her time? The great heroines of the Old Testament—Judith, Esther, Deborah—won a measure of human glory even here on earth, for they were acclaimed and exalted by the people. Mary's throne, by contrast, like that of her Son, is the Cross. During the rest of her life, until she was taken body and soul into Heaven, what most impresses us about her is her quiet presence. St Luke, who knew her well, describes her as being close to the first disciples, in prayer. This was the way she

[19] Jn 2:11.
[20] Lk 1:48.

lived to the end of her days on earth, she who was to be praised by all creatures for all eternity.

What a contrast between our Lady's hope and our own impatience! So often we call upon God to reward us at once for any little good we have done. No sooner does the first difficulty appear than we start to complain. Often we are incapable of sustaining our efforts, of keeping our hope alive. Why? Because we lack faith. "Blessed art thou for thy believing; the message that was brought to thee from the Lord shall have fulfillment."[21]

She teaches us to have charity. Remember 287
the scene of the presentation of Jesus in the temple. An old man, Simeon, "said to his mother Mary, 'Behold, this child is destined to bring about the fall of many and the rise of many in Israel; and to be a sign which men will refuse to acknowledge; and so the thoughts of many hearts shall be made manifest; as for your own soul, it shall have a sword to pierce it.' "[22] So great is Mary's love for all mankind that she, too, fulfilled Christ's words when he

[21] *Ibid* 1:45.
[22] *Ibid* 2:34-35.

affirmed: "Greater love has no man than this, that he should lay down his life for his friends."[23]

It is with good reason that the popes have called Mary Co-Redemptrix. "So fully, in union with her suffering and dying Son, did she suffer and nearly die; so fully, for the sake of the salvation of men, did she abdicate her mother's rights over her Son, and immolate him, insofar as it was in her power, to satisfy the justice of God, that it can rightly be said that she redeemed mankind together with Christ."[24] This gives us a deeper understanding of that moment in the Passion of our Lord, which we shall never tire of meditating: *Stabat autem iuxta crucem Iesu mater eius,*[25] ("there, standing by the cross of Jesus was his Mother").

I expect you have noticed how some mothers, moved by a legitimate pride, are quick to appear alongside their children when success comes their way, when they receive some public acclaim. But there are other mothers who, even at times like these, stay in

[23] Jn 15:13.
[24] Benedict XV, Letter *Inter sodalicia*, 22-III-1918, AAS 10 (1919), 182.
[25] Jn 19:25.

the background, showing their love silently. This was Mary's way, and Jesus knew it.

But when it comes to the scandal of the Sacrifice of the Cross, Mary is there, hearing with sadness how "the passersby blasphemed against him, tossing their heads, 'Come now,' they said, 'you would destroy the temple and build it up in three days, rescue yourself; come down from that cross, if you are the Son of God.' "[26] Our Lady is there listening to the words of her Son, united to him in his suffering, "My God, my God, why hast thou forsaken me?"[27] What could she do? She united herself fully with the redemptive love of her Son, and offered to the Father her immense sorrow, which pierced her pure Heart like a sharp-edged sword. 288

Jesus is comforted anew by the quiet, loving presence of his Mother. Mary does not shout; she does not run about frantically. *Stabat*: she is there, standing next to her Son. It is then that Jesus looks at her, and then turning his gaze to John he exclaims, " 'Woman, this is thy son.' Then he said to the disciple, 'This is thy

[26] Mt 27:39-40.
[27] *Ibid* 27:46.

Mother.' "[28] In the person of John, Christ is entrusting all men to his Mother, and especially his disciples: those who were to believe in him.

Felix culpa,[29] the Church sings. Happy fault, that has brought us so great and wonderful a Redeemer. Happy fault, we could add, which has merited that we should receive Mary as our Mother. Now we are safe. Nothing should worry us now, because our Lady, the crowned Queen of Heaven and earth, is omnipotent in her supplication before our Father God. Jesus cannot deny anything to Mary, nor to us, who are children of his own Mother.

Our Mother

289 Children, especially when they are small, give very little thought to what they should do for their parents and are much more concerned about what they hope to get from them. As children, we tend to be very self-interested, although our mothers, as we have already mentioned, do not seem to mind really,

[28] Jn 19:26-27.
[29] Easter Vigil, *Praeconium*.

because they have so much love in their hearts and they love with the best kind of affection: that which gives without expecting anything in return.

The same is true of Mary. But today, on the feast of her divine Motherhood, we should try to be more attentive than usual. If we find there have been times when we failed to be gentle and kind towards this good Mother of ours, we should feel sorry. I ask you now, as I ask myself, how are we honoring her?

Let us return once again to our everyday experience and see how we behave with our earthly mothers. What does a mother want most of all from her children, from those who are flesh of her flesh and blood of her blood? Her greatest desire is to have them close to her. When the children grow up and it is no longer possible to have them beside her, she waits impatiently for news from them, and everything that happens to them, from the slightest illness to the most important events, concerns her deeply.

Look: in the eyes of our Mother Mary we **290**
never cease to be little, because she opens to us the way to the Kingdom of Heaven, which will only be given to those who become little

children.[30] We should never separate ourselves from our Lady. How should we honor her? By keeping close to her, talking to her, showing her that we love her, pondering in our hearts the scenes of her life on earth and telling her about our struggles, successes, and failures.

When we do this we discover the meaning of the Marian prayers, which the Church has always used, as if we were saying them for the very first time. What are the *Hail Mary* and the *Angelus* if not loving praises of her divine Motherhood? And when we say the Holy Rosary, which is a wonderful devotion which I will never tire of recommending to Christians everywhere, our minds and hearts go over the mysteries of Mary's admirable life which are, at the same time, the fundamental mysteries of our faith.

291 The liturgical year is adorned with feasts in honor of Mary. The basis of this cult is the divine Motherhood of our Lady, which is the fount of all the gifts of nature and grace lavished on her by the Blessed Trinity. Anyone who fears that the cult of veneration given to the Blessed Virgin could in some way lessen the

[30] Cf. Mt 19:14.

cult of adoration given to God shows scant knowledge of his Christian faith and very little filial love. Our Mother, the model of humility, sang, "from this day forward all generations will count me blessed; because he who is mighty, he whose name is holy, has wrought for me his wonders. He has mercy upon those who fear him, from generation to generation."[31]

When the feasts of our Lady come round let us not be sparing in our tokens of affection. Let us raise our hearts to her more often, asking her for what we need, thanking her for her constant, motherly care and entrusting to her the people we love. Though, naturally, if we really want to act as good children, every day is a good day for loving Mary, just as every day is a good day for those who really love one another.

Perhaps some of you might be thinking that **292**
the ordinary comings and goings of your working day are not going to help you much to stay close to someone as pure as our Lady. But I would just ask you to reflect a little. What are we looking for all the time in things we do, even without thinking about it especially? If we

[31] Lk 1:48-50.

are motivated by the love of God and we work with a right intention, then we are seeking whatever is good and clean, whatever brings peace to our conscience and happiness to our soul. Yes, you might say, but don't we still have our faults? Indeed, but it is precisely by acknowledging our faults that we are able to see, more clearly than ever, just what our goal has to be. What we are looking for is happiness; not a momentary happiness, but one that is deep and lasting and both human and supernatural.

There is one creature who achieved such happiness here on earth because she is God's masterpiece: our most holy Mother Mary. She lives now and is protecting us. She is there, body and soul, with the Father and the Son and the Holy Spirit. She is the same person who was born in Palestine, who gave herself to God while still a child, who received the message from St Gabriel the Archangel, who gave birth to our Savior, and who stood beside him at the foot of the Cross.

In her, all ideals become a reality; but this should not make us think that her sublime greatness makes her inaccessible to us. She is the one who is full of grace and the sum of all perfections; and she is also our Mother. Her power before God is such that she can obtain anything we ask for, and, like any mother, she wants to answer our prayers. Like any mother also, she knows and understands our weaknesses. She encourages us and makes excuses for us. She makes the way easy for us and, even when we think there is no possible solution for our worry, she always has one ready to offer us.

If we truly got to know Mary our Mother, 293
how quickly the supernatural virtues would grow in us! Let us not be shy about repeating short prayers and aspirations to her throughout the day. There is no need to say them out loud, we can say them in our heart. Christian devotion has gathered together many of these loving words of praise in the Litany which accompanies the Holy Rosary. But each one of us is free to think up new ones, and address new praises to her, telling her with our hearts—with a holy bashfulness that she understands and approves—what we would not dare to say out loud.

Finally, I would recommend that, if you haven't already done so, you find out for yourself by personal experience the meaning of

Mary's maternal love. It is not enough just to know she is our Mother and to think and to talk about her as such. She is your Mother and you are her son. She loves you as if you were her only child in this world. Treat her accordingly: tell her about everything that happens to you, honor her, and love her. No one will do it for you or as well as you, if you do not do it yourself.

I give you my word that, if you set out along this way, you will quickly discover all the love of Christ: and you will find yourself drawn into the ineffable life of God the Father, God the Son, and God the Holy Spirit. You will draw strength from it to put the Will of God fully into practice, and you will be filled with desires of serving all men. You will be the Christian you have sometimes dreamed of being: full of works of charity and justice, happy and strong, understanding towards others, and demanding on yourself.

This, and no other, is the kind of faith we want. Let us have recourse to our Mother Mary; she will accompany us and help us make firm and constant progress.

TOWARDS HOLINESS*

We are deeply moved, and our hearts profoundly shaken, when we listen attentively to that cry of St Paul: "This is God's will for you, your sanctification."[1] Today, once again, I set myself this goal and I also remind you and all mankind: this is God's Will for us, that we be saints. 294

In order to bring peace, genuine peace, to souls; in order to transform the earth and to seek God our Lord in the world and through the things of the world, personal sanctity is indispensable. In my conversations with people from so many countries and from all kinds of social backgrounds, I am often asked: "What do you say to us married folk? To those of us who

* A homily given on November 26, 1967.

[1] 1 Thess 4:3.

work on the land? To widows? To young people?"

I reply systematically that I have only "one stewing pot." I usually go on to point out that our Lord Jesus Christ preached the good news to all, without distinction. One stewing pot and only one kind of food: "My food is to do the will of him who sent me, and to accomplish his work."[2] He calls each and every one to holiness; he asks each and every one to love him: young and old, single and married, healthy and sick, learned and unlearned, no matter where they work, or where they are. There is only one way to become more familiar with God, to increase our trust in him. We must come to know him through prayer; we must speak to him and show him, through a heart-to-heart conversation, that we love him.

Talking with God

295 " 'Call upon me and I shall hear you.' "[3] The way to call upon him is to talk to him, turn

[2] Jn 4:34.
[3] Jer 29:12.

to him. Hence we have to put into practice the Apostle's exhortation: *sine intermissione orate*[4] ("pray always, no matter what happens"). "Not only with your heart, but with all your heart."[5]

You may be thinking that life isn't always easy, that we all have our share of bitterness, sadness, and sorrow. I tell you again, with St Paul, that "neither death, nor life, nor angels, nor principalities, nor powers, neither things present, nor things to come, no force whatever, neither the height above us nor the depth beneath us, nor any other created thing, will be able to separate us from the love of God, which comes to us in Christ Jesus our Lord."[6] Nothing can take us away from the charity of God, from Love, from keeping up a constant relationship with our Father.

In recommending this unbroken union with God, am I not presenting an ideal so sublime that it is unattainable by the majority of Christians? Certainly then goal is high, but it is not unattainable. The path that leads to holiness is the path of prayer; and prayer ought to take

[4] 1 Thess 5:17.

[5] St Ambrose, *Expositio in Psalmum* CXVIII, 19, 12 (PL 15, 1471).

[6] Rom 8:38-39.

root and grow in the soul little by little, like the tiny seed which later develops into a tree with many branches.

296 We start with vocal prayers which many of us have been saying since we were children. They are made up of simple, ardent phrases addressed to God and to his Mother, who is our Mother as well. I still renew, morning and evening, and not just occasionally but habitually, the offering I learned from my parents: "O my Lady, my Mother! I offer myself entirely to you, and in proof of my filial love, I consecrate to you this day my eyes, my ears, my tongue, my heart..." Is this not, in some way, a beginning of contemplation, an evident expression of trusting self-abandonment? What do lovers say when they meet? How do they behave? They sacrifice themselves and all their possessions for the person they love.

First, one brief aspiration, then another, and another...till our fervor seems insufficient, because words are too poor...: then this gives way to intimacy with God, looking at God without needing rest or feeling tired. We begin to live as captives, as prisoners. And while we carry out as perfectly as we can (with all our mistakes and limitations) the tasks allotted to us by our situation and duties, our souls long to escape. It is drawn towards God like iron drawn by a magnet. One begins to love Jesus, in a more effective way, with the sweet and gentle surprise of his encounter.

" 'I will release you from captivity, wherever 297
you may be.' "[7] We shake off slavery, through prayer: we know we are free, borne on the wings of a lover's nuptial song, a canticle of love, which makes us want never to be parted from God. It is a new mode of going about this earth, a mode that is divine, supernatural, marvellous. Remembering oft-repeated phrases of the Spanish Golden Age, we may like to taste for ourselves that truth: "I am alive; or rather, not I; it is Christ that lives in me!"[8]

One gladly accepts the need to work in this world and for many years, because Jesus has few friends here below. Let us not turn away from our duty to live our whole life—to the last drop—in the service of God and his Church. And all this, freely: *in libertatem gloriae filiorum Dei*[9] *qua libertate Christus nos liberavit*[10] ("with the

[7] Jer 29:14.
[8] Cf. Gal 2:20.
[9] Rom 8:21.
[10] Gal 4:31.

freedom of the children of God which Jesus won for us by dying on the tree of the Cross.").

298 It may be that, even from the beginning, dark clouds will appear and, at the same time, the enemies of our sanctification may employ techniques of psychological terrorism so vehement and well orchestrated—it is a real abuse of power—that they drag in their absurd direction even those who for a long time had behaved in a more reasonable and upright manner. Yet though their voices sound like cracked bells, that have not been cast from good metal and have a very different tone from the shepherd's whistle call, they so distort speech, which is one of the most precious talents ever bestowed on men by God, a most beautiful gift for the expression of deep thoughts of love and friendship towards the Lord and his creatures, that one comes to understand why St James says that the tongue is "a whole world of malice."[11] So great is the harm it can do: lies, slander, dishonor, trickery, insults, tortuous insinuations.

[11] Jm 3:6.

The Sacred Humanity of Christ

How can we overcome these obstacles? How can we strengthen our initial resolve, when it begins to seem a heavy burden? Let us take inspiration from the example of the Blessed Virgin Mary, our Mother. She shows us a wide and open road, which necessarily passes through Jesus. **299**

In order to draw close to God we must take the right road, which is the Sacred Humanity of Christ. This is why I have always advised people to read books on the Lord's Passion. Such works, which are full of true piety, bring to our minds the Son of God, a Man like ourselves and also true God, who in his flesh loves and suffers to redeem the world.

Take the Holy Rosary, one of the most deeply rooted of Christian devotions. The Church encourages us to contemplate its mysteries. She wants to engrave upon our hearts and our imaginations, together with Mary's joy and sorrow and glory, the spellbinding example of our Lord's life, in his thirty years of obscurity, his three years of preaching, his ignominious Passion, and his glorious Resurrection.

To follow Christ—that is the secret. We must accompany him so closely that we come to live with him, like the first Twelve did; so closely, that we become identified with him. Soon we will be able to say, provided we haven't put obstacles in the way of grace, that we have put on, have clothed ourselves with our Lord Jesus Christ.[12] Our Lord is then reflected in our behavior, as in a mirror. If the mirror is as it ought to be, it will capture our Savior's most lovable face without distorting it or making a caricature of it; and then other people will have an opportunity of admiring him and following him.

300 I have distinguished as it were four stages in our effort to identify ourselves with Christ: seeking him, finding him, getting to know him, loving him. It may seem clear to you that you are only at the first stage. Seek him then, hungrily; seek him within yourselves with all your strength. If you act with determination, I am ready to guarantee that you have already found him, and have begun to get to know him and to love him, and to hold your conversation in Heaven.[13]

[12] Cf. Rom 13:14.
[13] Cf. Phil 3:20.

I beg our Lord to help us make up our minds to nourish in our souls the one noble ambition that matters, the only one that is really worthwhile: to get close to Jesus, like his Blessed Mother and the Holy Patriarch St Joseph did, with longing hearts and self-denial, without neglect of any kind. We will share in the joy of being God's friends—in a spirit of interior recollection, which is quite compatible with our professional and social duties—and we will thank him for teaching us so clearly and tenderly how to fulfill the Will of our Father who dwells in Heaven.

But do not forget that being with Jesus **301**
means we shall most certainly come upon his Cross. When we abandon ourselves into God's hands, he frequently permits us to taste sorrow, loneliness, opposition, slander, defamation, ridicule, coming both from within and from outside. This is because he wants to mold us into his own image and likeness. He even tolerates that we be called lunatics and be taken for fools.

This is the time to love passive mortification which comes, hidden perhaps or barefaced and insolent, when we least expect it. They can even go so far as to strike the sheep with the very stones that should have been thrown at the wolves: the follower of Christ experiences in his own flesh that those who have a duty to love him, treat him instead in ways that range from mistrust to hostility, from suspicion to hatred. They look upon him with misgiving, as if he were a liar, because they do not believe it is possible to have personal dealings with God, an interior life; and all the while, with atheists and those who are indifferent to God (people who are usually impertinent and rude), they behave in a most amicable and understanding manner.

Our Lord may even allow his followers to be attacked with a weapon that never does honor to its user, the weapon of personal insult; or to be subjected to a smear campaign, the tendentious and indictable result of a massive campaign of lies: for not everyone is endowed with a sense of fairness and good taste.

When people favor a doubtful theology and an easy-going "anything goes" morality, and engage in dubious liturgical practices following their own whims, with a "hippy" discipline which is answerable to no authority; then it comes as no surprise if they spread envy, suspicion, false allegations, insults, ill-treatment, humiliations, gossip, and all kinds of outrage against those who speak only of Jesus Christ.

This is the way Jesus fashions the souls of those he loves, while at the same time never failing to give them inner calm and joy, because they are fully aware that, even with a hundred lies, the devils are incapable of making a single truth; and he impresses on them a living conviction that they will only find comfort when they make up their minds to do without it.

When we really come to admire and love the 302
most sacred Humanity of Jesus, we will discover each of his Wounds, one by one. When we undergo periods of passive purgation, that we find painful and hard to bear, periods when we shed sweet and bitter tears, which we do our best to hide, we will feel the need to enter into each one of his most Holy Wounds: to be purified and strengthened, rejoicing in his redeeming Blood. We will go there like the doves which, in the words of Scripture,[14] find shelter from the storm in the crevices in the rocks. We hide in this refuge to find the inti-

[14] Cf. Cant 2:14.

macy of Christ. We find his conversation soothing and his countenance comely,[15] because "those who know that his voice is gentle and pleasing are those who have welcomed the grace of the Gospel, which makes them say: 'You have the words of eternal life.' "[16]

303 Let us not think that because we are on this road of contemplation our passions will have calmed down once and for all. We would be mistaken if we thought that our longing to seek Christ, and the fact that we are meeting him and getting to know him and enjoy the sweetness of his love, makes us incapable of sinning. Though your own experience will tell you, let me nevertheless remind you of this truth. Satan, God's enemy and man's, does not give up nor does he rest. He maintains his siege, even when the soul is ardently in love with God. The devil knows that it's more difficult for the soul to fall then, but he also knows that, if he can manage to get it to offend its Lord even in something small, he will be able to cast over its conscience the serious temptation of despair.

[15] *Ibid.*

[16] St Gregory of Nyssa, *In Canticum Canticorum homiliae*, 5 (PG 44, 879).

If you want to learn from the experience of a poor priest whose only aim is to speak of God, I will tell you that when the flesh tries to recover its lost rights or, worse still, when pride rears up and rebels, you should hurry to find shelter in the divine wounds that were opened in Christ's Body by the nails that fastened him to the Cross and by the lance that pierced his side. Go as the spirit moves you: unburden in his Wounds all your love, both human and...divine. This is what it means to seek union, to feel that you are a brother to Christ, sharing his blood, a child of the same Mother, for it is She who has brought us to Jesus.

The Holy Cross

Be eager to adore, yearn to make reparation, **304**
suffering quietly and calmly. Then Jesus' words will come alive in your lives: " 'he who does not take up his cross and follow me, is not worthy of me.' "[17] Our Lord becomes more and more demanding with us. He asks us to make reparation, to do penance, and the time comes

[17] Mt 10:38.

when he makes us experience a fervent desire to want "to live for God, nailed on the Cross with Christ."[18] But "we have this treasure in vessels made of clay," which is fragile and brittle, "to show that the power that shines through us is not ours but God's."[19]

"We are afflicted in every way, but not crushed; perplexed, but not without hope," or sustenance; "we are persecuted, but not forsaken; struck down, but not destroyed; we carry about continually in our bodies the dying state of Jesus."[20]

We may even imagine that our Lord does not hear us; that we are being deluded, that all we hear is the monologue of our own voice. We find ourselves, as it were, without support on earth and abandoned by Heaven. Nevertheless, we have a real and practical horror of sin, even venial sin. With the stubbornness of the Canaanite woman, we go down on our knees as she did, adoring him and imploring " 'Lord, help me.' "[21] The darkness will vanish, vanquished by the light of Love.

[18] Gal 2:19.
[19] 2 Cor 4:7.
[20] *Ibid* 4:8-10.
[21] Mt 15:25.

The time has come to cry to him. Remember, Lord, the promises you made, filling me with hope; they console me in my nothingness and fill my life with strength.[22] Our Lord wants us to rely on him for everything: it is now glaringly evident to us that without him we can do nothing,[23] whereas with him we can do all things.[24] We confirm our decision to walk always in his presence.[25] 305

With God enlightening our intellect, which seem to be inactive, we understand beyond any shadow of doubt that, since the Creator takes care of everyone, even his enemies, how much more will he take care of his friends! We become convinced that no evil or trouble can befall us which will not turn out to be for our good. And so, joy and peace become more firmly rooted in our spirit, and no merely human motive can tear them from us, because these "visitations" always leave us with something of himself, something divine. We find ourselves praising the Lord our God, who has

[22] Cf. Ps 118:49-50.
[23] Cf. Jn 15:5.
[24] Cf. Phil 4:13.
[25] Cf. Ps 118:168.

worked such great wonders in us,[26] and understanding that God has made us capable of possessing an infinite treasure.[27]

The Blessed Trinity

306 We started out with the simple and attractive vocal prayers that we learned as children, prayers we want never to abandon. Our prayer, which began so childlike and ingenuous, now opens out into a broad, smooth-flowing stream, for it follows the course of friendship with him who said: "'I am the way,'"[28] If we so love Christ, if with divine daring we take refuge in the wound opened in his Side by the lance, then the Master's promise will find fulfillment: "'Whoever loves me, keeps my commandments, and my Father will love him and we will come to him and make our dwelling in him.'"[29]

Our heart now needs to distinguish and adore each one of the divine Persons. The soul is, as it were, making a discovery in the

[26] Cf. Job 5:9.
[27] Cf. Wis 7:14.
[28] Jn 14:6.
[29] *Ibid* 14:23.

supernatural life, like a little child opening his eyes to the world about him. The soul spends time lovingly with the Father and the Son and the Holy Spirit, and readily submits to the work of the lifegiving Paraclete, who gives himself to us with no merit on our part, bestowing his gifts and the supernatural virtues!

We have run "like the deer, longing for **307**
flowing streams;"[30] thirsting, our lips parched and dry. We want to drink at this source of living water. All day long, without doing anything strange, we move in this abundant, clear spring of fresh waters that leap up to eternal life.[31] Words are not needed, because the tongue cannot express itself. The intellect grows calm. One does not reason; one looks! And the soul breaks out once more into song, a new song, because it feels and knows it is under the loving gaze of God, all day long.

I am not talking about extraordinary situations. These are, they may very well be, ordinary happenings within our souls: a loving craziness which, without any fuss or extravagance, teaches us how to suffer and how to live,

[30] Ps 41:2.
[31] Cf. Jn 4:14.

because God grants us his wisdom. What calm, what peace is ours once we have embarked upon "the narrow road that leads on to life!"[32]

308 Asceticism? Mysticism? I don't mind what you call it. Whichever it is, asceticism or mysticism, does not matter. Either way, it is a gift of God's mercy. If you try to meditate, our Lord will not deny you his assistance. Faith and deeds of faith are what matter: deeds, because, as you have known from the beginning and as I told you clearly at the time, the Lord demands more from us each day. This is already contemplation and union. This is the way many Christians should live, each one forging ahead along his own spiritual path (there are countless paths) in the midst of the cares of the world, even though he may not even realize what is happening to him.

Such prayer and behavior do not take us away from our ordinary activities. In the midst of our noble human zeal they lead us to our Lord. When men offer up all their cares and occupations to God they make the world divine. How often have I reminded you of the myth of King Midas, who turned all he touched

[32] Mt 7:14.

into gold! We, despite our personal failings, can turn all we touch into the gold of supernatural merit.

This is the way our God does things. When 309
the prodigal returns, having squandered his fortune in riotous living and, worst of all, having forgotten about his father, his father says: " 'Quick! Bring out the best robe, and clothe him in it; put a ring on his finger, and shoes on his feet. Then bring out the calf that has been fattened, and kill it; let us eat, and make merry.' "[33] Our Father God, when we come to him repentant, draws, from our wretchedness, treasure; from our weakness, strength. What then will he prepare for us, if we don't forsake him, if we go to him daily, if we talk lovingly to him and confirm our love with deeds, if we go to him for everything, trusting in his almighty power and mercy? If the return of a son who had betrayed him is enough for him to prepare a banquet, what will he have in store for us, who have tried to remain always at his side?

Far be it from us, therefore, to remember who has offended us or the humiliations we

[33] Lk 15:22-23.

have endured—no matter how unjust, uncivil, or unmannerly they may have been—because it would not be right for a son of God to be preparing some kind of dossier, from which to read off a list of grievances. We must never forget Christ's example; besides, our Christian faith is not something to be put on and off like a suit of clothes: it can grow weak or more robust or be lost. With this supernatural life our faith grows strong and the very thought of how wretchedly naked man is without God is enough to terrify the soul. And so one forgives and gives thanks. My God, when I look at my own poor life, I find no reason to be vain and still less to be proud: all I see are abundant reasons why I should be always humble and contrite. I know full well that a life of service is man's noblest calling.

Living prayer

310 "I will arise and go through the city; through its streets and squares I will seek my love."[34]...And not only through the city; I will

[34] Cant 3:2.

run from one end of the world to the other—through all nations and peoples, through highways and byways—to find peace of soul. And I discover this peace in my daily occupations, which are no hindrance to me; quite the contrary, they are my path, my reason to love more and more, and to be more and more united to my God.

And if we are waylaid, assaulted by the temptation of discouragement, opposition, struggle, tribulation, a new dark night of the soul, the psalmist places on our lips and in our minds these words: "I am with him in the time of trial."[35] Jesus, compared to your Cross, of what value is mine? Alongside your wounds, what are my little scratches? Compared with your Love, so immense and pure and infinite, of what value is this tiny, little sorrow which you have placed upon my shoulders? And your hearts, and mine, become filled with a holy hunger and we confess to him—with deeds—that "we die of Love."[36]

A thirst for God is born in us, a longing to understand his tears, to see his smile, his

[35] Ps 90:15.
[36] Cf. Cant 5:8.

face...The best way to express this, I would say, is to repeat with Scripture: "Like the deer that seeks for running waters, so my heart yearns for thee, my God!"[37] The soul goes forward immersed in God, divinized: the Christian becomes a thirsty traveller who opens his mouth to the waters of the fountain.[38]

311 Along with this self-surrender, our apostolic zeal is enkindled and grows day by day; it also sets others on fire with its desire, because goodness is diffusive. It is not possible for our poor nature to be so close to God and not be fired with hunger to sow joy and peace throughout the world, to spread everywhere the redeeming waters that flow from Christ's open side,[39] and to begin and end everything we do for Love.

I was speaking before about sorrow and suffering and tears. Without contradicting what I said then, I can affirm that the disciple who lovingly seeks the Master finds that sadness, worries, and afflictions now taste very differently: they disappear as soon as we truly accept

[37] Ps 41:2.
[38] Cf. Ecclus 26:15.
[39] Cf. Jn 19:34.

God's Will, as soon as we carry out his plans gladly, as faithful children of his, even though our nerves may seem to be at breaking point and the pain impossible to bear.

Ordinary life

I would like to confirm once more that I am not talking about an extraordinary way of living as Christians. Let each of us meditate on what God has done for him and how he has responded. If we are courageous in examining our behavior, we will perceive what still needs to be done. Yesterday I was very moved when I heard that a Japanese catechumen was teaching the catechism to others who did not yet know about Christ. I felt ashamed. We need to have more faith, much more faith and, with faith, contemplation. 312

Go over, calmly, that divine admonition which fills the soul with disquiet and which at the same time tastes as sweet as honey from the comb: *redemi te, et vocavi te, nomine tuo: meus es tu*[40] ("I have redeemed you and called you

[40] Is 43:1.

by your name: you are mine")! Let us not steal from God what belongs to him. A God who has loved us to the point of dying for us, who has chosen us from all eternity, before the creation of the world, so that we may be holy in his presence;[41] and who continually offers us opportunities to purify our lives and give ourselves to him.

If there were still the slightest doubt in our minds, we receive yet another proof from his own lips: "It was not you that chose me, it was I that chose you, to go out and bear fruit, fruit which will endure," the fruit of your work as contemplative souls.[42]

What we need, therefore, is faith, supernatural faith. When faith weakens men tend to imagine that God is far away and hardly cares for his children. They come to regard religion as a kind of appendage, something to have recourse to when there's no other remedy; they expect, with what justification one cannot say, spectacular manifestations, unusual happenings. But when faith is really alive in the soul, one discovers instead that to follow Christ one

[41] Cf. Eph 1:4.
[42] Cf. Jn 15:16.

does not have to step aside from the ordinary pattern of everyday life, and also that the great holiness which God expects of us is to be found here and now in the little things of each day.

I love to speak of paths and ways, because 313
we are travellers, journeying to our home in Heaven, our Father's land. But don't forget that, though a path may have some particularly difficult stretches, and may occasionally involve wading across a river or passing through an almost impenetrable wood, as a rule it will be quite passable and hold no surprises for us. The danger lies in routine, in imagining that God cannot be here, in the things of each instant, because they are so simple and ordinary!

There were two disciples on their way to Emmaus. They were walking along at a normal pace, like so many other travellers on that road. And there, without any fuss, Jesus appeared to them, and walks with them, his conversation helping to alleviate their tiredness. I can well imagine the scene, just as dust was falling. A gentle breeze was blowing. All around were fields ripe with wheat, and venerable olive trees, their branches shimmering in the soft glowing light.

Jesus joins them as they go along their way. Lord, how great you are, in everything! But you move me even more when you come down to our level, to follow us and to seek us in the hustle and bustle of each day. Lord, grant us a childlike spirit, pure eyes and a clear head so that we may recognize you when you come without any outward sign of your glory.

314 The journey ends when they reach the village. The two disciples who, without realizing it, have been deeply stirred by the words and love shown by God made Man, are sorry to see him leaving. For Jesus "made as if to go on further."[43] This Lord of ours never forces himself on us. He wants us to turn to him freely, when we begin to grasp the purity of his Love which he has placed in our souls. We have to hold him back ("they pressed him") and beg him: " 'Stay with us; it is towards evening, and it is far on in the day,' "[44] night is coming on.

That's just like us. Always short on daring, perhaps because we are insincere, or because we feel embarrassed. Deep down, what we are

[43] Lk 24:28.
[44] *Ibid* 24:29.

really thinking is: "Stay with us, because our souls are shrouded in darkness and you alone are the light. You alone can satisfy this longing that consumes us." For "we know full well which among all things fair and honorable is the best: to possess God forever."[45]

And Jesus stays. Our eyes are opened, as were those of Cleophas and his companion, when Christ breaks the bread; and, though he vanishes once more from sight, we too will find strength to start out once more—though night is falling—to tell the others about him, because so much joy cannot be kept in one heart alone.

The road to Emmaus: our God has filled this name with sweetness. Now the entire world has become an Emmaus, for the Lord has opened up all the divine paths of the earth.

With the Holy Angels

I ask our Lord that, during our stay on this **315**
earth of ours, we may never be parted from our divine travelling companion. To ensure this, let us also become firmer friends of the holy

[45] St Gregory Nazianzen, *Epistolae*, 212 (PG 37, 349).

Guardian Angels. We all need a lot of company, company from Heaven and company on earth. Have great devotion to the holy angels! Friendship is a very human thing, but it is also very much a thing of God; just as our life is both human and divine. Don't you remember what our Lord says? "I no longer call you servants, but friends."[46] He teaches us to have a lot of confidence in those friends of God who are already in Heaven, and also in the people who are living with us on this earth, including those who seem to be far from the Lord, so as to attract them to the right path.

I would like to end with some words of St Paul to the Colossians: "We have been praying for you unceasingly. Our prayer is that you may be filled with that closer knowledge of God's will which brings all wisdom and all spiritual insight with it."[47] Wisdom, which is the fruit of prayer, of contemplation, of the infusion of the Paraclete in the soul.

"May you lead a life worthy of the Lord, fully pleasing to him, bearing fruit in every good work and increasing in your knowledge

[46] Jn 15:15.
[47] Col 1:19.

of God. May you be strengthened with all power, according to his glorious might, for all endurance and patience with joy; giving thanks to the Father, for making us fit to share in the inheritance of the saints in light, for rescuing us from the power of darkness, and transferring us to the kingdom of his Beloved Son."[48]

May the Mother of God and our Mother **316**
protect us, so that each one of us may serve the Church in the fullness of faith, with the gifts of the Holy Spirit and with our contemplative life. May each one of us joyfully honor the Lord by carrying out his own duties, those which are properly his; each one of us, in his job or profession and fulfilling the obligations of his state in life.

Love the Church; serve the Church with the conscious gladness of one who has committed himself to this service for Love's sake. And if we should see anyone travelling without hope, like the two men on the road to Emmaus, let us approach them full of faith—not in our own name but in Christ's name—to reassure them that Jesus' promise cannot fail, for he is always watching over his Spouse and he will never

[48] *Ibid* 1:10-13.

abandon her. The darkness will pass away, because we are children of the light[49] and have been called to life everlasting.

"And God will wipe away every tear from their eyes, and there will be no more death, or mourning, or cries of distress, no more sorrow; those old things have passed away. And he who sat on the throne said, 'Behold, I make all things new.' He said to me, 'Write it down, for these words are most sure and true.' And he added, 'It is done. I am Alpha, I am Omega, the beginning of all things and their end; those who are thirsty shall drink—it is my free gift—out of the spring whose water is life. He who wins the victory shall possess all this; I will be his God, and he shall be my son.' "[50]

[49] Cf. Eph 5:8.
[50] Apoc 21:4-7.

INDEX TO QUOTATIONS FROM SACRED SCRIPTURE*

OLD TESTAMENT

* The reference numbers refer to the numbers printed in the margin of this volume.

PROVERBS

ECCLESIASTES

CANTICLE OF CANTICLES

WISDOM

ECCLESIASTICUS

MARK

LUKE

ACTS OF THE APOSTLES

ROMANS

INDEX TO QUOTATIONS FROM FATHERS AND DOCTORS OF THE CHURCH AND OTHER ECCLESIASTICAL WRITERS

SUBJECT INDEX